PENGUIN BOOKS

WHEN CHILDREN WANT CHILDREN

Leon Dash is a member of the investigative news staff of *The Washington Post*. As a foreign correspondent, he once spent over seven months and walked twenty-one hundred miles with anti-government guerrillas in Angola. From 1979 to 1984 he covered West Central and East Africa. On returning to Washington, he covered the State Department. He is a winner of the Overseas Press Club's George Polk Memorial Award, and his six-part series for *The Washington Post* about teenage childbearing was a finalist for the Pulitzer Prize. He lives in the Washington, D.C., area.

WHEN CHILDREN
WANT CHILDREN

*An Inside Look at the
Crisis of Teenage Parenthood*

LEON DASH

PENGUIN BOOKS

PENGUIN BOOKS
Published by the Penguin Group
Viking Penguin, a division of Penguin Books USA Inc.,
40 West 23rd Street, New York, New York 10010, U.S.A.
Penguin Books Ltd, 27 Wrights Lane,
London W8 5TZ, England
Penguin Books Australia Ltd, Ringwood,
Victoria, Australia
Penguin Books Canada Ltd, 2801 John Street,
Markham, Ontario, Canada L3R 1B4
Penguin Books (N.Z.) Ltd, 182–190 Wairau Road,
Auckland 10, New Zealand
Penguin Books Ltd, Registered Offices:
Harmondsworth, Middlesex, England
First published in the United States of America by
William Morrow and Company, Inc., 1989
Reprinted by arrangement of William Morrow and Company, Inc.
Published in Penguin Books 1990

1   3   5   7   9   10   8   6   4   2

Copyright © Leon Dash, 1989
All rights reserved
All photographs are copyright © by
Fred Sweets of *The Washington Post*.

LIBRARY OF CONGRESS CATALOGING-IN-PUBLICATION DATA
Dash, Leon.
When children want children: the urban crisis of teenage
childbearing/Leon Dash.
p.   cm.
Reprint. Originally published: New York: William Morrow, ©1989.
ISBN 0 14 01.1789 X
1. Afro-American teenage mothers—Washington, (D.C.)—Case studies.
2. Teenage pregnancy—Washington (D.C.)—Case studies.   3. Afro-American
teenagers—Washington (D.C.)—Sexual behavior—Case
studies.   4. Washington Highlands (Washington, D.C.).   I. Title.
HQ759.4.D37   1990
306.7'0835—dc20   89-28458

Printed in the United States of America
Designed by Bernard Schleifer

Except in the United States of America, this book is sold subject to the condition that it
shall not, by way of trade or otherwise, be lent, re-sold, hired out, or otherwise circu-
lated without the publisher's prior consent in any form of binding or cover other than that
in which it is published and without a similar condition including this condition being
imposed on the subsequent purchaser.

For my parents,
Leon and Ruth,
and my daughters,
Darla and Destiny

ACKNOWLEDGMENTS

DURING THE RESEARCH for the original *Washington Post* series, the subsequent research in North Carolina, and the writing of this book, I received encouragement from friends, colleagues, and people who wanted to know why so many black adolescents are having babies. Some crucial support came from foundation officials who are supporting programs to prevent adolescent pregnancy and childbearing.

First among this group was *Post* investigations editor Bob Woodward. Bob insisted on the methodology of repeated interviews over the seventeen-month period of the Washington Highlands project, an approach that I initially resisted. Investigations desk deputy editor David Maraniss kept me going at critical junctures of depression and anxiety by acting as a sounding board and pointing out clear patterns of human behavior that I was too close to to perceive. Steve Luxenberg, who replaced David in September 1985, structured the entire series and, by so doing, made the major editorial contribution to this book. Steve was particularly perceptive in picking out the major theme for each of the six families at a point when the data I collected had overwhelmed me.

There also were friends who acted as sounding boards and offered interpretations of what I witnessed and heard. They kept me going when I reached points of frustration and thought that I would never get to know the genuine motivations of the people I interviewed. They are Karen Williamson, Dyann Waugh, Brenda Connor-Bey, Taft "Chuck" Broome, John Hope Franklin, John W. Franklin, Paula Giddings, Melita Karalic, Junette Pinkney, Eric Robertson, and Ronald P. Walker.

James O. Gibson, director of equal opportunity for The Rockefeller Foundation, was supportive during the project. Gibson also encouraged my desire to go further and research the antecedents of black-adolescent childbearing among black tenant farmers. He and associate director of equal opportunity Bruce Williams were instrumental in arranging a Rockefeller Foundation grant to help support me and my family during a year's leave of absence from *The Post.*

Peter Bell, president of the Edna McConnell Clark Foundation, provided a grant that made up the majority of the money needed to shuttle between Washington, D.C., and Oxford, North Carolina, and live in Granville County to conduct the field interviews with retired tenant farmers. New World Foundation president Colin Greer also contributed to my living and research expenses.

Gerry and Tammy Bender are two friends who recognized the importance of getting at some of the real reasons children are choosing to become parents. Gerry is a political science professor at the University of Southern California and approached USC's School of Public Administration dean, Ross Clayton, to provide me with a student researcher. Michelle Mallory was the tireless USC student researcher who worked with me for the fall 1986 semester.

Bruce Lee, my editor at William Morrow and Company, made invaluable suggestions and contributions to the structure of this book; without his guidance and patience this book might never have been published.

I am eternally indebted to all of the above-mentioned people and the many others too numerous to mention.

LEON DASH
Mt. Rainier, Maryland
March 6, 1988

*P*ROLOGUE

I BEGAN MY RESEARCH into adolescent childbearing burdened with adult presumptions. I assumed that the high incidence of teenage pregnancy among poor, black urban youths nationwide grew out of youthful ignorance both about birth-control methods and adolescent reproductive capabilities. I also thought the girls were falling victim to cynical manipulation by the boys, although the numbers of babies born to adolescent girls appeared to be awfully high for this to be the dominant pattern.

I was wrong on all counts.

Among the adolescents in Washington, D.C., whom I interviewed, I found that teenage boys and girls as young as eleven knew more about sex, birth control, and their reproductive abilities than I had known at the same age. Others had had extensive school courses in sex education in the sixth or seventh grades.

I found that the girls, far from being passive victims, were often equal—or greater— actors than their boyfriends in exploring sexuality and becoming pregnant. The girls were as often the leaders in their desire to have a child as the boys were. I did not find one adolescent couple where both partners were ignorant about the results of sexual activity without the use of contraception.

In time it became clear that for many girls in the poverty-stricken community of Washington Highlands, a baby is a *tangible* achievement in an otherwise dreary and empty future. It is one way of announcing: I *am* a woman. For many boys in Washington Highlands the birth of a baby represents an identical rite of passage. The boy is saying: I *am* a man.

The desire for a child was especially acute among adolescents who were doing poorly in school. They knew implicitly and had been told explicitly that they were not likely to graduate from high school. These were the youths, ages fifteen to seventeen and still in the seventh grade, who were at highest risk to get pregnant or father a child. While the better students strove for a diploma, the poorer students achieved their form of recognition with a baby.

If the crisis of black teenage parents were simply a matter of ignorance, then it might be a relatively easy problem to solve. But poor academic preparation that begins in elementary school, the poverty that surrounds them, and social isolation from mainstream American life motivate many of these boys and girls to have children.

CHAPTER ONE

I MET TAUSCHA VAUGHN for the first time on the hot, sunny afternoon of September 7, 1984, and we talked for several hours in her family's living room. She appeared to be a tough, extroverted, self-assured girl. She knew where she was going and what she wanted out of life. She was sixteen. In three days she would enroll for her junior year at Ballou High School, in the far-southeast corner of Washington, D.C.

For an hour I kept asking questions about what teenagers know, don't know, or misunderstand about contraceptives. Obviously tiring of my probing, Tauscha leaned forward over the coffee table and looked at me as if I were a naïve child.

She spoke in a husky voice: "Mr. Dash, will you please stop asking me about birth control? Girls out here know all about birth control. There's too many birth-control pills out here. All of them know about it. Even when they twelve, they know what [birth control] is. Girls out here get pregnant because they *want* to have babies! You need to learn what's going on inside people's homes these days!"

Her words shocked me into silence. I tried to regroup my thoughts. This was only my second interview for *The Washington Post* with an adolescent on the subject of teenage childbearing. And it was not what I had expected. I thought to myself: Stop! Drop all assumptions, presumptions, and extrapolations from your childhood. It's time to listen.

"What do you mean?" I asked. I thought I sounded awfully lame.

"*None* of this childbearing is an accident!" Tauscha replied.

"When girls get pregnant, it's either because they want something to hold on to that they can call their own or because of the circumstances at home. Because their mother doesn't pamper them the way they want to be pampered or they really don't have anyone to go to or talk to or call their own. Some of them do it because they resent their parents. Right?"

Her "Right?" was less a question than an exclamation. I was now the pupil. Tauscha had taken charge of the interview.

"A good example is my brother, Adrian, and his ex-girl friend," she continued. "They went together for about two years. Her mother used to keep her in the house all the time. Never let her out. She and my brother used to do some crazy stuff to see each other. It caused problems for both families. She told him she wanted to get pregnant. She wanted a little boy.

"My brother was like, 'Hey look, I can't take care of a child. I don't have no money. I don't have a job. You gonna have to wait.' And she was like, 'Fine, but I still want one.' She would bring it up half of the time." At the time, Adrian and his girl friend were sixteen.

"My brother would come and ask me, 'What should I do?' I'd say, 'Don't give it to her. Because all it's going to do is mess up her life.' She used to talk to me about having a baby, and I'm like, 'Why are you bringing a baby up all the time?' She was like, 'I just want to have something cuddly and something I can hold on to and just kiss all the time. I want to treat it the way my mother didn't treat me. I want to give it all the love my mother didn't give me.' "

Shortly after they broke up, the girl called Tauscha. " 'I'm *pregnant*!' And I was like, '*Dawg,* I hope it ain't my brother.' She said, 'No, it's not.' And I said, 'OK, now why did you do this? Are you scared? Are you afraid?' She was like, 'I'm happy and I'm excited about it. I got a job and everything.' Which was good because most of them don't!" Tauscha said the last remark sarcastically.

"Then she say, 'I can't wait to get *fat*! I can't wait to see it blow up in my stomach. I can't wait to see it come out, and I hope it's a boy.' She was very happy about it. It wasn't no *accident*!"

Another girl friend of Tauscha's had a child at fifteen. When the girl was thirteen, her mother "used to take nude pictures of her[self] and her daughter together to show guys. That was off to me. I said, 'Why did your mother make you do something like that?' She said, 'Cause ——— likes me, and she wants him to like her, too.' That's just a wild family." Her girl friend became pregnant after the mother forced her daughter to have sex with older teenagers, boys seventeen to nineteen.

In her ninth-grade class, "a perfect young lady popped up pregnant," continued Tauscha. "Everybody was like shocked. The guys would talk about her, 'Aw man, I could have gotten that. I didn't know she was like that.' And stuff like that."

She was a bright girl whose mother was never home. "She was from a broken home. She would see her father, but her father wouldn't come around that often."

The pregnant girl's classmates "gave her a lot of attention. Positive. Used to hang around her all the time. But then some of the girls started feeling like, if she gets all that attention from people then maybe if I get pregnant I can get a lot of attention. And you know what? Two girls wound up being pregnant after she was, but they didn't get as much attention."

One of the two girls asked Tauscha, "What did I do wrong? I thought I was suppose to get all this attention." But the novelty had worn off.

"I don't want *no* babies!" Tauscha told me. "I don't want a child because there is so much I want to give my child. So much love. So much attention. So much of me that I'm not able to give right now. I'm not financially fit. I don't really have an education. I'm lacking in skills. I can't get out of my mother's house. To me that's just like bringing a child into a world where all he's going to see is a lot of pain. I don't want it to have pain. All I want it to feel is a lot of joy. You old enough to have a child when you can take care of it!"

My conversation with Tauscha took place five weeks after I had moved into a basement apartment in one of Washington, D.C.'s poorest neighborhoods: a run-down, isolated community called Washington Highlands.

What followed was one of the most stressful, intense professional and personal ordeals I have experienced.

I had planned for a six-month stay in Washington Highlands on assignment for *The Washington Post* searching for the causes of the high rates of teenage pregnancy and childbearing among the black urban poor. What I discovered was a total surprise. I stayed a year.

During this time I was able to observe how family life, economic circumstances, environment, and third parties act in concert to influence, if not determine, an individual's behavior.

I found people of extraordinary endurance and people of exceptional destructiveness. There were people who were suicidal. None of their strengths or foibles had been created in a vacuum. There was a reason, a past and a present reason, for each decision a person chose to make.

I first learned of the nationwide problem of teenage pregnancy one cold, sunny January day in 1984 after returning to Washington after working almost five years as a *Washington Post* correspondent in Africa. On this day, I was visiting a black American friend, Vernita P. Fort, in her apartment in the affluent Washington neighborhood that borders the campus of American University.

In our conversation, Fort shocked me by saying that more than one half of the black children born in America today are the children of single mothers. "More than one third of those mothers are poor teenage girls," she added.

I was staggered. The high percentage rates foretold of generational cycles of poverty for thousands—if not millions—of newborn black babies. These infants would be linked to a chain of conduct that begins with an adolescent mother and would be passed on to most of her children and, thereafter, her grandchildren. Many of these childlike parents are burdened already with inadequate educations. With the added responsibility of children, I reasoned, these adolescent parents would have only the slightest chance of rising above lifelong privation. Their children would have even less of a chance of escaping urban poverty's minefield.

At a time when middle-class blacks are making significant strides in upward economic mobility and all areas of American life, it seems that all too many poor, black youths are reducing their chances in life and adding to their burdens by having children much too early in their lives.

Why are so many of them caught up in this syndrome?

I set out to find some answers. I began to ask relatives, friends, and colleagues, black and white, why they thought so many young black children are having children. Some of the responses were cynical. "Black girls are having babies to qualify for welfare payments," some said. Others responded with sympathy, saying the girls are having children in order "to have someone to love" in their otherwise bleak lives.

"Then why are the boys fathering children?" I asked.

Irresponsible, macho boys, I was told, "are taking advantage of ignorant, emotionally needy girls." The boys, some people added, are following familiar patterns of behavior set by the men they know and put the burden of contraceptives on the girls. Others claimed the girls are largely uninformed about the consequences of sexual activity without birth control.

As it turns out, not one of these responses is true.

But at that moment, I had begun to believe that large numbers of today's poor, sexually active boys and girls must have been producing babies out of a widespread ignorance about contraception. Yet, I was worried by the fact that the numbers seemed to be awfully high for all of these babies to be the result of naïveté. So I carried these two unresolved thoughts with me into Washington Highlands.

Months after moving in, I learned that for many of Washington Highlands' adolescents, having a child meets basic human needs that have nothing at all to do with girls qualifying for welfare payments. Monthly public-assistance checks never meet the needs of one child —much less those of the adolescent mother of the child or the other children who all too often follow the first.

The concept that smart, macho boys were manipulating dumb, emotionally needy girls also turned out to be a myth. None of the girls I met were easily manipulated by anyone, especially a boyfriend, although they were quite willing and able, when they perceived it to be to their advantage, to play the *role* of a used, abused female victim. The girls I came to know well were cynical about their relationships with *everyone* and very savvy about what their boyfriends were capable of. One thing was clear. The boyfriends could not convince their girlfriends to have children unless the girls *wanted* them.

In seventeen months of intensive interviews with adults who had become parents as teenagers and the adolescent parents in six families, I did not find a single instance in which procreation had been accidental on the part of *both* sexual partners. While there was some profession of ignorance about birth control among adults forty years old and older, not one of the adolescents that I met and interviewed had been ignorant about contraception *before* becoming a parent.

By living in Washington Highlands the investigation I conducted proved to be a unique approach for *The Washington Post,* in particular, and journalistic practice, in general.

Before I could set up the assignment, I had to run it past several layers of key editors. No project can be started up by a reporter at *The Post* without a lot of preliminary discussion with any number of editors. The inevitable play of personalities, perceptions, personal histories, and past relationships between editors and reporters is interwoven into this process. My situation was no different.

I had ended my tour in Africa in the fall of 1983—while in the midst of moving *The Post*'s West Africa bureau from Abidjan, Ivory Coast, to Nairobi, Kenya, in East Africa—because I wanted to come home. I had not tired of Africa. In fact, the move to Kenya was a happy one and would have brought me full circle, back to the first African country I had lived in. During 1969 and 1970, I had been a Peace Corps volunteer rural high school teacher in western Kenya.

I changed my mind about returning to Kenya because of the needs of my younger daughter, Destiny. (My older daughter, Darla, had begun attending Howard University and her needs were minor compared to her younger sister's.) Destiny had been born prematurely in Abidjan in 1979. Her mother and I had met at *The Post*. We married in 1978, moved to Africa six months later, separated in 1980, and then divorced. It was learned after Destiny and her mother returned to the States that Destiny had cerebral palsy.

So when I took a two-week vacation in Washington in July 1983, I spent every day with Destiny but the following month found me in Chad covering the renewed fighting in that tortured country's perennial civil war. This time, the neighboring Libyans and the French, the former colonial power, were directly involved in the fighting. Their troops were stalemated in the desert several hundred miles north of the Chadian capital, N'Djamena.

For the dispirited press corps, the daily August coverage of the war consisted of running around the hot and dusty capital from one press briefing to another. The front was several hundred miles away. Reporters were not allowed to go there. So we wrote every day about a war we could not see.

I often thought of Destiny during the cool of the Chadian evenings after the telex machines were shut down and the Chadian censor had gone home. The two weeks in July had been the longest time I had spent with her since she was seven months old. And it was then that I made the decision to come home.

I told Jim Hoagland, the assistant managing editor of the foreign desk, that I no longer wanted to travel. Instead, I wanted to establish a stable, steady schedule with Destiny. Hoagland said that that decision meant I would have to leave the foreign desk. He told me to take my time and write some wrap-up African feature stories while I looked for a new slot in the newsroom.

I did an extensive story on the spreading famine in Africa just before the calamity of 1984 began to receive widespread attention in the media. I also did, over the next three months, political and economic reporting on Africa out of the State Department, the U.S. Agency for International Development, the World Bank, and the International Monetary Fund. I was anxious to move on, however. Writing about Africa from Washington was boring, and it was my conversation with Vernita Fort that started me thinking that an investigation into teenage pregnancy would be of significant value. But how to get into it?

The Post is a newspaper top-heavy with talent. Few openings are left vacant for long. I now had to find a place for myself within this crowded field.

I had to find out, therefore, what if anything had been already written in *The Post*'s news columns about teenage pregnancy and childbearing. I began to talk about the subject with other reporters and editors. I learned that they were aware of the problem, had discussed it with other journalists, or had mulled it over individually. But no one on *The Post* had done the definitive piece on the subject. What had been written about it, up to that point, had come mostly from press conferences and studies issued by government and private organizations.

I had been a reporter at *The Post* since 1966, long enough to know that not every editor has the ability to conceptualize how to tackle such an abstruse subject. I also believed that the daily publishing pressures at *The Post* would make it difficult to pursue the reporting end of the story for long. Editors at *The Post,* at all levels, routinely ask, "When do you expect to finish?" This unsubtle pressure forces you to complete your assignments at the most frenetic pace possible.

I had been through some bruising battles in the past with editors who had forced me to finish my reporting and sit down to write. Nothing that I had been through, however, was to compare to the internal tensions I experienced during the teenage-pregnancy assignment.

First, I had an enlightening lunch with Richard "Dick" Harwood, then the *Post*'s deputy managing editor. Meals with editors are an essential part of getting along at *The Post.* The daily stream of incoming stories and important telephone calls in the newsroom make it a necessity to have a meal at a nearby restaurant if an editor and reporter are to have an uninterrupted conversation. It is generally during lunch or breakfast with editors when reporters work out story ideas, find out what their standing is in the big fishpond of *The Post*'s newsroom, and receive the details of a staff decision that happily moves them forward on their career trail or shunts them aside to Siberia with the office drones. Office politics at *The Post* is some of the best hardball around. Sadly, some of the losers never recover.

The lunch with Dick, a man whom I had always seen as one of *The Post*'s most conservative newsmen, proved to be important. Dick suggested, without any prompting from me, that I take a look at black teenage pregnancy. He counseled that I might check out the investigations desk, a new section that had been created while I was in Africa, as a logical place from which to do the teenage-pregnancy project.

Bob Woodward, whom I had physically worked alongside but did not know, had been made assistant managing editor in charge of the investigations desk. Woodward and Carl Bernstein had done *The Post*'s famous 1972–74 Watergate investigation that toppled President Richard M. Nixon. After Watergate, Woodward had moved through several positions at *The Post* and ended up as the head of investigations. With Dick's suggestion in mind, I began to ask newsroom colleagues about Woodward's operation.

I developed the impression from those conversations that the investigations desk was a small, elite group of reporters doggedly tracking down malfeasance by public and private officials. I was skeptical about whether Woodward or his deputy, David Maraniss, would be interested in the subject of teenage pregnancy among the black poor, because my perception of Woodward was of an energetic, hardworking journalist who was keenly interested in the workings of all branches of the federal government and, most especially, the Central Intelligence Agency. I was unsure if he would see the merit in plunging into a crisis of adolescent childbearing among America's black poor.

The day after my lunch with Harwood, I had lunch with Peter "Pete" Silberman, who was the cigar-chomping assistant managing editor for the national desk and was known to his colleagues as a hard-nosed newsman. I think the last conversation I had had with Silberman was sometime in 1972, a year after my return from the Peace Corps. A group of reporters and editors, Pete and I among them, had been drinking in a bar nearby *The Post*. I had been drunk and railing against institutional racism at *The Post*. I didn't remember what he had had to say that night or if he had said anything.

A month or so later, I and six other black reporters filed a racial-discrimination complaint against *The Post* with the federal Equal Employment Opportunity Commission. The commission later issued a report finding *The Post* to be a discriminatory employer. *The Post*'s management retorted there were errors of fact in the report and refused to conciliate an agreement resolving the issue. The matter has rested there since then after the commission voted not to take the newspaper into court to arbitrate a remedy.

Ever since, I had been labeled a "troublemaker" by several of the newsroom's editors, but my directness on matters of racial inequities at *The Post* did not change.

Now, I was going to lunch with a man with whom I had not had a sober conversation in twelve years. Another editor had forewarned me that Pete would not think much of my story idea on teenage pregnancy and that he did not think a reporter should work on *any* story longer than one day.

I told Pete about my project, and I repeated the warning I had been given that he would be lukewarm to the idea. Pete responded that he had been misjudged.

"I don't think a reporter should work on *any* story longer than three months," Pete said. Then he added in his deadpan manner: "I happen to think your story idea is a good one."

Yet Pete made it plain he was not eager for me to come into his operation to do the story.

Five days later I had lunch with Woodward. I was totally surprised. He was enthusiastic about the idea, the need to take a deep look at this problem, and about me doing it and coming onto his staff. I had completely misread him. I had not realized how broad his interests were.

Next, I had to get on to managing editor Howard Simons's calendar to clinch the move. The earliest available date Howard had open was breakfast on March 16—the morning of my fortieth birthday. I knew from years of working with him that Howard would be receptive to what I wanted to do. His curiosity on a variety of subjects gave reporters the margin for probing way beyond the immediate details of a story.

"Where do you intend to start your reporting?" asked Howard.

I said I would probably begin with some experts, such as sociologists who have studied black life in urban poverty. Then I would add interviews with social workers who worked every day with teenage mothers. At the same time, I would gather statistics from the federal Department of Health and Human Services and then interview some teenage parents, mothers and fathers.

Howard said that the best place to start was the U.S. Census Bureau.

"You'll learn a lot more by beginning with Census Bureau stats," is how I recall his advice. "You should identify where the problem is greatest, among which part of the population, and how it is affecting both blacks and whites."

I thought there was merit in Howard's suggestion. First, I would work through all of whatever raw data existed. I would then interview experts for descriptions of the sociological setting for the project. Only then would I begin interviewing adolescent parents *within the framework of what I had already learned* from the specialists.

Now I see that conventional technique as totally pedestrian.

Neither Howard nor I had thought of moving into a poor community where teenage childbearing is part of the local social fabric. That approach was introduced later.

Next, Howard had to decide to where in the newsroom I should go to do the story.

"If you're going to do it right, you'll have to go to Bob's [Woodward] staff," said Howard. "That's the place to do something like this. Bob is very good at handling something like this. That's settled then. I will tell Bob you're coming to his staff to do it. Finish it in four months. Make it dramatic!"

I moved my papers, books, and notes from the foreign desk over to the investigations desk. I was excited. This assignment was tough and important. Within minutes my enthusiasm evaporated. I was sidetracked to another story.

During the few minutes it had taken to move my files, Ben Bradlee, *The Post*'s charismatic executive editor, came into the investigations section all charged up. He had a story about a slightly built young black woman in St. Louis whose conviction of murdering a six-foot-tall gas-station attendant left many lingering questions about the quality of Missouri justice.

Bradlee suggested that I join a team of three reporters to dig into the facts behind the case. I was not interested in a lengthy investigative piece about the criminal-justice system in St. Louis, but Bradlee described it as a "quickie." David Maraniss, the deputy editor of investigations, overrode my objections. In half an hour, I was making arrangements to leave for St. Louis.

A "quickie" it turned out not to be. Six weeks later, after long days of legwork in Missouri reading through piles of court documents, perusing lengthy trial transcripts, and interviewing numerous people connected to the case, we did a two-part series on St. Louis's criminal system that raised issues of questionable prosecutorial procedures linked to an ineffectual defense.

Of greater concern was that during two brief conversations in the office, Woodward had indicated that he thought my approach was the wrong way to begin examining adolescent childbearing. Woodward said we would discuss his ideas after the St. Louis project was completed.

By mid-June I was ready to begin. But now it was Woodward who blindsided me.

"I think you should move right into a neighborhood and rent a room there," was how Woodward began. I sat upright on the edge of the beige upholstered couch in his small office.

What the devil is he talking about? was my first thought.

Woodward was talking about a methodology that would require much more time than I had anticipated or even wanted to spend. He was insisting that I move into and become a resident of a poor Washington neighborhood to do the story from the ground up, instead of using the orthodox journalistic approach of interviewing experts and then continuing from the top down.

"I think you ought to find a neighborhood in Washington that has what we're looking for and live there," said Woodward without pausing for breath. "You ought to move in and start interviewing people right away. Become known in the neighborhood. Meet people. Talk to people. That is how we ought to do this one!

"Stay away from the experts until you've finished your reporting. Don't talk to *any*! Talk to the people who are experiencing the problem. Find out what they want out of life. What hopes they may have had that they can no longer realize. Everything about them."

The usually phlegmatic Woodward began talking excitedly as he went on. I should limit myself to twelve principal teenagers and do extensive interviews with each, he said. Then interview them again. And again. And again.

It was a technique that Woodward had used successfully in uncovering Watergate and in subsequent investigations. (A year later, Ben Bradlee told me that for his book on the workings of the Supreme Court, *The Brethren,* Woodward had interviewed the clerk of the court sixteen times before the man opened up with some meaningful anecdotes. The clerk probably concluded that Woodward would not leave him alone unless he gave the dogged reporter some information, laughed Bradlee.)

"You should disengage from *The Post,*" continued Woodward. "Don't come in here! Don't come into the office! Don't let me see you in any more pinstripe suits. The next time I see you, you should be wearing jeans!"

I felt a flash of excitement. This was an approach that I had always wanted to use on a domestic story. But the initial enthusiasm was gradually replaced with apprehension. While one part of me wanted very much to do this story in the way Woodward was laying it out, another part of me reacted fearfully to many imagined pitfalls. This method would consume a lot of time. Woodward was still talking, but he seemed to be very far away.

What if this unorthodox method failed? I was asking myself. I would be months into the story before I would know it was not working and at a point where it would be too late to start over with the more conventional technique.

I broke in on Woodward's monologue. "What of Howard's [Simons] warning to have it done in four months?" I asked.

"I think Howard is wrong about four months," said Woodward. "It should take you six months."

This was getting worse. If anyone got the sack for the project taking six months or longer, it would be me! And if the story did not make a significant impact, my effort would be judged a failure. What Woodward was insisting on was very risky. For me!

Chad's fratricidal war suddenly looked inviting. In Chad, I would have been on familiar ground. Here, with Woodward, I was stepping over the edge of a precipice.

"And there was this look you got on your face of like, 'You go there!' " Woodward recalled about my reaction some time later. "What are you talking about?" was written across my face, he remembered. "And talk about resentment," laughed Woodward. My face must be easier to read than I thought it was.

Eight months were to pass from that conversation until the first girl shed her adopted version of accidental pregnancy and told me the truth. Those eight months were among the most stressful of my seventeen years as a reporter. I did not know until that moment that the technique Woodward had outlined for me would work.

Meanwhile, I had started gathering statistics on adolescent child-bearing from the National Center for Health Statistics. They revealed much I had not known. Teenage childbearing among all segments of the American population has been at high levels for quite some time.

I began with 1940 and looked for trends over the years, especially to see if there were demographic links to the rural-to-urban migration of job-hungry blacks from the agricultural South during World War II. Among whites and nonwhites (blacks were not counted as a separate statistical category until 1969), there was a pivotal jump in the birthrates to all teenagers in the postwar years through the early seventies. Significantly, the birthrates for adolescent black girls were disproportionately high in every year.

Almost 55 of every 1,000 American girls under the age of 15 and up to the age of 19 had had a child in 1940. In the same year, there were 45 infants born to every group of 1,000 white teenage girls under the age of 15 and up to the age of 19.

For nonwhite adolescent mothers of the same age range (the overwhelming majority of whom were black), the rate was a disturbingly high 125 babies born to every 1,000 teenage girls.[1]

Thirty years later, in 1970, 58 of each group of 1,000 white teenage girls had babies compared with 153 infants born to every group of 1,000 black adolescent girls. A decade after that, there were 45 infants born to every group of 1,000 white teenagers and 104 born to each group of 1,000 black adolescents. By 1984, the birthrates had fallen further to 43 infants born for every group of 1,000 white teenagers compared to 100 babies born for each group of 1,000 black teenagers.[2]

While the birthrates for both white and black teenagers have steadily declined since 1970, the figures revealed that black teenagers are affected in larger proportions by adolescent childbearing than white teenagers. To me, the birthrates meant that large numbers of black teenagers were adding to their burdens early in life in a world that held them at a disadvantage from birth.

The consequences of this adolescent childbearing appeared to be more devastating than I had imagined. According to official sources: "Babies born to teenagers are more likely to be premature, to have low birth weights, to have low [cognitive] scores and to die within

TABLE 1 *Adolescent Birthrates, 1940–84*
(Births Per 1,000 Women)

YEAR	All Races		Whites		Blacks (and Others*)	
	UNDER 15	15–19	UNDER 15	15–19	UNDER 15	15–19
1940*	0.7	54.1	0.2	45.3	3.7	121.7
1941*	0.7	56.9	0.2	47.6	4.0	128.3
1942*	0.7	61.1	0.3	51.8	3.9	131.8
1943*	0.8	61.7	0.3	52.1	4.0	133.4
1944*	0.8	54.3	0.3	45.3	3.9	121.5
1945*	0.8	51.1	0.3	42.1	3.9	117.5
1946*	0.7	59.3	0.3	50.6	3.7	121.9
1947*	0.9	79.3	0.4	69.8	4.6	146.6
1948*	1.0	81.8	0.4	71.1	4.9	157.3
1949*	1.0	83.4	0.4	72.1	5.1	162.8
1950*	1.0	81.6	0.4	70.0	5.1	163.8
1951*	0.9	87.5	0.4	75.9	5.4	166.3
1952*	0.9	86.0	0.4	75.0	5.2	162.2
1953*	1.0	88.1	0.4	77.1	5.1	164.4
1954*	0.9	90.4	0.4	78.9	4.9	169.2
1955*	0.9	90.3	0.3	79.1	4.8	167.2
1956*	1.0	94.4	0.3	83.1	4.7	171.2
1957*	1.0	96.1	0.5	85.1	5.6	171.4
1958*	0.9	91.2	0.5	80.9	4.3	165.8
1959*	0.9	90.2	0.4	79.7	4.0	165.5
1960*	0.8	89.1	0.4	79.4	4.0	158.2
1961*	0.9	88.6	0.4	79.2	4.0	155.2
1962*	0.8	81.4	0.4	73.2	3.9	147.1
1963*	0.9	76.7	0.3	68.2	4.0	142.6
1964*	0.9	73.1	0.3	63.4	4.0	141.5
1965*	0.8	70.5	0.3	60.6	4.0	138.4
1966*	0.8	70.3	0.3	60.4	4.0	136.4
1967*	0.9	67.5	0.3	56.9	4.1	135.0
1968*	1.0	65.6	0.4	54.9	4.3	132.3
1969	1.0	65.5	0.4	54.7	4.5	131.3
1970	1.2	68.3	0.5	57.4	5.2	147.7
1971	1.1	64.5	0.5	53.6	5.1	134.5
1972	1.2	61.7	0.5	51.0	5.1	129.8
1973	1.2	59.3	0.6	49.0	5.4	123.1
1974	1.2	57.5	0.6	47.9	5.0	116.5
1975	1.3	55.6	0.6	46.4	5.1	111.8
1976	1.2	52.8	0.6	44.1	4.7	104.9
1977	1.2	52.8	0.6	44.1	4.7	104.7
1978	1.2	51.2	0.6	42.9	4.4	100.9
1979	1.2	52.3	0.6	43.7	4.6	101.7

	All Races		Whites		Blacks (and Others*)	
YEAR	UNDER 15	15–19	UNDER 15	15–19	UNDER 15	15–19
1980	1.1	53.0	0.6	44.7	4.3	100.0
1981	1.1	52.7	0.5	44.6	4.1	97.1
1982	1.1	52.9	0.6	44.6	4.1	97.0
1983	1.1	51.7	0.6	43.6	4.1	95.5
1984	1.2	50.9	0.6	42.5	4.3	95.7

*Blacks not counted as a separate statistical group until 1969.

SOURCE: National Center for Health Statistics, *Vital Statistics of the United States,* annual volumes.

the first month and first year of life. Low birth weight (less than five and one-half pounds) is a major cause of infant mortality and also contributes to serious long-term medical conditions such as mental retardation, cerebral palsy, epilepsy, and other birth injuries and neurological defects."[3]

Beyond human and medical costs, teenage childbearing has a direct impact on local and national public-assistance budgets. For example, it has been calculated that approximately 60 percent of the children who are born to unmarried teenagers are the recipients of welfare.[4]

I found other extensive research within the Child Health and Development section of the National Institutes of Health, where Wendy Baldwin, chief of the Demographic and Behavioral Sciences Branch of the Center for Population Research, and her staff annually put together a collection of the center's research findings, entitled "Adolescent Pregnancy and Childbearing—Rates, Trends and Research Findings."

Some of the findings were shocking to me. They were:

- While the overall rates of adolescent childbearing have steadily dropped over the past decade, there was a threefold increase in the number of infants born to *unmarried* teenagers between 1960 and 1983, a frightening leap from a total of 91,700 up to 270,076. Moreover, at least 23 percent of teenage mothers said they intentionally became pregnant. Forty-eight percent of adolescent mothers said later that they regretted the timing of the birth of their first child.

- Early unmarried parenthood is generally tied to reduced educational achievement, marginal income-earning capacity, and welfare dependence. Teenage mothers tend to have larger families by the time they are in their thirties and forties compared to women who had their first child after age twenty. Married teenage couples tend to break up at a higher rate than married adults.

- The consequences of early childbearing become alarming when you look at the impact of teenage pregnancy on the infants of adolescents. The children of unmarried teenage mothers are generally in poor physical health. There is a consistent tendency for the children of teenage mothers to have slightly lower IQ scores than do children of older mothers when the children are measured at several years of age up to age seven. The children of girls seventeen years old and younger are less likely to adapt to the disciplines of school than the children of older mothers. The children of adolescent mothers are at higher risk to be born at a low birth weight and, therefore, at a higher risk to suffer lifelong learning disabilities.

- Children of parents seventeen and younger have lower cognitive scores than children born of parents eighteen years old and older. The children of teenage mothers have a greater chance of living in a disrupted home while in high school, have lower academic aptitude as teenagers, and are at high risk of repeating their parents' pattern of early parenthood. The best predictor of a teenage mother's age at first birth is her adolescent mother's age at first birth.

- Since the early 1970s, an increasing number of adolescents have become sexually active before marriage and at earlier ages. Research reveals that the average lapse of time between the beginning of sexual activity for a teenage girl and her first appearance at a family-planning clinic is six months to a year. For an average of 36 percent of the girls, the inducement for their first clinic visit is the fear that they may already be pregnant. There are more than four hundred thousand abortions for teenagers in America each year.

I also studied data from Washington, D.C.'s Human Services Department on household income levels, rates of births to teenage girls, and welfare-recipient statistics throughout the city to see which neighborhood I should move into. The department's statistics showed a direct tie-in between high rates of teenage pregnancy and poverty levels.

In 1984, among eight city council districts, Wards 7 and 8 had the highest teenage childbearing rates and the largest percentages of residents living in poverty. Here then was one link: Where there was a concentration of the poor, there were high rates of teenage childbearing.

Since the end of World War II, most of Washington's public-housing construction had been crammed into the far corners of these two wards on the east side of the city's Anacostia River. Both wards are geographically isolated from the rest of the city. Most of Washington's lifelong residents do not consider the two wards to be a part of the city. To them, it is another world, where poverty and crime are endemic.

It is a part of Washington that is rarely seen by the congressmen who fly in and out of the capital every day. It is an area of the capital that is virtually unknown to the million tourists who visit each year.

Although the two wards were relatively close in their teenage populations, slightly over 10,200 in each, Ward 8 had the highest birthrate for teenage girls.

In Ward 8 in 1984, 72 infants were born to every 1,000 teen-age girls. Ninety percent of its population was black. Twenty-six percent of its residents were living in poverty, the largest concentration of poor people in the city. The median household income, $12,747, was the lowest in the city. It was obvious: Ward 8 then was the section of the city in which to do the project.

Ward 3, by comparison, was the most affluent ward in Washington with a median household income of $25,167. Only 8 percent of this section's population lived in poverty, 5 percent of the population (in 1980) in this area was black, and the birthrate to adolescent mothers was an extraordinarily low 1.6 infants born to every 1,000 teenage girls.

I looked up neighborhood census data on Ward 8. Within Ward 8, I found a cluster of census tracts where 26 percent of the neighborhood's 19,123 residents were receiving some form of public assistance. I had to look up the community's name, Washington Highlands, on a city map.

It must be one of the most isolated communities in Washington, I thought. I had lived in Washington since 1965, but I had never heard anyone refer to Washington Highlands by that name.

In the same month of June, I attended a speech given by Howard

TABLE 2 *Teenage Births and Poverty in Washington, D.C.*

Areas	Median Household Income in Dollars (1979)	Number of Teens 14–19 (1980)	Birthrate per 1,000 Female Teens (1984)	Percent of Residents in Poverty (1979)	Percent of Black Population
WARD 8	12,747	10,291	72.2	26	90
WARD 1	12,997	7,529	55.3	20	70
WARD 7	14,470	10,340	61.0	23	95
WARD 5	15,262	9,585	50.2	18	89
WARD 2	15,567	6,218	41.7	21	47
WARD 6	16,365	7,424	63.9	19	77
WARD 4	18,970	8,440	36.0	10	87
WARD 3	25,167	6,863	1.6	8	5
D.C.	16,210	66,690	51.4	18	70

SOURCE: Indices, a Statistical Index to District of Columbia Services, U.S. Department of Human Services.

University psychologist Harriette Pipes McAdoo, who spoke about her recent research on teenage childbearing among Washington adolescents.

Two points from her talk stuck with me. One of her two points influenced my choice of where to rent an apartment.

First, McAdoo said that between 50 percent and 70 percent of the teenage mothers in Washington had a second child within two years of their first child. Second, after the birth of their second child many adolescent mothers joined a church for the first time. These child-mothers were seeking an escape from the high stress levels they experienced in raising two babies with very limited means. Religious spirituality provided the emotional release the girls needed to keep them from having a nervous breakdown.

"The girls realize," McAdoo said, "after the birth of their second child that their dreams of the future and their lives [in terms of personal growth] are at an end. Many of them relieve the stress of that realization with religiosity."

Two weeks had passed since Woodward had told me to select a neighborhood and move into it. Now, after gathering the research and poring over city maps, I was ready to begin looking for an apartment in Washington Highlands.

But Woodward was angry. He felt I should have rented a room, preferably furnished, and moved into a poor community the day after he told me that that was how this story was going to be done. Instead, several weeks after that discussion, I presented him with an estimated budget to buy secondhand furniture for a one-bedroom apartment. I did not intend to live in a room in just any poor neighborhood. Tension rose between us.

When reviewing the details of any assignment with Woodward, if his eyes go vacant, you've lost his attention. Forget trying to recapture it. Move on to something else. His attention span became shorter and shorter with me when I explained the details of selecting the neighborhood. On one occasion he became visibly angry and I felt my own temper rise.

Rather than clash, we avoided each other. We put the investigations desk's news aide, Barbara Feinman, between us. Anything that I had to tell him, I told to Barbara over the telephone. She would tell Woodward what I was doing and what I had said. She would pass his polite responses back to me and told me nothing of his angry reactions.

Woodward recalls, "It was the slowest process because you [had] to get an apartment, you [had] to pick the area, get furniture, and it just seemed to go on for weeks and weeks and weeks. And I would say to Barbara, 'Hasn't Leon moved into that goddamn place yet? Tell him to get some furniture and get moved in there and get going on this thing.' "

When I was in *The Washington Post* office building, I would avoid Woodward and talk at length with David Maraniss, the deputy head of investigations, whose glass-walled office was next to Woodward's glass-walled office. Sometimes, after I walked out of David's office, Woodward would go into David's office. If Woodward wanted more details, he could get them from Maraniss. But after I moved into the apartment on July 30, Woodward and I gradually got back on good terms.

Two occurrences later in the assignment illustrate Woodward's tenacious techniques at their best. To be honest, I responded negatively to both of his proposals. Part of the problem was my state of mind. I desperately wanted to finish the story and get it published. I reacted viscerally to Woodward's insistence on additional reporting, a process I thought was wasting time.

From the first weeks of my moving in, my Washington Highlands neighbors reacted to me with the indifferent looks reserved for any stranger in an urban community. But within days of the move, I learned from an upstairs neighbor, one Charles A. "Willie" Hood, that I had attracted attention, that people were wondering who I was and what I was doing in Washington Highlands.

They knew, even from a distance, that I was different. Although I am black, although the neighborhood is overwhelmingly black, it was immediately clear from my clothes and my speech that I was "not from Southeast" Washington, as Hood pointedly put it.

My old jeans and my brightly colored African shirt marked me as someone from another place. And Kimberly Hood, Willie's pregnant wife, thought I was from overseas or perhaps the Caribbean.

Willie and his wife and infant daughter lived on the first floor in the three-story, fourteen-unit building. I lived below them in the basement apartment. They were the first couple I met, the first couple I spoke with. In time, I won their trust, and Willie and I would spend hours walking around Washington Highlands and other parts of Southeast Washington in summer's waning days.

During these walks, Willie, twenty-one, began gradually to open up about his life and his past. He had grown up in the neighborhood, and on one of those long walks, Willie revealed his thoughts about when he first became sexually active in the mid-seventies. He had been sixteen.

"When we hit our teens, everybody got to fucking, fucking, fucking," Willie said. "But that Pill. That Pill hurt our women. That Pill wouldn't let my seed penetrate" to impregnate his fifteen-year-old girl friend a second time following an abortion. Because she would not become pregnant, he said, "I couldn't feel like a man!"

Could adolescents believe that to become a *man* or to become a *woman* one must have a child? I asked myself.

I did not know if Hood's feelings were unique or widespread, but I knew it was not isolated behavior. One Center for Population Research study had found that at least 23 percent of adolescent mothers admitted to intentionally becoming pregnant. When you add to that figure the many adolescents who mask the choice they made behind tales of ignorance and accidents, the final figure on how many of the 420,000 American adolescents who had babies each year actually chose to become parents would be disturbingly high. When even 23 percent of these children *want* children, for whatever collection of reasons, we have a serious crisis facing our nation.

My experience with Hood was repeated, but not as quickly. Hood had been very honest and open about wanting to be a father at age sixteen. The members of the six families that I became close to were not so forthcoming about their motivations as teenage parents. Each person had a false, *adopted version* of how the pregnancy had occurred—something they felt would be accepted by parents and others who were not close friends or peers.

The most common *first* types of excuses, I discovered, were ignorance of how to use birth control, inability to buy birth control, fear of birth control, and a faulty comprehension of how their reproductive powers functioned. Months after the parents had told me the *adopted version,* they would contradict themselves, admitting that the first story had been untrue. They would then unload, going back over hints they had given in their first biographical sketch of their lives. The second or third time, they would tell me the story that was closer to the truth. In the end, I discovered that not a single one had become pregnant out of ignorance or by accident.

Some of the people I interviewed were couples. Some were single parents. Some were people living on welfare stipends. Some were working people living on what little they earned each day. One was an adolescent mother who had been abandoned by her family. What they all shared was poverty and a long legacy of racial oppression.

I had believed, even before I moved in, that the patterns of alienation acted out in Washington Highlands every day parallel the behavior patterns of innumerable other poor Americans. Their poverty is the dominant factor of their lives. Their poverty produces predictable responses, predictable choices.

I also knew that among black Americans I would find another dimension of antagonism. Our American experience has added layers of alienation, starting three and a half centuries ago with slavery, followed by a de jure system of ethnic oppression, then de facto discrimination, and rejection at every level of the larger, white society.

I do not believe any black American, even one born into comfortable levels of economic well-being or privilege, has completely escaped the feeling of alienation. Blacks of different income groups and of varying economic mobility handle the alienation differently, more because one's class often governs one's behavior and outlook, but all blacks can readily agree on the source of the alienation.

In Washington Highlands, one of the many black-adolescent symptoms of alienation from mainstream America is having a child, a rejection of the larger society's value system regarding what is *rational* and *irrational* behavior. The patterns of childbearing were laid down long before the children of Washington Highlands were born. The patterns are viewed by many of them as *rational* responses to human needs, requirements that cannot be met by other means.

Six months later, by January 1985, I was beginning to develop a general understanding of what was going on in Washington Highlands. I was interviewing the members of thirteen different families. Among them were two large families of eleven children, several of whom were teenage parents. I had developed a rapport with the members of six of the thirteen families and a lukewarm relationship with the members of the other seven. It was too much. The project had become unwieldy. I decided to cut the project down to the six families with whom I had the closest relationships.

I set up a luncheon powwow between Woodward, deputy investigations editor David Maraniss, and me at the basement apartment. Neither had been there before. I fixed lunch.

We ate on my rickety, metal-top secondhand kitchen table, which was covered with a cheap red-and-white oilcloth. I made had a large mixed salad with beets (David refused to eat his beets), sliced-turkey-breast sandwiches on bran bagels, and Amaretto-flavored coffee (I ground the beans, a habit developed in Africa).

I told Woodward and Maraniss that I had approached about twenty families. Thirteen had agreed to participate, and seven had refused. Of the thirteen, I had completed most of the interviews with the members of six families. They agreed that I should drop the other seven families and concentrate all of my energy on the six.

Then Woodward told me what he wanted me to do next.

"Leon, you've got to go and interview each person four more times," he said.

"What?" I continued with mounting exasperation: "Bob, each interview is about eight hours and takes up to four weeks to finish. I've gotten them to agree to one two-hour session a week. I can't go any faster!"

"I'm not saying anything about going faster," Woodward continued. "As long as it takes, just keep going at it. Go over the same material, the same anecdotes with them. See what comes out."

I did not know how I should feel as I looked at Woodward. I wondered what more he thought I could possibly get from these sources. If he wanted four more interviews from each of the eleven principal people in the six families, I reasoned, then I could be out here for months more. I was. Twelve months more.

I also had reams of material that I had been personally transcribing. Early in the project, the dictationists at *The Post* had been transcribing my taped interviews, but one of them was offended by the explicit sexual discussions I was having with adolescents, all of whom were either sexually active, pregnant, or parents.

The detailed discussions were necessary to determine at what stage they had a complete understanding of their reproductive abilities. When did they really understand what coitus is? What or who were their information sources?

The discussion of sexuality always came in the last two hours of the eight hours of interviews, in the fourth week. I would start each person from their earliest childhood memory. Each two-hour segment would follow along four lines: homelife, school life, church life (if any), and social life, which included sexual development.

By the time we reached the last category, I had established a friendly relationship with the adult or the teenager. Each person had become comfortable with me and grown accustomed to my style of interviewing and the explicitness of my questions.

In the interviews on sexual development, I would use formal and clinical terms, but was not always understood. When this happened, I would use whatever colloquial word was appropriate.

Generally, there was no embarrassment in this part of the interview. But the dictationist's supervisor complained to Woodward and gave him a copy of a transcription instead of returning it to me. Usually unflappable, Woodward was agitated by the direction in which I was going and wanted to know the purpose.

I explained that if we were going to establish what these children knew or did not know in terms of sexual activity, the questions could not be vague or the responses would be equally so. I felt I had to pinpoint, as best possible, the adolescents' understanding of their sexuality. Woodward agreed, but was not completely convinced I was on safe ground.

I became paranoid. Immediately after that conversation with Woodward, I took back from the dictationists the tapes of interviews with three other teenagers, locked them up in a file cabinet, and decided to transcribe all future tapes myself. At the end of the assignment, I had transcribed 205 hours of taped interviews.

The January day that Woodward told me that I had to conduct four additional interviews with each of the principal people, I still had hours of interviews that I had not yet transcribed. Some of the most intimate details of the lives of the adults and adolescents in these six families were on the tapes. There was nothing more to gain from going over and over and over the same life passages, or so I believed.

I was wrong. I did not know it, but none of the people I had already interviewed had told me the truth. I was still a month away from the first person, Sherita Dreher, telling me the truth in the fifth hour of the third interview. It was an honest, if unflattering portrait of herself that Dreher painted that February afternoon.

I was so excited, I wanted to jump up and shout.

Here it is, I thought. What she is telling me now about manipulating her boyfriend is probably as close to the unflattering truth as I will ever get. The method had worked!

By the second, third, and fourth interviews, all seven of the principal adults and teenagers had begun to contradict their original stories. It had taken four to six months with each person to reach the point at which he or she could tell me the truth.

But Woodward is a very demanding journalist. It is one of the secrets of his success. His last demand came after I had finished all my interviews.

It was now January 1986. A year later. We were days away from publishing my articles. I was uptight. I correctly anticipated a very critical reaction to the pieces from many members of the black middle class who would feel that the stories should not have been published. Blacks believe that whites cannot distinguish differences in class behavior among us. Therefore, they would be angered by a public discussion of behavior that they felt whites would attribute to all blacks.

In those last days before publication, I was on edge, and I had begun to lash back at the sarcasm I had been getting for months from colleagues and editors about how long it was taking to bring the investigation to a close. Most of them did not realize what I had managed to achieve under considerable duress and in the most depressing of circumstances.

David Maraniss, with whom I had shared all of the first twelve months of anxiety, tension, and discovery, had left the investigations desk in August to open *The Post*'s bureau in Austin, Texas. A new deputy editor for the section, Steve Luxenberg, who had been lured away from *The Baltimore Sun* by Woodward, had been reading, editing, and rewriting my material since September. I accepted long ago that I am a reporter who needs an editor, and four months of the process had left me a bundle of nerves.

I had had misgivings about Luxenberg, because he had not been with the project from the beginning and I did not know him. My apprehension had been replaced by trust and admiration. He had turned out to be a superb, sensitive editor. His abilities added considerably to the articles.

Woodward interrupted Luxenberg and me at work one day and called us into his office. I idly wondered what he wanted to talk about. Most of the articles had been reworked and were ready to go. Once more, I was sitting on the edge of Woodward's beige upholstered couch facing the side of his desk. Luxenberg was sitting directly opposite Woodward. Then Woodward began to talk. Again I could not believe what I was hearing.

Woodward said I should do one more interview with at least four of the seven principal personalities. He wanted to close the pieces with the thoughts that these adolescents had about their futures. What were their dreams and hopes, if any? What did they plan to do in the immediate future?

I felt my face flush. This was too much. After months and months of interviews. Months and months of anxiety. He wanted me to do another set of interviews. I know I blurted something unpleasant, but I have not been able to remember what I said. Woodward looked sheepish, but insisted the pieces needed those endings.

I said no more. I went out and did the interviews. After I had included that material at the end of the articles, I saw that Woodward had been right. Those four pieces had needed those endings. I told him so.

On the day *The Post* published the first article, Woodward and I were able to laugh about what had passed between us. And as I paused at my desk to ponder what the future might bring, I reflected on the long, emotionally draining assignment that I had just finished, an assignment that had forced me to do in months what academics spend years working out. Yes, the work had been grueling. But it had been worthwhile, because I had learned a lot from my interviews in Washington Highlands. I had grown professionally, and I had a better understanding of human behavior and characteristics. I could never forget the suffering I was witness to. Now all I could do was hope and pray that I could put what I had learned to good use.

CHAPTER TWO

I REMEMBER THE evening that a soft tapping on the apartment door interrupted an interview. Charmaine Ford, twenty-nine, stopped talking about how she had become a teenage mother, opened the red metal door as far as the chain lock would allow, and peered cautiously into the hallway.

There stood one of Charmaine's neighbors, a six-year-old girl, her cheeks stained with tears, crying so hard that her pigtails shook. Charmaine unlatched the door and knelt down to calm her. Sobbing, the girl said that she had been taking care of her seven-month-old sister since her mother had left early that morning. It was then eight-thirty.

The weeping girl said her mother had just telephoned, but only to say that she was spending the night out. Before hanging up, the mother told the girl to fix a bottle of formula for the baby. Confused, unsure how to make the formula, the girl had panicked.

It was not the first time this had happened. Charmaine often argued with the girl's mother, twenty-three, about leaving the children home by themselves in an apartment on Condon Terrace SE that was only two blocks away from one of Washington, D.C.'s most dangerous street-corner drug markets. Her arguments failed. The woman always said the six-year-old girl was "big enough" to care for herself and the baby. Now the girl was standing in the hallway, her cream-colored dress hopelessly wrinkled and her face contorted by her crying.

Charmaine took the girl back to her own apartment to make the formula. Charmaine's mother, Rosalee Ford, who lives in Charmaine's apartment and had been listening to the little girl's story, turned to me and said: "Left that baby in there by herself. . . . Left that baby with no milk or nothing. I think it's a shame. These young girls having these babies."

It was October 4, 1984, and two months after I rented the one-bedroom basement apartment in Washington Highlands to start my investigation into teenage childbearing. As the scene between Charmaine and the sobbing girl unfolded, I began to understand what had happened. Charmaine filled in the rest.

The mother of the crying girl had become pregnant when she was sixteen. She gave birth to her first child at seventeen. At nineteen, she had a second child, a boy, by the father of the first child. The past March, the young woman delivered a third child by another father who is one of Charmaine's cousins.

Charmaine's mother, Rosalee Ford, had been sitting in on the interview and said it all in her comment: "These young girls having these babies." What I had just witnessed is one of the disturbing consequences of teenage childbearing—children raising themselves.

Several people in Washington Highlands had told me that many adolescent or young-adult parents left their very young children at home to fend for themselves for hours or days at a time. It is a pattern, like much else linked to urban underclass life, with a history stemming from the fact that some young black mothers in the rural South—left alone through divorce, desertion, or death—were forced to leave their children to care for themselves at ages as young as four while they worked in the fields. The practice has followed black country-to-city migrants into America's urban slums.

Up until that October night, I had been somewhat skeptical about this phenomenon of "children raising themselves." But now I had seen it. Later, I was introduced to two other families in Washington Highlands in which the children were raising themselves. I was told by the people who introduced me that these families were merely a small sample of what is happening every day in Washington Highlands.

To me, the long-term implications of leaving children on their own to raise themselves were unnerving. Generations of children were being lost. So, over the course of the year, I searched for answers to turn this situation around.

I had always thought of myself as a hard-bitten reporter who had seen much of the miserable side of human nature in seventeen years of journalism. I felt there wasn't much else that could leave me astonished. I was wrong.

I learned a great deal about what the stresses of a desperate poverty and alienation is producing in America's cities. Teenage childbearing and children raising themselves are but two elements of this alarming story. I discovered seamy parts as well, elements that were difficult to absorb and accept. As hard as it was to write about it, none of it, I believe, should be hidden from the public.

In order to confront it, you have to know what is there. In order to stop it, you have to know what to change. In order to do something about it, you have to know what in the past created it. In order to turn it around, you have to know what continues to feed it. The solutions are not easy, but there is hope.

I entered the community of Washington Highlands on the hot, sunny morning of July 30, when an Anacostia free-lance mover with a rented truck picked up some furniture from my home in Marbury Plaza in Washington and made two stops at nearby secondhand stores for the remaining items I had purchased.

"I know this neighborhood," the mover said a short time later as his two helpers unloaded the furniture in front of 3900 Fourth Street SE. "[Washington Highlands] is an area of lots of young girls and very few men."

After I was moved in, I straightened up the apartment and then left to visit a friend in upper Northwest Washington in the black-middle-class section known as the Gold Coast. I stayed at the friend's house until very late, delaying my return to the basement apartment until after midnight. When I went back, I went straight to bed.

This was my pattern for the next several days. Up early in the morning, take a three- to seven-mile jog followed by a shower, spray the apartment for roaches, and leave immediately, not returning until it was late enough to go directly to bed.

My adjustment to life in the basement apartment was not easy. I felt isolated. I detested the apartment. I was obsessed with exterminating the apartment's roaches. Their crawling presence was a daily irritation. The sooty grayness of the bathtub's center, where the porcelain was worn, gave me the uncomfortable feeling of standing in dirt when I showered.

What would have been just normal anxiety was heightened by the unanswered questions facing me: Would this unorthodox method really get me to some bottom-line answers? Would the people of Washington Highlands accept me?

I was no stranger to poor communities. I had grown up in New York City in a middle-class Harlem enclave called the Riverton, which was surrounded by a public-housing development and dingy, old walk-up tenements. Many of the people in public housing and in the tenements I knew then lived at distinguishable levels of poverty. None of my past had prepared me, however, for my first few days of living in apartment B-1 at 3900 Fourth Street SE. Months later I was able to look back and see why I had felt so alone.

The mile-square Washington Highlands neighborhood is a world unto itself, cut off from even the rest of Southeast Washington by a crescent-shaped swath of grassland called Oxon Run Park. It is a neighborhood of hardworking people, struggling to protect themselves against the drug dealing and street crime that plague the community.

The community is physically and socially far from the areas of Washington that I knew. On a city map, it is in a far corner of the city bordering Maryland. It is dominated by three sprawling public-housing developments. There are several privately owned rent-subsidized housing complexes. A substantial percentage of the run-down public-housing and private-apartment complexes, those that have not been boarded up and abandoned, are slowly being renovated with federal and city funds.

There are numerous churches and day-care centers, but not one supermarket. There are several small stores and two fast-food restaurants, but there is not one industry. There is one elementary school, one junior high school, and one combined elementary-junior high school.

One of every three people living in Washington Highlands exists below the poverty level. It is a community where more families receive welfare payments than in almost any other community its size anywhere else in Washington. It has more teenage parents than almost any other Washington neighborhood. In 1984, one of every four babies in Washington Highlands was born to someone between the ages of thirteen and nineteen.

Drug trafficking is the community's major affliction. The illicit but popular drugs of use at that time, in order of preference, were the following: phencyclidine (commonly known as PCP), marijuana, cocaine, and heroin.

In the first week in the apartment, I could not sit still. I paced the short distance between the apartment door and the bedroom. Outside the apartment's ground-level windows was the bright August sunshine, but little of it shone into the apartment. The apartment was dark and cool, and the coolness did provide welcome relief from the oppressive heat. But the darkness gave me a feeling of being jailed in some murky dungeon of penance.

The daily battle with the roaches added to the tension, although I did manage to laugh at my reaction. Their presence was one of the reasons I chose this apartment. The day I unlocked the steel door to inspect the empty apartment, the roaches did not run. Their reaction told me I was in the right place.

In my Harlem childhood, the presence or absence of roaches was directly tied to the housing you could afford. There were roaches wherever poor people lived. In addition, there was a critical difference between the way families tolerated or did not tolerate them.

The poor families that held on to their personal pride, no matter that their material possessions were few, kept their apartments immaculate. The building they lived in might be infested, but roaches were not seen often inside these spotless apartments. On the rare occasion when a roach sauntered into sight, it usually had to flee for its life.

Other families appeared to be overwhelmed by the conditions of their poverty. The soiled and unkempt condition of their homes reflected a deep despair. Roach infestation was always heavy in these homes and the roaches so numerous that little energy was expended in trying to exterminate them. The roaches were ignored.

In turn, the roaches in the poorly kept apartments became so bold that you had to brush them off a pile of dirty dishes in a kitchen sink to get to a drinking glass. They would appear at any time of day and strut across any piece of furniture, occupied or not. They were not afraid of people.

On the day I inspected apartment B-1, the roaches didn't even run when I walked up close to them!

I waved my right hand over a group of them bunched up on the living-room windowsill. They did not even stir. I pushed them with the blunt end of a pen. They scattered, but didn't run far.

Lines of roaches hung down in single files on the vertical cords of the Venetian blinds. Large roaches crawled slowly across the freshly painted cream-colored walls. The dark hardwood floors, shiny with a new coat of varnish, camouflaged them so well that I didn't see one until I stepped on it.

Roaches like these will crawl up under a pant leg or walk across the back of your hand, I thought. The roaches said it all. They brought to life Washington Highlands's poverty statistics. The person who had lived here before me had been beaten down. That person had given up the struggle and had lived alongside of these roaches. There were now generations of roaches in the apartment that were unafraid of people.

The fearlessness of the roaches was one reason I rented the apartment. The second was the apartment building's location, just two buildings down the street from the Paramount Baptist Church.

Harriet Pipes McAdoo had made a point in a speech that I remembered. Large numbers of adolescent mothers, McAdoo said, turn to religious spirituality for release from the stress they experience after the birth of their second child. McAdoo estimated that considerably more than 50 percent of the teenage mothers in Washington have a second child within two years of giving birth to their first. If such large numbers of adolescent mothers turned to the church, a large number of them must attend Paramount Church, I reasoned. Paramount Church could be my best avenue into the Washington Highlands community of teenage parents.

I did not inspect the apartment long and decided within a few minutes that I would rent it. When I went to let myself out, the inside doorknob turned without releasing the latch. I was locked in.

I fiddled with the knob for a few minutes, but could not get the door open. I yelled for several minutes to see if anyone would come downstairs and open the door from the outside. B-1 was the only apartment in the basement. The only other compartment at this level was the small furnace room next door. No one in the other thirteen units in the three-story building could hear me.

I finally pulled up one of the living-room windows, knocked down the flimsy antiburglar metal grating that covered it, and crawled out of the apartment onto the grass just under the outside ledge. So much for the burglar protection, I chuckled. This was clearly the place I needed to be.

The drive back to the William J. Davis Realty office, in a far corner of Northwest Washington, covered a distance of twelve and a half miles and took forty minutes in non-rush-hour traffic.

As I drove, I wondered how many buses the residents of Washington Highlands would have to take to reach the same realty office. I figured that a one-way bus trip to the Davis Realty office, the company that appeared to manage many of the privately owned low-rent apartment buildings in far-off Washington Highlands, might take all of a morning.

Much of Washington's new rapid transit metropolitan rail system was completed, but construction of the line that would serve Washington Highlands, one of the city's poorest communities, had just started. By contrast, the rail lines serving the affluent Washington communities and the middle-class suburbs in Maryland and Virginia had been operating for almost a decade. Rail service for the residents of Washington Highlands was scheduled to begin in 1990, if local and federal funding was available.

At the realty office, I made out an application to rent the apartment for $267 a month and reclaimed the $35 deposit I had had to leave to get the keys to inspect it. A clerk said they would have the door fixed the next day and that I could move in after they had run a credit check on me. That would take about a week, he said.

I bought a bed, a rickety metal kitchen table with four chairs, a small dresser, and four ugly lamps at two secondhand furniture stores in the nearby Southeast Washington community of Anacostia. At Woolworth's, I bought white plastic end tables for the lamps, a red-and-white oilcloth for the kitchen table, dishes, flatware, and glasses. I donated a brown-and-white checked couch and two chairs of my own for the apartment's small living room.

I kept my two-bedroom apartment in Anacostia at the comparatively luxurious Marbury Plaza complex on Good Hope Road, a fifteen-minute drive from Washington Highlands, because of my younger daughter, Destiny. She stayed with me every other weekend. At my Marbury Plaza apartment, Destiny had her own room. And there were no roaches there.

As part of the project, Bob Woodward and David Maraniss had suggested that I write a weekly letter about the experience. The letters would keep both of them informed of my progress and help me to unload my thoughts. During the year, I wrote thirty letters entitled "Letter from a Basement Apartment." I came into the office late on Sunday night, usually, and wrote a letter for them to read on Monday morning.

Maraniss became worried about me after the first letter. I wrote:

> *I am alienated from the apartment. The battle against the roaches is a constant aggravation. The apartment's windows are at ground level and are just around the corner from the building's*

rat- and roach-infested garbage-can area. The roaches crawl in across the windowsills from the garbage-can area. The hallway also is roach infested, and they come into the apartment under and around the apartment doorframe.

I've accepted that they will always be there—were there before I arrived (in great numbers) and will be there when I move out (must shake out all my clothes). They are accustomed to coexisting with humans. I hope I do not weaken and begin to coexist with them. The new arrivals run from me on sight, so they are not part of the generation I found when I first looked at the apartment. That generation has been, I suspect, wiped out.

The rats don't come into the apartment. They just scurry around out back, running from can to can or into the back of the building when I empty my garbage. There is always garbage spilling out of the cans onto the muddy ground around the garbage-can area.

The building is full of small children stuffed into thirteen one-bedroom apartments. There are a number of apartments with two single women with four or five children between them. The garbage pickup is probably not as often as it should be. Children use the stairways and hallways as a playground. They leave stairways and hallways dirty with bits of hamburger, greasy fried-chicken cardboard cartons, candy wrappers, and melted ice-cream drippings. There is no other place for them to play unless a parent takes them out. Hallways are a great breeding ground for the roaches.

By the first Friday night (August 3), I had adjusted to the oppressive atmosphere of the apartment and did some early evening reading. My choice, of all things, was Franz Kafka's "The Metamorphosis," a short story about Gregor Samsa, who one morning awakes to find himself transformed into some sort of bug. All I could see Samsa as was a brown roach, although the Samsa family's charwoman called him a dung beetle.

My sense of isolation has begun to diminish, I think, because my neighbors have begun to acknowledge me as part of the landscape. This acknowledgment comes in nods and gestures, but not much else as yet. Those neighbors who are seeing me for the first time greet me with noncommittal, open-eyed stares or glances of hostility. Hostility and surliness is the standard greeting for a stranger in this world until one gets the measure of the new person. This experience is like crossing a tribal border.

Male machismo is alive and well in this poor section of Washington. It probably gives the females a much needed boost as well as no end of grief from the males that approach them in public places and on public transportation. I've been watching the encounters with some amusement. They take me back to my childhood in Harlem and what peer pressure taught us we were supposed to be able to do with a smooth line. I think machismo may play a strong role on the male side of teenage pregnancy. The self-questioning about the need for male machismo seems to be a middle-class phenomenon and may have little to do with poor males.

The male youths are sporting a new style of haircut that I have not seen anywhere else in Washington. This is truly a community apart from the rest of the city. Must find out what its name is. The cut is close on the sides and gradually sweeps up into a squared-shaped pompadour. The girls have taken the cornrow hairstyle of Africa and included bangs and brown beads, the ubiquitousness of which reduces it to the boring.

I hope to invite one or more of my neighbors into my place next week, but will choose an opportune moment. I don't want it to appear forced or rushed. I imagine I will have to offer them something to drink, so I'll have to put some beer in the refrigerator and buy a couple of bottles of whiskey. I do not drink alcohol, but I would like to have it available for neighborhood visitors.

This project is turning out to be very exciting. I'm looking forward to getting into the meat of it. I just hope that like Kafka's hero, Samsa, I don't wake up one morning to find that I have been transformed into a roach (smile).

After Maraniss read my letter, he went to Woodward to say that sending me to live in Washington Highlands might not have been such a good idea.

"Why?" Woodward replied.

Maraniss said, "Because, you know, Leon here has worked his way up the ladder to a position of stature and respect and economic income, and we have asked him to go back to, well, to move into the worst neighborhood, into a terrible apartment and kind of adopt all of the accessories of poverty."

Maraniss came up to me in the office several days later on one of the weekdays I was in the office. He looked genuinely worried. I did not know, at that time, about his conversation with Woodward.

"Leon, are you too isolated out there?" Maraniss asked.

"No, Dave," I said, laughing.

I told him that I had felt that way in the first week. I apparently had been successful in capturing my dark mood in that first letter, but I assured him that I was now comfortable in the apartment, had killed almost all of the roaches, and was beginning to establish relationships with people in the neighborhood.

Maraniss looked relieved.

Still, throughout my yearlong residency, there were many moments of deep frustration and near despair. At times, I felt that Washington Highlands was so locked and hidden away that I would never get to its core. Worse, almost every person I met or introduced myself to reacted to me with anger and suspicion.

At times later on, I wanted to turn off the flow of information and not learn any more than I already knew. One night I got a splitting tension headache after listening to one high school girl's story of a brutal rape she had endured. Her story was followed that same night by another tale of rape. In pursuing the second story, I learned about the trauma of incest and sexual abuse—more that I wanted to know. My transcript of the interview with the high school girl reads as follows:

> Tony tugged gently on her arm. Disbelieving at first, then angered, she jerked away from him. Thirty-year-old Tony was like a brother to the sixteen-year-old Ballou High School sophomore. What is he trying to do? she asked herself, beginning to worry about his behavior. Tony had just finished smoking his third home-rolled cigarette of "loveboat."
>
> Earlier that day, after her classes at Ballou, Tony volunteered to drive her from southeast Washington to the suburban Maryland Landover Mall so she could do some shopping. When she finished, Tony asked her to ride with him over to his cousin's nearby apartment. Tony said he wanted to get something. She easily agreed. Tony was her oldest brother's best friend, a man she trusted.
>
> The something Tony wanted turned out to be "loveboat," cigarettes of marijuana sprayed with phencyclidine, commonly called PCP. The potent marijuana-PCP combination is known as "loveboat," "lovely" (pronounced "lülē"), "boat," and "buck naked," among many other names, on the streets of Washington.

Tony began to act strangely after his second cigarette. She had turned down his offer to join him. Although she smoked marijuana occasionally, she did not like to smoke PCP because of its reputation of radically altering the behavior of the user. She had seen too many friends lose control of themselves and take an unpleasant "trip" after smoking "lovely." She preferred to smoke marijuana because she felt she remained in control of herself.

By the time Tony had lit up the third cigarette, she had asked him several times to drive her back home. It was getting late. The winter twilight was darkening into night. It was January 1983. She tried again to get Tony to leave. To take her home. He ignored her. She became angry.

She got up from the couch without a word and strode purposefully toward the apartment's front door. She could catch a taxi outside, she thought. She didn't hear him, but rather felt his powerful grip on both her arms. She did not have time to turn, speak, or scream.

Tony threw her to the floor. The earlier gentleness was gone. She sensed a desperation in him. He tightened his hold with an intensity that hurt. He twisted her arm behind her back, pushing her face into the floor's wooden squares. Fear washed over her. She pleaded with him not to hurt her. She had $250 in her pocketbook. She told him to take it. She would walk back home.

Tony was not interested in her money. "You're so sexy and fine!" " she heard him hiss through her mounting hysteria. "You've got a fine shape. A fine body. I want you. I've been wanting you ever since I first seen you" several years before. The girl now understood that Tony had been waiting for this moment for a long time, had won her trust over the years, and now had her trapped in this apartment. She asked what would happen if his cousin walked in. Tony told her his cousin was out of town.

She tried to remind him of what he was to her. "I've always looked up to you," she wailed. "What's wrong with you? Is the stuff [phencyclidine] getting to you that bad?" His response was a hard slap to the side of her face. Tony was suddenly someone she did not know. "I started to cry. I was so hysterical. I didn't know what was up."

She told him that she was a virgin, that she could not do

anything with him. "Well, I'm going to do something," Tony
hissed. He ripped her shirt off. He pressed his knee into the
base of her spine. He put the blade of a knife against the
back of her neck, threatening to cut her throat if she
screamed.

He pulled her by her hair into the apartment's one
bedroom. "A lot of my hair came out," she recalled. There
was a mattress on the floor. He threw her down on it. "And,
you know, he had took and pulled my pants off. And I
kicked him in the mouth. And he took his fist and knocked
me out. He just punched and punched me. I didn't know
anything until, you know, it was daylight coming in."

She was naked. Her face felt swollen and her scalp
throbbed where the roots had been ripped out. She moved to
get up, then doubled over. There was a searing pain in her
womb. She looked down at the sheet. She was bleeding.
Hemorrhaging. "It hurt. It hurted me so bad!"

Tony threatened her. "He told me that if I say anything,
just remember him. That he will always be around." She
notified the police anyway. An aunt who had accompanied her
to the hospital had insisted. A police detective warned her and
her aunt of the courtroom situation the girl would face. He
said that she could be blamed, that Tony could say she came
into the apartment and willingly went to bed with him. "So I
didn't press charges. I just let it go."

She spent two and a half weeks at Georgetown University
Hospital, where the brutality of her ordeal was replaced with
an acute fear. Doctors told her her internal injuries were
severe enough to keep her from having children. After her
release from the hospital, the fear persisted. It was a worry
that plagued her day and night. It was unfair that she should
be left barren, she pouted. She had not done anything wrong.
She had been the victim. She began to wonder if she would
ever conceive.

In April, three months after the rape, she began dating a
twenty-one-year-old man. She saw him as a friend. They
made love. She knew about contraceptives, but chose not to
use any. She became pregnant after the first time. The
pregnancy lifted her fear of being barren, of being less than a
woman. The pregnancy meant she was whole. She turned
seventeen in May.

> *As the pregnancy grew, she lost interest in the father of her child. She had never had deep feelings for him. He was light-skinned and handsome, so her child would probably be a lighter shade than her coffee-brown complexion. And that was OK with her. As a couple, they drifted apart. She stayed in school, completed her sophomore year, and in the fall, moved on to her junior year. At the end of November 1983, she became the mother of a baby boy.*

This interview occurred during my third two-hour interview session with the girl.

I had asked her, "So when was your first sexual experience?" She began telling me of the rape. I interrupted her. "I can see by your eyes this is very painful for you. Let's talk about that some other time. Why don't you tell me about your first sexual experience," I said.

"This *is* my first sexual experience!" she replied, saying she had been looking for a confidant for some time. After our second interview session, she had decided that I was the person she could share some of her pain with.

Her family's apartment was always in chaos. There were thirteen people squeezed into a small four-bedroom apartment in the housing development. Besides the girl, her mother, and her stepfather, there were six small children—her eleven-month-old son and five others —a thirteen-year-old younger sister, and three unmarried older sisters. Two of the older sisters were the mothers of the five children. Each of these two mothers had dropped out of Ballou High School several years earlier when pregnant. The girl had four older brothers, but they had moved out of the home in their early teenage years.

Within the family, only the girl's mother and the aunt who helped the girl knew about the rape. The girl's mother had warned her that her brothers might kill Tony if they learned about the rape. Keeping it secret from the brothers meant keeping one or several of them out of jail for murder. She could not trust her sisters to keep the story to themselves, so they also were not told.

During her narrative of the rape, whenever anyone came into the kitchen, I would have to shut off the tape recorder and we would begin talking about something else. The girl's son would wander in and out, periodically demanding his mother's attention. The television was blaring in the adjacent living room. Her two sisters repeatedly slapped, pinched, and yelled at their progeny. One of these five children was always crying. The general bedlam made it difficult to hear and record the girl's narration, and what could have been told in twenty minutes in a private setting took us two hours to get through. When I stepped out of her apartment building that night my head was throbbing painfully.

Only a few days earlier, I had received an award for international reporting in Africa from the Capitol Press Club. Marian Wright Edelman, director of the Children's Defense Fund and also a recipient of an award that evening, was seated next to me on the dais. Edelman said Donald Graham, publisher of *The Post,* had told her to make me tell her what I was doing. I did so, and she encouraged me to see the project through. She explained that her fund is in the forefront of trying to turn around the incidence of teenage pregnancy in all communities as well as alerting the American public to the needs of adolescent parents and their children.

"Don't rush it!" I remember her telling me. "Take as long as you need to get to the bottom of it. The reasons are very complicated."

But on the night I finished the interview about the rape, I wondered just how far I should go. By this time, I was dividing my time among the members of thirteen different families. In two families alone there were eleven children, several of whom were teenage parents. My headache was telling me that I could not be everyone's confidant.

Moreover, if the rape victim was willing to tell me about such a brutal aspect of her life so early into the interview process, what more would I learn as I began to peel away the layers of her public self and get more into the private person? She had hinted there was a lot more she wanted to tell me, to unload onto me, some of which she would not mind seeing published and some of which would have to remain between the two of us. However, we never went any further. Soon afterward she dropped out of the project on her own volition.

After leaving her apartment, I went to dinner with one of the first women I had interviewed to celebrate the completion of the first eight-hour interview. She was in her early thirties and had given birth at age fifteen. We went to a popular Szechuan Chinese restaurant in downtown Washington.

After the waiter took our order, I told the woman that I might not be the best of dinner company because of my headache. I explained that one of the girls in the project had told me earlier of a rape she had endured.

"Well, I didn't tell you, but I was raped, too!" she responded. I groaned.

While we ate, the woman plunged into a harrowing story of a gang assault on her and four of her junior high school girl friends. Several weeks later, I recorded the tale during an interview session. She had been thirteen years old. It was a rape that plagued her life almost two decades later.

I did not want to hear the cruel tale, but I could not stop her from talking. She had chosen to share some of the really unpleasant parts of her life, matters she had kept hidden from me in the first interview. She was just beginning to feel comfortable enough to peek from behind her mask. I could not stop her now!

The five schoolmates decided to "hook" afternoon classes after lunch one beautiful, blue-sky spring day. They agreed to walk one of their girl friends into another neighborhood to pick up a sweater at the home of one of the girl's mother's friends. After they were invited into the house by a young man, they discovered that none of the women of the house were home. All five were attacked by a group of young males, the woman told me.

Over the background screams of her girl friends, the woman continued, she was attacked in the blacked-out kitchen of the house by one of the men. "This is what happens to young girls when they play hooky from school," she said he told her. She kept pushing him away. He began to slap her with the open palm of his right hand across her face. Tiring of that, he punched her with his fist and knocked her to the dirt-stained linoleum-covered floor. The two tussled as he tried to pull her dress up and she pulled it down. He hit her with his fist again and she passed out.

"I don't know anything after that," she said. "When I woke up, my girl friends had on their clothes. I think they helped me up. I was a little sore."

The man who had let them into the house and had attacked her threatened to "kill us" if they told anyone about the attack. It was already close to 3 P.M. Her mother was due home at 4 P.M. so she rushed home and got into a hot tub. "I remember scrubbin' myself so hard, I was scrubbin' the skin off," she said.

> *At school the next day, all five girls agreed not to tell anyone because "people [would] think it our fault 'cause we were there in his house" when they were supposed to be in school. Several months before the attack on her, another young girl had been gang raped at night in a playground near her house. The neighborhood girl got pregnant after the rape.*
>
> *So rape, incomplete or not, meant pregnancy and perhaps venereal disease to her as a thirteen-year-old, the woman said. She went to a free city clinic next to her school for an examination. A doctor there told her that she was "just a little torn," gave her a cream to aid the healing, and said she was not pregnant and had no diseases.*

She sought help from a female school counselor whom she trusted as a big sister. Later, I tracked down the counselor, Allean Brown, who had retired in 1977 but remembered the girl coming to her. Brown did not remember the particular details of the attack. (Up to the time the woman told her story to me she had never told her mother.)

"There were so many girls who came to me with so many problems," including sexual assault, Brown said. More girls suffered assaults than were willing to seek help, said Brown. "The main thing about it, the girls didn't tell. There was something wrong with you if it were known you were the victim of a sexual attack. You'd been spoiled. You couldn't tell it," she said.

According to Brown, the boys accused of raping a girl would say, "Oh, I was just playing with her" or "Her dress was too short. She parades herself." Often, the boys got away with assault, Brown recalled.

Almost all of the children at Brown's junior high school came from very poor homes. These were homes in which the mother was struggling from day to day to make ends meet. And it was here that a seamier side of sexual abuse surfaced, because in these homes a working man, husband, or boyfriend was all there was between shelter or being put out on the street. In a number of cases, if the man chose to sexually abuse the family's children, the mother would turn a blind eye toward the abuse or "totally deny to herself" that it was happening.

The girls would come to Brown, "but many times you had to coax it out of them." They wanted to talk but would start out very vaguely about what was bothering them.

"Many times I would suspect, and so often it was the father. Blood father. That's a mess! And sometimes the mother was in the home, but she was unsympathetic to what was happening. [The mother] didn't want to break up her home. Here was a man who was supporting that home." The mother would be aware that the daughter was being abused. "And sometimes [the mother] was afraid to say anything."

Sometimes, the mother would tell the girl that she did not believe her or tell the girl not to parade herself in front of the father. "Mothers made no attempts to prosecute. He was taking care of the family, and this was her living. Sometimes, the mother would ask if we could take the girl outta the home! Take *her own daughter* out of the home so she could stay with *that* man!"

In one case, Brown said, a mother had a nervous breakdown before it was revealed that her daughter's father would make the daughter disrobe, beat her, and then rape her. "[The] authorities seemingly were reluctant to even handle cases like that. Because there was no place to send the girl. The city was not taking on the responsibility."

There also was a case of young, pre-school-aged boy being abused by the boyfriend of his mother, Brown continued. The boy's older brother was at the junior high school and went to a male counselor about it. The boy had been taught to commit fellatio on the boyfriend, and the boy would cry when not allowed to do it. The child was taken out of the home through court intervention because the mother would not intercede to protect her son.

After the woman I interviewed came to Brown about the gang assault, Brown took her to see a black female psychiatrist. After school, sessions with the psychiatrist were continued once a week for about two months. Toward the end of the sessions, the girl grew increasingly angry with the psychiatrist, who was a brown-skinned black woman.

The woman said she sensed the psychiatrist looked down on her because she is dark-skinned and is from a poor family.

"The psychiatrist made me feel that it wasn't the guy's fault," the woman told me. "It was my fault. As if I had enticed him on." She said she told the psychiatrist, "It never entered my mind that this shit would ever happen to me. I was as cautious as cautious could get" about protecting herself from sexual assault. "Hell, you here to make me feel worse

than I am. That's the reason I didn't want to come here in the first place."

The psychiatrist responded, "Well, you know how little black girls are!"

After that session, the girl complained to Brown about the psychiatrist's attitude, and the counseling sessions were ended.

Former counselor Brown said she did not remember the girl's complaints but added that the experience she related is consistent with the "attitude at the time," even for a black female psychiatrist. "The girl would end up at the brunt of the thing," said Brown, sighing.

When I met her, the woman was still having flashbacks to the attack in the blacked-out kitchen, particularly when men of short acquaintance tried to hug her or became sexually suggestive. "They put me on edge," she said. Is this man gonna pull this shit this other one did? she begins to think.

The attack has stayed with her all through her adult life. During sexual intercourse, she said, she insists on the lights being on. On occasion, she suddenly has begun to scratch, bite, and punch the male if he turns out the lights without forewarning her. Darkness brings back the strongest memories of the rape.

My relationship with my two daughters and close friends became a welcome respite from the misery and pain I had begun to record. With the passage of time, the biographies of the people of Washington Highlands did not get any better. What changed was my ability to handle the information.

Destiny, my younger daughter, was four going on five in the summer of 1984. I visited her at her mother's home in the Maryland suburb of Silver Spring one night each week and brought her to my home every other weekend. I was able to forget the project and focus just on her whenever we were together. On the weekends she stayed with me, we lived at my legal residence at Marbury Plaza, where she had her own bedroom, rather than at the basement apartment. We often visited the basement apartment. I had explained to her that this was an office I was using to do a story, in order not to confuse her about where I lived. She accepted that explanation in the way little children accept a direct, simple explanation. In fact, she said my office was "the best office" she had seen. It had a record player, a radio, a kitchen, and a shower to wash off the chlorine from the neighborhood swimming pool.

One of Destiny's favorite activities is swimming, and we went to the Oxon Run Park city pool, located just two blocks from the basement apartment. On Saturdays, we went after lunch and stayed until the pool's 6 P.M. closing. We then went back to "my office" to shower and eat dinner. Destiny thought I was fortunate to have such a pool so near to my office.

Periodically, I was invited by any one of the six families to participate in a family event at their homes or to come by to share a special holiday meal, as Destiny and I did with Charmaine and Rosalee Ford Christmas Eve. Moreover, on different Sundays, Destiny and I attended all three churches frequented by the six families. In this manner, she met everyone in the project.

Our social visits were a welcome break from the routine of the project.

I did not see Darla, my older daughter, as much. She was living in a dormitory near Howard University's campus. When we were able to spend time together, however, Darla's interests provided a different type of release from the project for me.

She was entirely focused on her college life, of course, and the experiences she recounted caused me to reminisce, pleasantly, about my days at Howard. On a number of occasions, I had to break off from what I was doing in Washington Highlands to go help Darla through one of her passages. Two of the most upsetting occasions for her—the temporary breakup with a boyfriend and the rejection of her first application to join a sorority—I saw as important learning experiences about handling life's disappointments. On these occasions, I repeated one of my mother's favorite sayings: "It's a great life if you don't weaken!"

I shared with Darla the details of the lives and histories of some of the people I was interviewing. The experiences I chose to share with Darla were the truly traumatic events, usually the most recent stories I had been told. Alongside these tales, her difficulties appeared minor. She was able to compare what she was undergoing with some grim possibilities.

Sharing the details of what I was learning with friends became extremely important to me. I gradually realized that retelling the stories allowed me to unwind and reduce the tension in me.

One friend, Taft Howard "Chuck" Broome, is as insatiably curious about human behavior as I am. Chuck was one of my college roommates and is an engineering professor and an assistant dean at our Howard University alma mater. His lady friend was a Baltimore social worker. She already knew much of what I was just learning about teenage childbearing and the lives of the urban poor. The three of us talked for hours about my project one frigid winter night.

Ronald P. and Jackie Walker are two other friends with whom I could talk about the project. Ron and I grew up in the same Riverton building in Harlem, 2235 Fifth Avenue. I had moved in with my parents at age three, and Ron had moved in days after his birth in Harlem Hospital just across the street. He was now a certified public accountant in Washington.

One Sunday morning, driving down Connecticut Avenue Northwest, I suddenly felt an urge to talk and turned onto their street. I banged on their front door, and later over a brunch of coffee and pancakes, Ron and Jackie plied me with questions about the lives of the people of Washington Highlands. I unloaded. I left their house in the early evening.

Karen E. Williamson was another helpful questioner and listener. We spent many hours talking by telephone, something I do not usually do. Karen had grown up in St. Louis in a middle-class black family and often was shocked by what I told her, but she listened.

Numerous discussions with Dyann A. Waugh, my first wife and one of my best friends, provided examples of identical behavior on the part of poor people—white and black—whom she treated in a Baltimore clinic. Dyann is an occupational physician, a relatively new medical specialty that includes preventing industrial accidents and treating on-the-job injuries. At the Baltimore clinic, her patients, especially the men working as general laborers in construction, exhibited the same customs and attitudes as the people in Washington Highlands. We were able to compare notes and anecdotes about her patients' attitudes toward time, dates, and the women in their lives.

My interactions with my daughters provided a periodic, needed retreat from the project. The lengthy discussions I had with friends, especially responding to their questions, helped me to analyze much of the material I was gathering. When I explained the underlying motivations for adolescent childbearing I put myself at a distance from the material, and my ability to handle some of the trauma of their lives improved.

CHAPTER THREE

OCCASIONALLY, I FELT the need to discuss what I was doing and learning with someone else. I sought to include as many people as possible, thinking I would gather a range of intelligent interpretations, observations, and responses to the anecdotes I recounted. I discovered, however, that I was not able to discuss what I was learning in Washington Highlands with a wide circle of friends and acquaintances. Only a few middle-class blacks were interested in conversing about black teenage childbearing and the life-styles of the black poor.

A number of people were just angered by the subject of black-adolescent childbearing. Their reactions caused me to grow increasingly selective about the people with whom I shared my information or from whom I sought feedback. I found most middle-class professional people, white and black, opinionated, judgmental and antagonistic toward the people I was describing. Part of their reaction was linked to any open discussion of sexuality, an area of human behavior about which people have a host of hang-ups. I knew a number of my friends would not understand the need to write about teenage childbearing among the black urban poor. I foresaw that many of the black middle class would be upset by this inquiry. They would feel vulnerable: tied to the behavior I would be describing. Their worries were justified because the larger, white society would identify the behavior of the underclass with them.

I expected a heavy load of criticism given the subject, but it would come later, after publication, and probably produce a bandwagon effect among the many who would argue that mine was "negative" information rather than a journalistic portrayal of life.

In the meantime, I sought out kindred people of inquiring minds and open personalities; people with whom I could discuss case histories and learn from their analyses. People who could listen and ask the right questions, forcing me to go deeper into what I was seeing in order to arrive at an interpretation. There were very few.

One of these rare people was a man I knew only casually, James O. Gibson of The Rockefeller Foundation. We had had one previous conversation of several hours in the early seventies. That talk had ranged from the possibility of financing a local Washington newspaper to the redevelopment of the city's neighborhoods left in lingering ruin by the 1968 riot.

I ran into Gibson in the street in the winter of 1984, a time when he was an official with the Meyer Foundation. I told him what I was doing. Immediately, Gibson wanted to know what the adolescents I talked to were thinking about. His questions were open-ended and did not reflect any biases picked up from previous studies he may have read or prior conversations he may have had. Outside of his questions, Gibson did little talking and mainly listened. I remember thinking, Here is a man who is not contemptuous of open inquiry. He wants answers even if these answers contradict the findings of the experts. It's amazing. He does not have an agenda!

We ended up talking in his office.

Gibson is intensely interested in closing the traps of poverty for the black underclass. He is not self-conscious about being black and, therefore, unconcerned about the labels whites may draw from the desperate actions of poor blacks and then apply to all blacks.

The first time we talked, I shared with Gibson the adolescent attitude of Charles A. "Willie" Hood: that one becomes a man by having a child. Gibson said he wanted to know more. He wanted to set up monthly meetings with me; him; Marian Wright Edelman, director of the Children's Defense Fund; and Eleanor Holmes Norton, former head of the Equal Employment Opportunity Commission, to discuss my findings. Edelman and Norton are actively involved in programs to turn around the incidence of adolescent childbearing. But Gibson's idea was unworkable given our schedules. He did manage to put together one evening meeting for three of us —Gibson, Norton, and me—one year after his monthly-meeting proposal.

Nevertheless, Gibson's enthusiasm and the support of a few other people were important to me because I knew that there were some people who would be interested in what I published.

In other instances, I blundered, misjudging what the person's reaction would be. After a number of my approaches only angered people, I shared less and less of what I was grappling with with fewer and fewer people. Most people were not even curious, and too many were offended by the details.

A black female free-lance photographer I know asked me casually one day in *The Post* cafeteria what I was working on. I replied, "Teenage pregnancy." She was curious at first but became incensed when she realized I was interviewing black families. She attacked my right to do so by asking, "Were you a teenage father?"

Color consciousness, an antipathy among light-skinned blacks toward dark-skinned blacks, is another sensitive area. This prejudice began as far back as slavery when the offspring of a white master and slave woman, generally lighter in complexion than the field hands, automatically qualified for better treatment. If these children retained the status of a slave, they became house servants and saw themselves as a cut above the field hands. They might even be emancipated by their father and become members of the town-dwelling "free coloreds" of the antebellum South.

Among poor urban blacks—those who were generally passed over by the internal self-evaluation the civil rights movement of the 1960's and 1970's—color consciousness, or being "color struck," continues as an overt social consideration.

When I began circulating among the families of Washington Highlands, I was surprised by the prevalence of color consciousness. I also was surprised by how people discussed their preference for a light-skinned or a dark-skinned mate, ascribed particular negative behavior toward people of specific shades of color, regardless of gender, and used skin color conspicuously as a manipulative tool.

I discussed this persistent color consciousness one March day in 1985 with an old friend, a man I have known since the mid-sixties in New York City. He had raised himself from age eleven in Farmville, Virginia, and had worked hard to earn a master's degree in psychology from New York University. A widower, he was raising his three children in middle-class comfort outside Washington in Fairfax County, a high-income northern Virginia suburb.

Our habit had been to discuss, disagree, and argue about anything and everything in American or international life. We often loudly disagreed with one another.

I contend that his analysis is always faulty because it is fear-laden and, therefore, blocks his ability to listen to anyone but himself. For his part, he feels I expend too much energy pushing beyond the conventional limits of journalism, intruding on dangerous situations just to satisfy my curiosity with a close-up view of anything I am interested in and exposing too much of what I have learned, seen, gathered, and experienced for the public to read.

He feels that black journalists should be willing to withhold information perceived as detrimental to the interests of our ethnic group. In the past, he has become infuriated with me for saying that the public has every right to know everything I know about any given subject and there is *no* area in which I would practice self-censorship.

To do so, I had told him, would be to follow in the footsteps of the self-serving Negro journalists of a generation ago. They prided themselves on keeping news about blacks to themselves, more as gatekeepers of the black community and powerbrokers in both black and white society.

This winter day, as we fixed dinner for ourselves and his children in his kitchen, he asked, "What are you going to tell me about teenage pregnancy that I don't already know? I lived it in Farmville. I saw it with kids I worked with in New York. What more can be said about it?"

I thought he might know more than I had learned, since he had worked with a large group of poor adolescents in New York in the 1960s as part of his master's degree study. Without telling him her name, I began with Sherita Dreher's story, a girl who just a week before had told me how skin color had played the deciding role in her conscious choice to get pregnant at fifteen. She had tried to hold on to a light-skinned boyfriend with her pregnancy.

"What's new about *that*?" he sputtered over the salad bowl. "Girls and women have always gotten themselves pregnant to hold on to a man. Sometimes it works, and sometimes the man walks away. That's not behavior limited to poor blacks. Women all over the world do it!"

Once again, I told him, he had not listened. "But if you're going to sputter over the salad, why don't you let me mix it before we get into our argument." As he passed me the salad bowl, I continued.

This girl, I said, wanted to hold on to not just any man, but to a light-skinned man because that provided her status and prestige in her Washington Highlands community. She has a visceral dislike of dark-skinned black men. She is attractive, but has low self-esteem because she is dark-skinned. She and one of her sisters feel that dark-skinned men lie more often than light-skinned men and that light-skinned men with straight hair are better looking than dark-skinned men with kinky hair. Light-skinned men, however, are more apt to manipulate girls and women because they are highly prized, Sherita and her sister said.

"You're sure she just didn't want a light-skinned child?" my psychologist friend asked. "That is what was done in the past. You married someone lighter so your children would be lighter and could more easily make it in the white man's world."

I knew all of that, I responded. "No, the color of the child did not matter to this girl," I continued. "She wanted a child, a child of any color, a child who she thought would help her hold on to her boyfriend."

"Oh, you're going deep," my friend quietly responded. And then came the explosion. "Wait a minute! You're not going to write that, put that in the [news]paper?" he demanded.

"On the front page, if I can get it there!" was my answer.

"But you can't," he shouted. "White people know enough about us without knowing that, too. You're doing damage to us, man." I had been wondering how long it would be before I heard the "damage-to-the-race" pressure tactic.

Whites already made color-conscious distinctions. I reminded him of newspaper employment ads for domestic help of years past wherein it was specified, "Dark-skinned Negroes Need Not Apply." Such color-conscious discrimination among white employers had made lighter skin an economic premium. The lighter your shade, the more chances you had of being employed.

"I was raised in the South. I know more about that than you do, but if you write that about those girls you'll just be adding to it," my friend continued.

"I'm writing about something that already exists," I said. "By writing about it, I do not add to it. If I know that a person's low self-esteem, even self-hate, leads that person to the conscious choice to have a child, don't you think the public should? Don't you think the public should know that it is not welfare payments that are motivating these children to have children? That it has more to do with the alienation blacks feel? More to do with blacks looking at themselves through the eyes of whites? Don't you want the myth of welfare payments debunked?"

"Yes," he shouted, "but not by telling them about color consciousness among blacks. Anything but *that*!"

By now, we were into our standard heated argument. His three children, having witnessed this scenario before, ignored the two of us and sat down to dinner. We served the dinner, cleared the table and washed and put away the dishes without missing a beat—except to respond to some query from one of the children—in our relative positions. We argued far into the night; our positions remained unchanged.

When the series was published almost a year later, he became furious with me all over again. Our friendship did not survive, and as I write this section, I have not been in touch with him for almost two years.

SHERITA DREHER

On the morning of October 30, 1984, Sherita Dreher said goodbye to her two-year-old son, Marquis, and walked through the streets of Southeast Washington to tell her story of despair to the Mayor's Blue Ribbon Panel on Teenage Pregnancy Prevention.

If she was nervous, she did not show it. She rose to face the crowd of eight hundred in the Ballou High School auditorium—classmates and friends who remembered when she was a chubby, outwardly hostile fifteen-year-old—and spoke clearly, directly, and with a kind of cynicism and pragmatism often found in teenage mothers.

She began having sex, she said, at the age of fifteen, succumbing to the advances of her sixteen-year-old boyfriend. They did not use any kind of birth control because she did not believe she could get pregnant; she blamed her ignorance on her mother, who died of cancer without telling Sherita much about sex or birth control.

That is how she ended up pregnant. "I laid and I paid," said Sherita, eighteen.

Sherita's story had all the well-known elements of teenage pregnancy. But the story she told to the Ballou audience that day was not the full story. Sherita, like countless other people, had adopted an account of her life—a version she told to friends as well as the teenage pregnancy panel—that differed dramatically from reality.

After her October testimony before the mayor's teenage pregnancy panel, I set up an appointment for the evening of November 8 to meet Sherita at her Bellevue Street SE apartment.

Sherita sat on the living-room couch, her eyes expressing a deep anger, her right hand covering her mouth most of the time. Her manner with her son, Marquis, was severe, although I did not think he was more active than any other two-year-old.

Jacqueline Sherrod, Sherita's adult guardian, did most of the talking, starting with an understatement. "Sherita is a very hostile person today. She has a chip on her shoulder. Her hostility is ready to explode at whomever crosses her path." Sherita was then under threat of expulsion from Ballou for arguing with a teacher. "Sherita is hostile to all authority figures."

Sherita, looking down into her lap at her hands, interjected her feelings about school officials and teachers: "They ain't none of them my mother or father."

I had looked over at her from my seat in a corner of the living room when she spoke. I was beginning to get a picture of a girl so hostile I did not know if I could reach her about the steps that had led to her pregnancy. I said to myself it was worth a try.

Jackie continued. "It is difficult for her to smile. No matter where she stayed [after Marquis was born], she was spoken to as 'Bitch this' or 'Bitch that.' "

I made a date to return in five days to begin my interviews. I told Sherita, "I don't bite!" She smiled for the first time during my hour-long visit.

During a months-long series of lengthy interviews, Sherita gradually discarded parts of the version she had told at Ballou that day. Then one day, the last day of February 1985 in the fifth hour of the third interview, the full story tumbled out, unexpectedly, almost before she could stop herself:

Her pregnancy, she said, was no accident. She *wanted* to have that baby, *needed* to have it. She said she had tried to get pregnant, hoping that it might help her hold on to to her boyfriend, William Wheeler, the same boyfriend who was her first sex partner when she was eleven and he was twelve.

She was afraid of losing William, she said, and afraid that if she did, she would never get another boyfriend as handsome and as light-skinned.

"My girl friends had a nice little shape and everything," Sherita said. "They don't worry about boys. They knew [that if] one is gone"

—she stopped and snapped her fingers—"here come another one. It wouldn't work like that with me because I was so fat. But even though I was real big, I wasn't gonna accept anything that came my way. You had to have some looks, be red [slang for light-skinned], and have pretty [meaning straight] hair."

But Sherita did not talk about these motivations when she testified before the panel of experts at Ballou. She did not tell them that her plan did not work, that her boyfriend was furious when he learned that she was pregnant, that he was too busy stealing cars and dealing drugs to help raise Marquis, and that he had ended up in prison.

The panel also did not find out that Sherita tried to commit suicide after her mother's death, that she had a deep phobia of using any form of birth control, that she got pregnant nine months later, that her brother hit her after learning she was pregnant, that her family eventually broke apart—and that, finally, she and her baby ended up in a run-down motel as temporary wards of Washington, D.C.'s government.

The Sherita who appeared before the mayor's panel portrayed herself as a victim, a casualty of seduction and her own ignorance. The Sherita who emerged after months of interviews is tough, sophisticated, and clearly aware of her motivations.

Early on, she told me she had had "a complex about dark-skinned men." Sherita said she did not know where her revulsion toward dark-skinned men had sprung from, particularly since she and most members of her family are dark-skinned.

When she was dating Marquis's father, "I thought the red boys were all the fine ones. Dark-skinned boys were very ugly. But now I find them to be the best ones because these red ones ain't about too much. The red ones got them looks, and they know it. And they use they looks as a weapon" to manipulate girls.

One of Sherita's sisters, Carol Sherrod, nineteen, had been sitting in on this interview. Carol said Sherita's negative attitude toward dark-skinned males had been the correct one. "All dark-skinned men lie more than light-skinned men," added Carol.

Carol did not know how this belief had been formed, but she said she believed that and a piece of earthy folklore she had been told by her grandmother: "Young girls should not do *it* [sexual intercourse] with old men because old men give young girls worms." I laughed and speculated that that had been a bit of folklore made up to keep young girls away from old men, but Carola and Sherita insisted that they believed it.

Sherita had a clear idea of what her future relationship would be with any man: strictly financial. He would have to give her money for herself and her son. In exchange, he would get companionship and sex from her. If the man was not forthcoming with money, there would not be any relationship. She had no interest in an unemployed man. She had no interest in love.

Sherita is not alone.

Washington Highlands and myriad other urban slums like it are sharply separated from mainstream American affluence, culture, and values. Within these despairing communities, many teenagers have sex, often reject birth control, get pregnant, and have children—not because of ignorance, but because they see those actions as ways to keep a vital relationship alive, escape from families or poverty, or achieve something *tangible* in lives filled with poor education, job-lessness, failure, violence, and a penetrating uncertainty.

The experts describe teenage pregnancy as just one more strand in an intricate, destructive web of poverty, neglect, drug abuse, alcoholism, violence, unemployment, and sometimes, child abuse. In their view, Sherita Dreher got caught in this web.

But these are the words of experts, not Sherita's words. She does not talk about the poverty and violence that surrounds her and has surrounded her since her earliest childhood memory to the point that she hardly notices it. Instead, she talks about the people in her life, mostly men, who she says abandoned her—people she calls "triflin'," her word for weak and irresponsible—and left her to face a kind of private hell, alone.

Learning the Hard Way

If Sherita was fat in her early teens—she said in one interview that she was "humongous"—she was not fat when she testified at Ballou. She will never be called petite, but her weight is normal, evenly distributed. In a crowd, she attracts attention for other reasons: She has a presence about her, a self-assurance that has come from being a survivor. When she talks, she says as much with her eyes as with her words; the eyes light up, then narrow, never resting longer than a few seconds, always alert and expressive.

She has a vivid memory and remembers even small details. For example, she remembers the first time her mother beat her, and the memory is still painful:

She was nine years old, home alone one summer day in 1976. A repairman came to the Dreher home, a two-story row house on Ninth Street SE, part of the sprawling public-housing development known as Highland Dwellings. The repairman was there to fix the fuse box; in Sherita's mind, he took too long. She picked up her cheerleader's baton and whacked him across the back, telling him to get out of the house, she said.

"I used to be terrible," Sherita said. "I used to act like a boy. Be wanting to fight. I can box good enough to protect myself. My brothers and sisters nicknamed me 'Bill.' " She could be as rough with her tongue as with her fists. Adults in the neighborhood who tried to discipline her would be told, "You ain't my damn mother."

She did not expect that the repairman would call her mother the next day and complain. Nor did she expect that her mother would come into her bedroom while Sherita was sleeping and begin beating her with a thick leather belt, yelling at her about hitting the repairman.

"I woke up, start crying," Sherita remembered. "I kept saying, 'I didn't hit him.' She was beating me something terrible. I was all up under the bed, and she was still beating me," she said. Her mother stopped when Sherita admitted that she had hit the repairman.

The beating left a lasting impression on Sherita. "My mother had never beat me like that," said Sherita, who is the youngest of Joyce Dreher's five children. "I used to get my way all the time. I was spoiled."

Joyce Dreher married young, had her first child when she was seventeen, and had three others before her husband died in 1965. Soon after, she began a relationship with a man she knew from her church's choir and became pregnant with Sherita. The relationship did not last, and Joyce Dreher raised her children mostly by herself while working as a cleaning woman at the National Archives.

There was little money in the Dreher household when Sherita was growing up. Sherita said she sometimes manipulated her mother, with tears and whining, to give her things that her brothers and sisters went without. Her mother would get angry, shouting, "Where the fuck ya'll think I be getting all this money?"

One thing they didn't talk about was sex, Sherita said. Her mother had strong feelings on the subject, but Sherita said she learned them the hard way—through another beating.

It happened this way, according to Sherita: Like many girls in Washington Highlands, Sherita belonged to a cheerleading squad, a group of girls from her housing project or neighboring buildings. The squads competed at community events, wearing uniforms sewn by their mothers. They also held secret competitions, attended only by other children and teenagers, where some cheerleaders wore short skirts and no underpants while doing flips and "doing those nasty cheers," sexually suggestive chants, one of which went like this:

> I did it once
> I did it twice.
> I took my time
> I did it right.

The girls learned the cheers in secret and did them in secret, but their mothers were not fooled. One day when Sherita was nine, her brother saw the three Dreher girls doing one of the suggestive cheers and told Joyce Dreher, who had warned her daughters not to perform them.

Her mother called the girls into the house, one by one. Sherita said she didn't realize what was about to happen. "I came into the house saying, 'I did it once, I did it twice. . . .' [My mother] said, 'Yeah, and I'm gonna do it three times,' took that switch, and tore me up," Sherita said. One of her sisters, Wanda, still carries a scar on her leg from that day. After the beatings, Joyce Dreher told her daughters: "I bet ya'll don't do any more cheers."

One midsummer day in 1978, when she was eleven, Sherita met William Wheeler, the boy who would become the father of her child. William was soon the best thing in her life, and she could hardly believe he was interested in her. She knew she was overweight and thought little of herself because of her dark skin; William was light-skinned and, therefore, she thought, handsome.

To Sherita, William's skin color made a big difference. She had a visceral dislike, at the time, for dark skin, a prejudice held by some black Americans. Going out with the lighter-skinned William, she said, gave her a higher status in the neighborhood. But she was frightened by his popularity with other girls and thought sex would help keep him interested. She made it clear to William that she was willing to have sex.

William, twelve, had become sexually active weeks before he met Sherita with a seventeen-year-old pregnant girl. He was attracted to

Sherita's dark complexion. "It was smooth," he said in a separate interview. He had several girl friends. "I like 'em mainly for the pleasure they give you. You know, sex."

His father is a good-looking man and had a lot of women, William told me. He did not see much of his father, but "people would tell me they seen my father with a good-looking female. Unconsciously, I could have been imitating my father." His mother and father had never talked to him about sex.

Sherita and William first had sex in William's large bedroom closet two months before Sherita's twelfth birthday and only seven months after Sherita had started menstruating. She was not ready for either experience, she said.

Sherita said she knew so little about sex that she thought she could get pregnant kissing a boy. She learned more over the next few months through friends and a sex-education class at Hart Junior High School, where she was a seventh-grader. She learned little from her mother, she said. "Only thing she said was, 'Don't be out here messing with no boys.' And that was it!"

"I just couldn't talk to my mother [about sex]," Sherita said, echoing the feeling of other girls interviewed in the project. "I ain't want her thinking about me like that, for one thing. . . . And when I started having sex and stuff, I still didn't tell her."

She tried to hide her sex life from her mother but not from her classmates at Hart Junior High. They saw the "passion marks" on her neck, which Sherita showed off at school and covered up at home. Two teachers confronted her, Sherita said, and offered to get birth-control pills for her. But Sherita denied to them that she was sexually active.

Somehow, Sherita did not get pregnant. It seems incredible to her now, but then, she said, she just did not think about it. William, in a separate interview, said he did not worry about it either, believing what a nineteen-year-old woman had told him: that at age twelve, he was "not mature enough" to produce a child.

Birth control was never an issue, they said. Sherita refused to consider it. The idea frightened her, a fear she finds difficult to explain but that was shared by others, girls and women, interviewed for the project. She said simply: "I ain't want to be using that stuff, because I was scared." Her teachers advised her to ask her mother for permission to go on the Pill, but that meant Sherita would have to discuss her sex life with her mother—which, she said, was out of the question.

A Pair of Promises

Joyce Dreher had other things on her mind, too. She was dying, slowly, inevitably, from cancer. For two years, Sherita watched her mother grow progressively weaker, the result of regular chemotherapy and the advancing disease. On the night of February 22, 1981, Joyce Dreher summoned fourteen-year-old Sherita and fifteen-year-old Lisa to her bedroom.

Her mother wanted to extract a promise, Sherita said. The other Dreher children had all dropped out of school. Lisa and Sherita were the only ones left, and Joyce wanted them to promise they would finish. The two girls promised.

During the night, their mother died in bed. Sherita found her the next morning. "When my mother died, there was nothing left for me," she said. "There was nothing left."

After her mother's death, her oldest brother, Steven, the new head of the family at age twenty-three, extracted another promise, this one from Sherita and both her sisters. According to Steven, the promise was this: no pregnancies, not until they were adults and no longer his responsibility.

Two days after her mother's death, Sherita found all her mother's leftover pills and swallowed them. A short time later, she began to hold her stomach. Steven rushed her to the local hospital emergency room, where her stomach was pumped, and Sherita recovered.

About the same time, her relationship with her boyfriend began to fall apart. William said Sherita became loud, was argumentative, stayed out late at night without telling anyone where she was going, and began to curse. Before her mother's death, he said, she was hard to get along with; afterward, she was downright hostile.

Sherita agreed with some of William's complaints, but said William made matters worse by "dogging" her—carrying on a number of affairs and then bragging about them publicly. One day, returning to William's apartment after doing his laundry, she found him in his bed with another girl. Sherita tried to attack the girl, but William held her back, telling Sherita it was his fault. The girl hurriedly dressed and fled from the apartment.

In October 1981—eight months after Joyce Dreher's death—the couple split up. By this time, William, sixteen, had dropped out of school and gotten involved in selling drugs, stealing cars, and committing burglaries. It was, he said, the only way to get money for clothes he wanted and "to be able to do what I want when I want to."

He described his criminal activity during two interviews inside Youth Center II at Lorton, Virginia, the location of Washington, D.C.'s prison facilities twenty-two miles south of the city. When interviewed in early 1985, William was serving a six-year term for armed robbery. He was dressed in prison-issued blue shirt and pants, a dark-blue knit cap, and drab green overcoat that disguised his muscular shoulders and arms. As he talked, he wore a deadpan expression, projecting the macho image of someone who is in complete control of himself—a tough, streetwise dude.

A Planned Pregnancy

Sherita pretended publicly not to care about their breakup. She would not admit to anyone, except herself, that she was distraught —mostly because she feared that she would never have another light-skinned boyfriend. So she developed a plan.

One day in November, two weeks after her fifteenth birthday, she arranged to see William at his grandmother's house. They shared a marijuana joint and went to bed. This time, she hoped, she would get pregnant. A few weeks later, William was sent to a juvenile institution, Cedar Knoll, on a burglary conviction. Before he left, Sherita told him she was pregnant. He did not believe her.

The next time he saw her, she was about five months pregnant. For as long as she could, Sherita hid the pregnancy.

One night, when she was four months pregnant, she got ready for bed, grateful that her loose-fitting nightgown disguised her rapidly changing figure. Suddenly, she heard her older brother Steven loudly cursing as he climbed the stairs to her bedroom. Sherita recalled: "He was calling me every name in the book but the child of God."

Sherita described what happened next:

Steven stormed into the room, accusing her of breaking her promise not to become pregnant. Sherita protested, but he snatched open her nightgown.

"Bitch, are you lying to me?" he screamed. "You *are* pregnant!"

He hit Sherita in the face three times with his right fist and told her that he would beat her again the next day and throw her out of the house if she did not have an immediate abortion.

Steven, too, remembers that night. He confirmed Sherita's account, saying he was angry and felt justified in hitting her. "I was pissed off," he said in an interview. He had just discovered that Sherita's sister, Wanda, then eighteen, was having a baby. Wanda had not pretended it was accidental, Steven said. When a neighbor told him that Sherita looked pregnant, something snapped, he said.

Two days after his confrontation with Sherita, he took her to the Hillcrest Abortion Clinic and Counseling Service on Pennsylvania Avenue SE. He sat in the waiting room while Sherita saw the doctor.

Sherita said she told the doctor, "I'm being forced to do this." That led the doctor to tell Steven that Sherita could not have an abortion—that at four months, she was too far along in her pregnancy. In fact, abortions can be performed at that stage.

Steven took the relieved Sherita home. But he was still angry. As far as he was concerned, Sherita was too young to have a baby. He knew other teenage mothers, and he feared that Sherita would turn out like some of them: "End up on welfare. Out of school. Settin' there, looking dumb for the rest of her life."

Not long after their visit to the abortion clinic, Sherita's family safety net, already badly frayed, began to unravel completely.

It started when Steven stopped paying the rent. He was paying for two apartments, the one where he lived with his girl friend and the longtime Dreher residence where Sherita was living with her sisters and her other brother, John.

The family had some income: Steven was working at a computer firm, making $22,000 a year, and John was working at the same firm. Steven collected money each month from Sherita, who got $440 a month from her mother's pension, and from Lisa, who got $213 a month from her father's social security fund.

But he fell behind in the rent, owing more than $2,000. On June 18, 1982, the city sent U.S. marshals to evict the Dreher family from public housing.

"I felt very taken advantage of," Steven said. "When my mother died, she had backed-up rent. I had to be they [my sisters'] momma and daddy and they brother. I was being it all, and it was breaking me bad. . . . I said, 'To hell with them all,' because they were worrying me to death. I couldn't have no more fun. I couldn't go out and just spend money like I would normally do."

Out on the street were John, twenty-three; Wanda, eighteen, who had dropped out of school and now had an infant son; Lisa, sixteen, who would soon be pregnant; and Sherita, fifteen, who was seven months pregnant.

During the next two years, Sherita moved sixteen times, shunted back and forth between her grandmother in Maryland's Prince Georges County, a boyfriend's aunt, and her brothers' friends.

It was a period that nearly drove Sherita to madness. She had her baby, but lost William for good. She met her father for the first time in her life, but lost him, too. She dropped out of school and ended up homeless—and might still be lost on the streets of Washington if it were not for a series of lucky breaks and a woman named Jacqueline Sherrod.

Having the Baby

Marquis Antoine Dreher was born on August 9, 1982, at George Washington University Hospital in Washington. As Sherita was going into labor, she called William. She had never told him when the baby was due because, she said, "It wasn't none of his business."

Her water broke while she was on the phone. Sherita hung up. An hour before she delivered, her brother John came and borrowed twenty dollars from her. He left immediately. As her contractions and pain increased, she began to cry. More from the loneliness than from the pain. No one was there with her.

A sympathetic nurse called her brother Steve's girl friend, a woman who would have to come to Sherita's rescue again, and she came.

Later, in the delivery room, Sherita watched Marquis's birth at 12:23 A.M. through a mirror set up in front of her. Steve's girl friend held Sherita's hand and was so happy she wet herself.

"After they cut Marquis's umbilical cord, they just put him up on me and I told 'em, '*Get* that ugly baby off of me!' He was all covered with blood. It upset me.

"They took him, washed him off, put him back in my arms. I was just so tired. All I could say, 'He look just like William.' And I turned my head to the other side. It took me a long time to get use to Marquis. I didn't want to accept at fifteen I have a baby. It took me about two months to get use, really get use to Marquis."

A few months before, William had been released from Cedar Knoll, the juvenile facility for delinquents, unaware that Sherita had told him the truth when she said she was pregnant.

One day, as he was walking in the neighborhood, something odd happened. He ran into one of Sherita's girl friends, who said: "I'll be glad when ya'll have your baby!" He was perplexed; when Sherita called him a few days later—still clinging to the hope that the baby might bring them back together—he decided to go see her. He had not seen her since getting out of Cedar Knoll.

When he arrived, he said, Sherita's sister Wanda hugged him and said, "Sherita's pregnant. Ain't you glad?" Wanda continued, "What you wanna have? A boy or a girl?"

William asked, "Where Sherita at?" William began to struggle with himself to remain cool. "I was in shock, but I ain't want to show it."

William remembers thinking: "Don't she know I'm too young to have a baby? I'm not ready to have no baby. Well, I ain't supporting it. I don't see why she ain't getting no abortion."

Sherita came slowly down the stairs wearing a maternity shirt. William could feel his anger rising. "She come down [the stairs] like we planned it," he said. "Her sisters were acting all excited. Jumping all around. Telling her to hurry and come downstairs so William could see her." He tried to stay cool on the outside, but inside he was seething.

Sherita called her sisters "stupid for rushing her" as she came down the stairs. When she reached the bottom of the stairs, William said, "She told me she was glad to see me and was wondering what had taken me so long to come and see her."

They went outside, William first. When the front door closed, he whirled on his heels and angrily faced Sherita. "Who you pregnant by?" he demanded. Sherita, not one to be intimidated by anyone, locked his eyes with a look of cold disdain. "Don't *even* try it!" she told him. "What you mean, don't try it?" William replied. "You *know* it's your baby," continued Sherita. "I told you I was pregnant!"

They stood silently for long minutes. Sherita broke the silence. "Is you mad?" William said something to the effect, "What you think?" Sherita mumbled something in reply. William started walking away. "I'll be back."

After that day, he avoided Sherita—until she called him to say that she was going into labor.

The night of his son's birth, William went to the hospital with his mother, his sister, and a male friend. He scrubbed his hands, put on a gown, and held his son in his arms.

William and Sherita hardly talked at all. She had watched him prepare with mixed emotions. "I ain't really want him to hold the baby. But I was like, 'I might as well. He came all the way up here.' He was just smiling the whole time he was up there. He didn't say nothing until it was time to go. He asked me if he could have my sandwich."

Later that night, though, they talked on the telephone, and William told Sherita that he wanted to name the boy for his brother. Sherita said she pretended to agree, but she knew what she wanted: The boy would be named Marquis Dreher. As far as Sherita was concerned, William had no rights.

They saw each other a few more times after that—and even had sex, without using any birth control. But William said he was not interested in being a father, and he drifted away. "I was into crime and money then," he said. When Marquis was a year old, William went back to prison.

An Unexpected Reunion

When school opened in the fall of 1982, Sherita did not go back. She could not get a baby-sitter for Marquis, and her life was in chaos. She had some income—$172 a month from her mother's pension, $263.85 in welfare payments, and $102 in food stamps—and she used the money to help pay rent in the various places she lived and to feed her baby.

She spent the school year moving around, still hostile, still staying out late at night. But she finally got herself together and hired a baby-sitter so she could go back to Ballou High School in the fall of 1983.

She did not finish the year. Tired, cynical, depressed, she dropped out in February 1984. The same month, she moved again, this time to her aunt's house. One night, they were talking about the family. Sherita mentioned her father and said she had never met him. At one point, Sherita said his name and her aunt cried out, "What? I think I know him."

The aunt said the man was in the hospital, being treated for lingering back problems from an industrial accident. The aunt went to the telephone and called him. Sherita said she listened on an extension as her aunt questioned him about his relationship with Sherita's mother.

The aunt said, "Didn't you have a baby by her?"

Sherita's father replied, "Yeah, I had a little girl."

The aunt said, "Do you remember the little girl's name?"

He said, "Shaa . . . something. Shaa . . . something."

Sherita recalls her reaction: "I dropped the phone 'cause I didn't know what to do. I was scared. I don't know why I got scared. Chills went all through my body. I was happy. I was *real* happy."

Her aunt hung up the phone. But Sherita, excited now, wanted to talk to him immediately. So her aunt called him back and explained that Sherita was living at her house. He asked to talk to her. Sherita remembers the conversation this way:

"Do you know who this is?" he asked.

"No," Sherita pretended.

"This is your daddy," he said.

"Uummppff," answered Sherita, with exaggerated disinterest.

He said he had been looking for her for many years.

"If you would've looked hard enough, you would have found me," Sherita said she replied. "Evidently, you wasn't looking hard."

They made arrangements to see each other. Sherita was excited about the prospect of finally getting to know her father and harbored hopes that it might change her life for the better. Her father seemed excited, too: After his first meeting with Sherita, he called his other two daughters and told them about Sherita. He had never told them of Sherita's existence.

One daughter, Carol Sherrod, went to see Sherita. It was a fateful meeting: A few months later, when Sherita found herself on the street with no place to go, Carol persuaded her mother, Jackie, to take Sherita in.

Shortly after Sherita and Carol met, relations began to worsen between Sherita and the aunt with whom she was living. In June 1984, her aunt told her to get a job or move out, and she criticized Sherita for dropping out of school. Upset about the ultimatum, Sherita left the next day and moved in with her brother John and his girl friend.

That did not last long either. John's girl friend complained it was too crowded. Sherita, who had been sleeping with Marquis on a makeshift bed on the floor, decided to move in with her other brother, Steven. He eventually left her with a family friend, who was told that Sherita would be staying only two weeks. At the end of the two weeks, no one came to take Sherita somewhere else. Helpless, she turned to her welfare social worker.

The response was bureaucratic. The city had no place for her either. Sherita refused to accept that answer and told the worker that she was going to call a television reporter. After she talked to a reporter at Channel 9, she got a call from Audrey Rowe, Washington's commissioner for social services.

From Relief to Depression

Unlike the others, Sherita said, Rowe tried to help. She arranged for Sherita to stay at the Pitts Motor Hotel in Northwest Washington. Rowe said Sherita's plight led the city to provide financial support to Sasha Bruce House, a privately run shelter for homeless and runaway youths.

But Sherita's relief quickly turned to horror. On the way to Pitts, a city social worker told her that because she was a minor, the city would probably take Marquis away from her and put him in foster care.

After two years and sixteen moves, Sherita was on the verge of losing her baby.

It was hot and humid, a typical mid-July night in Washington, when Sherita and Marquis arrived at the Pitts Motor Hotel. As she tried to close the door, she realized that the lock was broken. Marquis was sick, suffering from a fever and an ear infection. He was whining and uncomfortable, and as Sherita listened to his sniffling and crying, she thought about suicide, as she had tried once before just after her mother died.

But then she thought about what would happen to Marquis. If I do this [commit suicide], all they gonna do is put him in a foster home, she thought.

She went down to a pay phone in the lobby and called collect to a cousin, pleading with her to find her brothers. The cousin found them on Wahler Place SE, in Washington Highlands, a hangout for drug dealers. Her brothers came to the phone.

Sherita said she told them to come get her, but they did not want to come right away. "They told me, 'We out here trying to sell this lully [slang for the drug PCP]. Just call us back and then we'll come get you.' "

When she called back, she couldn't find them. Frantic, she did something that she had never done before. For the first time in her life, she turned to her father for help.

"Daddy, come get me," she told him on the phone.

Her father said, "Where you at?"

"On Belmont Street at the Pitts Hotel."

"What you doing up there?" he said. "You should never have gone to some motherfucking shelter. You should have come here to stay with me like I told you to."

"Daddy, come get me!" she replied.

"Well, I'm not coming to get you tonight because I'm getting ready to go out."

This is Sherita's version. Her father, during a twenty-five-minute conversation in his kitchen in which Sherita participated, said he did not want to talk about his relationship with Sherita.

A New Life

Sherita called other relatives from the Pitts Motor Hotel that night in July 1984, including Carol Sherrod, one of her father's other children. They had met only recently, but Sherita liked her and believed that she had nowhere else to turn. Carol said she could not go to get her that night but said: "When you get out of there, you coming to stay around *here!*"

The next day, Sherita called her brother Steven's girl friend, who picked her up and drove straight to a hospital to get medical treatment for Marquis. That night, Sherita moved in with the girl friend's mother, who had harsh words for Sherita's brothers.

"I know your mother done turn over in her grave, probably walked the whole cemetery, after she see all this stuff happening," she said, according to Sherita.

The next day, when Steven Dreher came over, the woman "cursed Steve out some kind of terrible. 'All you care about is out there selling that lully. Your little sister and her baby sitting up in the shelter, and one of her friends gotta come and get her. Ya'll talking about ya'll gotta finish selling lully." She called him "a motherfucker, bitch, and son of a bitch," said Sherita.

Steven just hung his head during the long tirade, Sherita said. "That lady was just so hurt." When the woman stopped to catch her breath, Steven asked Sherita, "Can I talk to you a minute?" But Sherita refused to talk to him. The woman told him, "Just get the *fuck* out of my house." Without another word, Steven left.

A few days later, Sherita went to see Carol Sherrod and her

mother, Jackie. Carol insisted that she and Marquis move in. Jackie said, "Well, we don't have much, but she's welcome to what we have."

Jackie had only one demand: Sherita would have to return to Ballou High School or go to work. In the fall of 1984, Sherita did go back; she graduated in May 1986.

Sherita brought tremendous change to the Sherrod household. Before she came, Jackie, forty-two, was living there with her five-year-old daughter, Nyieka, and with Carol, nineteen. The addition of Sherita and Marquis made things much more crowded in the two-bedroom apartment, which was built for a family of three, perhaps four.

The children had no real place to play; they were supposed to play in the smaller of the two bedrooms, but they often spilled out into the green-carpeted living room, which was furnished with a couch, a piano, a television set, a stereo, and a videocassette recorder. The kitchen is tiny, hardly big enough for one person. The bathroom is no larger.

Despite crowded conditions, the Sherrod household gave Sherita some stability after three years of turmoil. She clearly changed after she moved in. At first, Jackie said, "she had a chip on her shoulder." Often, when she talked, she kept her hand in front of her mouth so that a listener could hardly hear her. She still gets mad—sometimes at Marquis, sometimes at Jackie—but she is obviously happier.

When Sherita moved in, she told Jackie and Carol how her father —Jackie's ex-husband, Carol's father—refused to pick her up at the shelter. They said they were not surprised.

Jackie explained: "Sherita had built up an idea, romanticized, of what it would be like to be involved with the father she had never known. The reality hurt her deeply."

As for Sherita, she makes no effort to see her father. Whenever she is asked on a form for information about him, she writes in big, bold letters: DECEASED.

A Bitter Family Meeting

For two weeks, the tension had been building inside the two-bedroom apartment on Bellevue Street SE that Sherita had come to call home. It was early June 1985, but a heat wave had already hit Washington, and the cramped quarters grew hot and stuffy.

Casual conversations turned into shouting matches. Household chores became excuses for angry confrontations. Old grudges burst forth, creating new wounds. The head of the household, Jackie Sherrod, decided it was time to clear the air, before things got out of hand, before somebody got hurt.

It was time for another family meeting.

Jackie began the meetings in November 1984 as a kind of safety valve, a way for everyone to release anger. At that first meeting, Carol and Sherita expressed their personal resentments toward the two children of the household, Nyieka, five, and Marquis, two, and admitted they beat them too harshly. Their stressful interaction as a family and the pressures outside the house produced tensions that caused them to snap, they told Jackie.

Jackie counseled Carol and Sherita not to take out their personal frustrations on the two children. A month later, however, Sherita told of slamming Marquis's face and head into the kitchen wall when he annoyed her by repeatedly asking for a glass of soda. Carol said she would probably not have children because she did not have the patience for them.

By the time of the June 12 meeting, tension in the household had reached such a level of shrillness, rage, and bitterness that everyone —including me, attending as an observer—was left emotionally drained at its end two and a half hours later.

The meeting started out calmly enough.

"Can we pray before we start this meeting, please?" asked Therresia Sherrod Thomas, twenty-one, who is Jackie's eldest daughter. Therresia, married to a Marine Corpsman, had moved into her mother's apartment until her husband returned from Japan. She and her daughter, Quannette, slept in Jackie's bedroom.

"Therresia, *no,*" shouted her sister, Carol Sherrod, nineteen. "We ain't been praying and I ain't now."

"I don't know nothing about that," said Therresia. "I haven't been here."

"Well, *you* pray!" retorted Carol.

"OK. Go ahead," Jackie said.

"Dear Lord, our Father, please give us the strength, the wisdom, and the courage to carry on like *adults,*" said Therresia.

Carol shouted, "But I'm not [an adult]."

Another family meeting was under way.

Around the rectangular table, scarred and nicked from years of use, sat four women:

- Jackie Sherrod, divorced, employed from time to time in temporary jobs, and living in the rent-subsidized apartment with her two daughters, Carol and Nyieka.
- Jackie's daughter Therresia, who since May had been sleeping in Jackie's bedroom with Therresia's daughter, Quannette, two.
- Jackie's daughter Carol, a secretary at a downtown hotel, who had found out that she did not earn enough to afford her own place and was sleeping on a makeshift bed on her mother's living room floor until she could earn enough to move out on her own again.
- Sherita Dreher, mother of Marquis, who had moved in with Jackie and Carol Sherrod in July 1984 after her own family broke apart.

At the outset of the meeting, Jackie tried to set the tone.

"We're not here to point out 'He say, she say stuff. We here to lay a problem on the table and figure out a way to solve the problem that will be agreeable to everyone. We're not here to argue. We're not here to yell and holler," she said.

But her warning seemed in vain. Often, the discussion seemed to center on the mundane: who left dirty dishes in the kitchen, who left soiled children's clothes in the bathroom sink, who should sleep where. Early in the meeting, Carol announced, "I'm not cleaning up behind nobody's children because I don't have none."

Moreover, Carol said, she did not have any responsibility for cleaning the bathroom. "I don't really live here. All I do is sleep here, and as long as I pay rent, it shouldn't be nothing said about it because I don't use the bathroom."

An incredulous Jackie asked, "You don't use the bathroom?"

"I don't use nothing but the [living-room] floor," responded Carol.

At one point, her mother interrupted and said, "Do you think [there is] anything in this house you suppose to do?"

"If I don't mess it up, no," answered Carol. "I don't have *no rights in this house.*"

Meanwhile, Sherita was angry at Jackie, who had said she did not feel "obligated" to do any housecleaning.

"I think that is wrong to *the utmost,*" said Sherita. "That's why [I] came into the house with [a sullen] attitude practically every day.

But that was my only way that I could just take my frustration out, was to have an attitude and go outside. Go outside and get some fresh air and run the streets. It just do not make any kind of sense. Now, you," Sherita said, turning to face Jackie, "do you still feel like you ain't obligated?"

"I ain't obligated," Jackie replied calmly.

The conversation turned to other issues, but Sherita wouldn't let go.

"I'm still fired up because you ain't obligated" to clean up the house, Sherita said, with heavy sarcasm.

"I don't care about you being fired up," Jackie responded. "You know that."

"You don't care about nothing," Sherita said.

"Yes, I do," Jackie said.

"But them children [Nyieka and Marquis]," Sherita added.

"I care about you," Jackie said simply.

"Oh, come off that, baby," Sherita said.

"You don't think I care about you?" asked Jackie.

"No," said Sherita.

"You wouldn't be here if I didn't," said Jackie.

As the meeting began to wind down, Sherita said that their inability to come to any lasting agreement was a "sad" development.

"It's real sad," Sherita added. "Simple as that. All of us in here are sad. Helpless."

"I ain't gonna be helpless for long," Carol, still angry, said. When she got her own place, things would be different, she said. "My house will stay clean."

Then, suddenly, in a tired, dry voice, Carol said, "*Why* do we have these meetings?"

"The question have been asked," said Sherita.

Jackie spoke up. "Well, I'll tell you what. We won't have no more meetings."

And they didn't.

CHAPTER FOUR

TAUSCHA VAUGHN TOLD ME early in my project of an adolescent girl whose mother forced her to pose nude with the mother in Polaroid snapshots. Later, the mother forced her daughter to become sexually involved with older adolescent boys. Soon, the girl was pregnant. Soon thereafter, I was told of other instances of parental abuse of their children.

When I shared some of these sordid aspects of life in Washington Highlands with my small circle of confidants, I was surprised to learn that several of them had suffered childhood sexual abuse. The patterns of child abuse, at different class levels, were virtually identical.

They talked about their torment after I related the sexual abuse stories that retired junior high school counselor Allean Brown had told me. In Brown's telling, I told her that I assumed she meant stepfathers and common-law husbands when she talked about "fathers" abusing their adolescent daughters. Brown corrected my presumption. She said, "Blood fathers!"

On separate occasions, three female friends grew silent as I related to them the ordeals of the children Brown had known. I did not know beforehand that any of the three women had suffered any manner of childhood sexual abuse. After I finished talking, each of the three women told me of her suffering at the hands of her blood father. One of the three women grew up in rural poverty in South Carolina, a second came from a religious working-class family in an East Coast city, and the third was raised in obvious affluence in Washington, D.C.'s Gold Coast, a middle-class black enclave.

My friend from South Carolina was thirty-nine, but she had not resolved with herself the abuse she suffered. She had kept the family secret bottled up inside of her for twenty-three years. She began to cry uncontrollably when she started the tale of repeated rapes. I insisted that she stop. She later went to counseling and was partially successful in unbottling the awful memories.

The other two women spoke matter-of-factly about what had happened to them, as if they had come to grips with that part of their pasts and it no longer mattered to them.

The woman from an East Coast city was an only child in a working-class family. She said her father had tried to rape her in bed one night when she was fourteen. She fought him with all her strength and he desisted. Later the next day, he tried to tell her that he had been drunk, but she told him he was lying. She had seen enough of his alcoholic pattern for a decade to know when he was genuinely drunk. She told her mother, who spoke angrily with her husband about the attempted rape. While she lived with her parents, the woman never again entered or stayed in the family home when her mother was not there.

The third woman said she had been sixteen, the oldest of three children in an upper-middle-class family. Both parents fussed at her to wash more often than she did. One warm summer afternoon, when her mother, sister, and brother were out, her father came home unexpectedly. He walked by her in the kitchen "and all of a sudden blew his top. I had body odor," she said.

He angrily ordered her upstairs. She had never seen him in such a rage. He ordered her to undress and to get into the shower in the bathroom of the master bedroom. He stood and watched her, yelling at the top of his lungs the entire time. After she stepped from bathtub and began drying off, he continued to rant. Then he grabbed her, threw her onto her parents' bed, and raped her. She offered no resistance, but looked up at him and asked, "Daddy, what are you *doing*?" She never told her mother.

Eight years had gone by when she told me the story. Her father still carried the guilt of his attack, and she got everything she wanted out of him.

My friends' experiences indicated that father-daughter sexual abuse is not exclusive to the poor. It is the carnal side of family relationships, which is rarely talked about and almost always hidden.

Yet I was to learn that within the pattern of sexual child abuse lies one of the seeds of adolescent childbearing.

THE FAMILY OF LILLIAN WILLIAMS

Nearly every day, Lillian Manley Williams, forty-two, sat by the window of her house in Southeast Washington, her head bowed, her eyes fixed on the dog-eared pages of her Bible.

She highlighted passages with a yellow marker as she read. From time to time, she looked up, repeated a passage to a visitor or one of her eleven children, and explained its meaning. It was her way of saying that since becoming a born-again Christian four years before, she had left behind the first thirty-eight years of her life. Those had been years when she suffered sexual abuse and molestation, years when she said she "ran from man to man, looking for love," years when she often hit and cursed her eleven children, years she now regarded as sinful and shameful.

Her face reflected the accumulated years of unhappiness and pain. The corner of each eye was lined, as if her past had been etched there permanently. But when she smiled—as she frequently did when discussing the Bible and as she often did when she teased me during our interviews—her face lit up and her cheeks became prominent and shiny. She "witnessed" me over many hours about her God, his son, Christ, and the kingdom of heaven. It was her genuine effort to "save" me, to give me a chance to be "born again" in the spirit of the Holy Ghost.

Her new life gave her a new mission: to prevent her sins from becoming her children's sins, to rise above the abuse and violence that had characterized her family since the early days of this century, and to give her children the love that she says she never got and was unable to give before.

She acknowledged with a heavy voice that she had failed up to then, early December 1985: Two unmarried daughters had become pregnant as teenagers and now had two children each. Two unmarried sons had children who lived with their mothers. A third daughter, seventeen, had just delivered a baby on December 8. She prayed fervently that her fourth and youngest daughter, then sixteen, would not follow the same path as her three older girls. The three were imitating her behavior, she said. That was the deepest hurt of all.

Early childbearing had had a logical basis of economic survival among Lillian's sharecropping forebears, but for the urban poor it does not make sense. Still this obsolete practice persisted across generations, ensnaring first Lillian and then her children and threatening to trap even her grandchildren in cycles of urban poverty.

The custom of growing up early and taking on adult undertakings, such as having children, came with Lillian from the rural backwaters of Lenoir County, North Carolina, and traveled north to a run-down public-housing development in an isolated, crime-plagued corner of the capital of the United States. She had been too late, she felt, in recognizing the practice's destructiveness in the city; in understanding that she had unwittingly passed on a century-old legacy to her children. Few of those around Lillian knew how to break the pattern, and fewer still were able to avoid the pattern before they, too, were swept up by it.

Yet her mission continued, a personal struggle against forces and attitudes that dominate the poorest families of Washington Highlands, home to more teenage mothers and fathers than any other neighborhood in Washington, D.C.

At the same time, Lillian waged another kind of war, a daily battle to feed and clothe her eleven children and five grandchildren. In the twenty-four years she had waged that battle, many things had taken a backseat: her personal development, the education of her children, and the attention her offspring had desperately needed when they were young. Instead, Lillian had fallen back on what was the most familiar, something she could do automatically, behavior that does not require any self-doubting or self-questioning. She raised her children as she had been raised, showing them harshness identical to what she had experienced as a child, patterns that had developed within her family as far back as living memory could take them, ways of behaving she would come to believe had ravaged her and her family.

Six of Lillian's eleven children were older than eighteen, but none of them had finished high school or were earning enough from menial jobs to be able to rent an apartment, move out of her house to live on their own. Occasionally, two older sons stayed with friends, but most of the time seventeen people were crammed into two side-by-side row houses on Atlantic Avenue SE, part of the vast Highland Dwellings housing project owned by the Washington, D.C., government.

It was so crowded—the seventeen people shared six bedrooms, a living room, a kitchen, and two bathrooms—that a three-year-old girl and a two-year-old girl slept in the same bed with their mothers.

If the present was a struggle for Lillian, then the past was a burden, an emotional weight almost too heavy to throw off. She looked at her twenty-three-year-old daughter, who said she had gotten pregnant to prove her womanhood, and saw herself as a teenage mother.

It seemed she had done to her children what had been done to her. It seemed her children had witnessed in her what she had witnessed as a child.

She remembered the cruel beatings she received from her mother and grandmother, and she thought about how she used to hit her children. She had been harshly treated, and she had been equally harsh with her children, beating one child because she disliked the child's light skin color. Love had been withheld from her, and she had withheld love from her children.

But there was another part of her life that played an integral role in the lives of Lillian and her fifty-seven-year-old mother and her twenty-three-year-old daughter—a sordid part, difficult to talk about, which bound the three women together by more than just ties of blood. As the three women told their stories, separate patterns unfolded—patterns of sexual abuse, of family violence, of a harshness with children, of an absence of love, of poverty, and of teenage childbearing.

The patterns' history was still locked into the memories of the living when I met Lillian Williams and her family in September 1984. It reached back into the early days of this century, into the destitute existence of outcast black sharecroppers, into the tobacco and cotton fields of Lenoir County, into the universal customs and rigid rules of segregation woven into the fabric of the American South.

Lilliam Williams's family is just one of hundreds of thousands of black American households that carry that legacy today in living memory, custom, and culture. Some have escaped it and never looked back—never wanted to be reminded of that past as they clawed their way up into the black middle class and mainstream society. Others are still held by it, annually sowing the fresh seeds of a self-perpetuating American underclass.

Remembering: 1940 and 1954

It happened in 1940, but even forty-five years later, the memory comes into focus quickly. It stays and lingers, causing pain, hatred, fury. The memory belongs to Lillian Williams's mother:

> It is 1939. The room is dark. She is lying in her bed in the small two-story wooden farmhouse, exhausted from working all day on the farm. She can hear the breathing of her brothers and sisters, all asleep, in beds around her. A man comes in, no, not just a man, not just any man, but her stepfather, Isaiah Hill. She remembers, "He came to my bed, he put his hand over my mouth . . . and he told me if I tell it, what he did, that he was gonna do something to my mother." But she told anyway, told her mother that Isaiah had raped her, told again when the rapes continued. But her mother never believed her, told her she was lying. Until the skinny little girl got pregnant. She was eleven years old.

Lillian knows now that her mother was raped. She learned about the assaults in her mid-twenties from her mother's mother, the same woman who had rejected the girl's pleas for protection. Lillian knows where it happened and who did it. She even knows how it happened, because she has memories of her own. Childhood memories of another nightmarish incident, of being forced into a sex act by an older adolescent female relative. She still has memories of a frightening visit to her bed years afterward:

> It is 1954 on the same North Carolina farm, in the same narrow wooden farmhouse. Lillian, too, is in bed, in a room with her aunts. She hears a sound, someone moving quietly on the wooden floorboards, then feels well-callused hands reaching out for her, the hands of her step-grandfather, the same man who raped her mother, the man named Isaiah Hill. Before anything else happens, Lillian screams. Her grandmother hears her screams, rescues her, and moves her to the room where her uncles sleep. She, too, was eleven years old. Lillian remembers sobbing that night and saying to

> *herself with deep anguish, Oh God, I'll be glad when I grow*
> *up and get out of here!*

After recounting the tale, Lillian spoke with deep emotion. "My people are rough!" Isaiah Hill "was just a man who just didn't care."

Years later, Lillian would rescue one of her own daughters. For some time, Lillian had noticed that fifteen-year-old Theresa was sometimes withdrawn and at other times nervous and distant, but she did not know why. Then Lillian came into the house unexpectedly one day and it suddenly became clear:

> *It is 1977. Theresa, fifteen, was later able to say it had*
> *started when she was twelve. The man was a friend of her*
> *mother's, someone who stayed in the house, someone who*
> *touched her body when her mother wasn't around. Theresa*
> *was frightened, but she couldn't tell anyone and couldn't*
> *make him stop. She avoided him, but he persisted. She*
> *became withdrawn, edgy, but still hid the problem. One day,*
> *her mother came into the apartment and noticed the man*
> *standing close to Theresa, so close that her mother suddenly*
> *understood—from her own experience—why Theresa had*
> *become so withdrawn. Lillian began asking the man sharp,*
> *direct questions. He denied ever bothering Theresa. He told*
> *Lillian she was imagining things. Lillian questioned Theresa,*
> *gently this time, remembering her own pain. Theresa denied*
> *that she had been touched. Lillian persisted, just as softly as*
> *she had begun. Theresa broke and, in tears, told her mother*
> *about the secret she had hidden for years. Lillian turned her*
> *fury on the man. The abuse finally was ended.*

The Years in North Carolina

Isaiah "Sack" Hill died in November 1985 on a farm nine miles north of Kinston, North Carolina, at the age of seventy-one. Five months before his death, he calmly denied in an interview that he ever had raped or molested anyone. We were seated together on a two-person bench on the front porch of the small house he rented for sixty dollars a month, not far from the farm where Lillian's mother said the rapes had occurred.

"That's a lie," Hill said with a slight smile about the rapes of his stepdaughter, Lillian Williams's mother. It seemed that he had spoken about it before. He was not shocked or upset by the questions. "All lies. No, that ain't right," he said, laughing. "I don't know what [my stepdaughter] told you that for."

Asked about molesting that stepdaughter's daughter, Lillian, fifteen years later, Hill replied, "No. I don't remember that."

But Lillian Williams and her mother were emphatic about Isaiah Hill's sexual abuse of them. Lillian said the harassment went further than that one night he felt her in the dark. "He was someone that would try to approach me. I would go to my people and try to explain it to them, you know, but it was like they didn't want to believe me."

Lillian was indignant about Hill's denials. "Just like people. They always want to try and hide things, you know. They don't want anybody to know anything about their personal life."

The Hills's weathered clapboard farmhouse on the south side of rural Route 58 in Lenoir County no longer exists. Corn was growing in the June sun in the place where the house once stood, where Lillian Williams's family harvested and looped tobacco leaves, where Lillian Williams's family chopped and gathered cotton, where Lillian Williams lived before she came to Washington in 1954.

Just as the farmhouse has disappeared, it is difficult to find records of Lillian Williams's ancestors. They lived within their own closed society, as outcasts from the larger, white world of Lenoir County. It was a world that regarded them with disdain. It was a world that kept them in perpetual poverty and exploited their labor.

It was a world that the black sharecroppers feared and hated, a world to which they most often showed a disingenuous face, almost never letting outsiders know what they were really thinking, what they were really doing. That was for survival, too. Still, it was through the eyes of the outside world that these sharecroppers looked at themselves, and seeing themselves as the outside world did, they hated what they saw and were particularly brutal toward one another.

Lillian Williams's mother never thought of going outside her isolated sharecropping world to report the rapes. Even in her youth, she knew enough to understand that whatever the outside, white world offered in the form of protection was not to be extended to a little black girl, the daughter of dirt-poor sharecroppers.

Not much had changed in this racial relationship years later, when Lillian Williams was growing up in the fifties and was, in turn, molested by the same man.

The family did not own the land they farmed. They kept no

Tauscha Vaughn working at a downtown McDonald's restaurant

ALL PHOTOGRAPHS ARE COPYRIGHT © BY FRED SWEETS OF *THE WASHINGTON POST*.

Tauscha Vaughn and Reggie Wiley outside her house

Sherita Dreher and her son, Marquis, who was born when she was fifteen

A volatile family meeting that turned out to be the last of its kind. From left to right, Carol Sherrod, Sherita Dreher, Jackie Sherrod, and Therresia Thomas argue away.

Marquis Dreher gets a consoling kiss from his mother, Sherita. They moved sixteen times in the boy's first two years of life.

Lillian Williams with her Bible and a note that she wrote in her journal. She wrote: "My heavenly father, you said . . . that you shall supply all my needs . . ." and then listed the items necessary to care for herself and sixteen others in her household—seven sons, four daughters, and five grandchildren.

Oh my heavenly father you said in phil
that you shall supply all my needs,
father I need washing power, — Cloth rox
3 boxes of chicken wings 2 cans of shortning
1.5 pound bag of flour — 6 loaf of bread
1 large rice
2 margerine, 10 pound bag of potatoes
6 can of sweet peas

Lillian Williams, who has eleven children ranging in age from eleven to twenty-three, stands outside her home in Southeast Washington with six of her seven sons—all of whom have the last name Williams—Isaac, Ronnie, Leon, Earl, Anthony, and Charlie. Ronnie and Charlie have each fathered a child.

Lillian Williams, who says she grew up "looking for love," hugs her mother, Lillian Waters.

Author Leon Dash, left, interviewing Isaiah "Sack" Hill at his home in Lenoir County, North Carolina, just before Hill's death

Theresa Williams, second from right, at church with other members of her family. From left to right are Isaac, Leon, Lillian, Sherita, Theresa, and Jeremiah.

Melissa Williams, in the last month of pregnancy, with Dr. Chee Tse at the Congress Heights Neighborhood Health Center

financial records. They sometimes forgot to fill out birth certificates. Birth dates were logged into the family Bible by one of the few relatives who could write. Most of her family could not read or write. So they kept no diaries and wrote no letters.

Just two generations before them, their progenitors had worked for nothing as slaves and were counted as capital. The sharecroppers worked to bring capital to the South and provide a bare subsistence for themselves. Survival was a priority, education was not. Education was for the privileged, those who did not have to answer the farm owner's bell in the predawn darkness signaling for the work to begin in his fields. The bell rang again for the sharecroppers to come in for the midday meal. It rang in the early afternoon for the field work to start again. It was rung again, with a welcome finality, at dusk, indicating it was time to go home. Even for those who managed to go to school, theirs was the inferior education of segregation, the one falsely proclaimed to be "separate but equal."

The telling of much of this family's story depended on the memories of Lillian Williams, her mother, and other relatives, interviewed separately at their homes in Washington, Kinston, Lenoir County, Baltimore, and Harpers Ferry, West Virginia. It was not an easy story for them to tell. It is not an easy story to retell.

The Forebears

Those recollections, sometimes sharp, sometimes blurred by time, nearly always colored by emotion, begin in the early 1900's with Lillian Williams's great-grandparents, Lettuce and Frank Harper. The Harpers ruled over a large, extended family. Lettuce had two children as an unmarried teenager and then had twenty more after marrying Frank Harper. Like other marriages recounted by Lillian's family, the union of Lettuce and Frank Harper appeared to be one of economic survival rather than one based on love, a learned emotion.

Children were a welcome necessity among sharecroppers like Lettuce and Frank Harper. Infertility was a heavy social burden for a woman. A girl who had proven her fertility by having children had a higher value than one who had none. Moreover, an unmarried girl with children had not reduced her chances of marrying as she might in an urban setting. Her children and she had value in the farmlands of North Carolina. Young, landless black men, anxious to get a sharecropping arrangement on a white-owned farm, were not put off by a young woman with children. They were drawn to them.

A sharecropping contract went all the more easily to those share-croppers with large families. Some landowners refused sharecrop arrangements to couples who did not have children. These couples managed to get sharecropping arrangements by adopting the children of relatives and friends and raising the youngsters as their own. Children were put to work on the farm at early ages. They were economic assets.

These conditions gave root to patterns of early childbearing, which are clearly identifiable in Lillian's life today, although the economic imperative for them no longer exists.

So Frank Harper married Lettuce and adopted her two children. They were raised as Harpers. He subsequently was given farmland to sharecrop in exchange for all the labor he could provide. The farmer advanced Harper credit through the year in food and clothes for his family. After the harvest, Harper and the farmer split the cash crops fifty-fifty. The farmer also subtracted from Harper's half of the harvest the amount, in dollar equivalents, he claimed to have advanced Harper during the year, plus interest.

If Harper was like many other sharecroppers, he usually did not "pay out" of debt. Instead, he owed the landlord large sums of money both in years of a good harvest and in years of a bad harvest. The only acceptable manner Harper could protest the debt was governed strictly by Southern customs of black-white male relations—he could move to another farm. It was not acceptable for Harper to challenge the arithmetic that kept him in debt. Such a challenge would be treated as an affront to the veracity of a white man, a judgment a black man was not allowed to make. Retribution would be swift, if not final. Even if Harper knew enough to add and subtract, if he was *put off* the land, he would have had difficulty landing another sharecropping arrangement anywhere nearby. Few other farm owners would hire such an "uppity" share-cropper.

The Harpers ran their farm according to a well-established set of priorities that had governed the family dating from the post-Reconstruction period after the Civil War.

The farm came first, the family came next, and education came last. It was common for black boys and girls to miss most of any school year, if they attended at all, at the nearby segregated one-room schoolhouse. The farm demanded their constant attention and labor. Girls were not expected to finish the inferior education available to black children, but rather, to begin to bear children early in their lives—children who could eventually be put to work on the farm. Children would assure a sharecropping contract. Children would assure the family's survival.

The regular replenishment of a sharecropping family's human labor, through procreation or adoption, guaranteed them a place on the land. Elderly sharecroppers were forced to move off the farm by the owner once all their children had grown up and left. Cotton and tobacco are hard taskmasters. They demand youthful, backbending labor from seedling to market.

Among the Harpers and families like them, patterns began to emerge. Teenage pregnancy was one, abandonment another, absence of love a third, and family violence yet a fourth.

Lettuce Harper gave birth to a daughter and a son before she met Frank Harper. Both children were raised as Harpers after Lettuce married Frank.

Eva Bell Harper, Lettuce Harper's eldest daughter and the grandmother of Lillian Williams, is buried at the Shady Grove Free Will Baptist Church in Greene County, North Carolina. The church, a red brick structure, sits on Route 1091 not far from the family's old North Carolina homestead in adjacent Lenoir County. Her headstone records her birth date as May 28, 1908, and her date of death, after a long, debilitating bout with cancer, as February 3, 1985.

Lillian Williams said only her grandmother's date of death is accurate. No one really knew exactly when Eva was born, not even she. But all who knew Eva agreed that she was a *severe,* closed woman.

Her granddaughter, Lillian Williams, said, "She was a *hard* woman."

Her grandson, William Earl Manley, who goes by the name Bill, remarked, "She was a *hard, mean* woman and unfair."

Lillian and Bill's mother said, "My mother was hard, but she had to be that way. That's the way she come up. My mother was raised by Frank Harper, her stepfather. He was mean to all the children, even his own. She said her momma was mean, too."

One hot summer day, Frank Harper trussed up his adolescent son Marvin with a plowline as punishment for some childish infraction. Frank affixed the leather straps "so that if Marvin moved, Marvin would choke," remembered Lillian's mother. "Left him like that from six in the morning until after midnight. I couldn't understand how [Lettuce Harper] would let this man do her child like that. I guess she did not want to challenge his role as head of the household."

The witness to Frank Harper's brutality toward his son was Lillian Harper Waters, who was born on July 12, 1928, the first of Eva's children. Waters said she knows her mother was young when she gave birth to her, but she does not know her mother's actual birth date.

Early in her life, Waters felt the pain of rejection. Her grandmother, Lettuce Harper, "raised me. I called her 'Momma.' She was the only one that did love me in the house."

She called her step-grandfather, Frank Harper, "Poppa," but he had little time for her. "He didn't want nothing to do with me. He rejected me. It hurted me! He didn't like me so good 'cause he didn't like my father, Ike Washington."

Ike Washington, who lived on a nearby farm, was not allowed to cross the doorstep of the Harper home. "Poppa didn't like him to come there." Frank Harper would say to Washington, *"Don't* come in my yard! I know you got a young'un here. If you want to see her, she'll come outside to see ya."

The love Waters wanted from Frank Harper was not made up by her father. "My father bought me one pair of shoes when I was coming up. That's all he ever did for me. He didn't never show me no love," although she saw him often in the countryside or in Kinston.

The deepest wound, however, was cut by her mother, Eva. "I called my mother, 'Bee Baby,' never 'Momma.' I don't know where I get that name from for her. My mother, she didn't like me either. I guess my mother rejected me because my father didn't marry her. He married another woman."

Within a short span, her mother gave birth to a second child, a boy, by another man. After the birth of her son, Eva started "keeping company" with a third man, Isaiah Hill. They married in 1932. Eva took her son with her when she moved to the farm along Route 58 with her husband. She left four-year-old Waters with Lettuce and Frank Harper.

Years later, Waters also would walk out on her children on three separate occasions.

In late 1938, Frank Harper took ill. He would ask his wife, Lettuce, to bring him a glass of water. Lettuce, tired from a day's work, would send Waters or one of her other children. "That man was so scared that some of [his children] was gonna poison him, he wouldn't even drink the water we brung to him. He was scared 'cause he was so mean, mean, mean" to all the children. Frank Harper did not recover and died the next year.

Moving in with Eva Bell

While Waters lived with the Harpers, she managed to get to the second grade in school. She decided to move to her mother's house on a farm three miles away after Frank Harper died. "I wanted to get to know my mother." She arrived unannounced, and her mother, without a greeting, asked her what she wanted. She told her mother that she wanted to get to know her and her sisters and brothers. Eva grudgingly consented to letting her stay.

She was eleven years old. "Then I had to stay out of school. Take care the rest of [my mother's] children. Baby-sitter, housekeeper, cook" is what she became.

She was motivated to do the work in her mother's house by a secret hope. "Maybe, just maybe, she'll get to love me like she do the rest of" her children. "That's what I was looking for from my mother. She had love for my other sisters. Why can't she have some for me?" she asked herself. "She didn't never buy me no clothes. I would always get hand-me-downs. My other sisters got new clothes. She got new clothes. But I didn't never get new clothes."

Soon after Waters moved in with her mother, the rapes began. Isaiah Hill often followed her home from the fields—she left early because it was her job to cook dinner—and trapped her in the cookhouse alone. (The rapes are part of the family's lore. Two other family members, both men, discussed the attacks in separate interviews.)

As she talks about the rapes, her face becomes drawn, her eyes turn sad, a tear starts to form. She was born a Harper, changed her name to Hill after moving in with her mother, took the name Manley from her first marriage, and her name is Waters now from her second marriage. She lived in Baltimore when I met her in May 1985 in a room that she rented in a two-story row house. She rarely saw her family, visiting her daughter Lillian two or three times a year.

Waters was a plump woman with a round face and dark brown
eyes that were clear and steady, until she started talking about the
rapes. Then she looked down, her eyes filling with tears as she
remembered how her mother had refused to believe her.

"Every time I come home to cook, my stepfather always followed. Somehow or another, he could get away from my mother and
come to the house. And then at night he would come to my bed."
Isaiah Hill told her, "If I tell it, what he did, he was gonna do
something to my mother." She felt "he would've, too, because he was
[always] fighting my mother."

But the frightened girl told her mother in spite of the threats. "I
was telling my mother that he come to my bed, you know, at night,
and she didn't believe me." She told her the first time it happened.
Her mother replied that she did not believe her, "and I don't want
you to say that no more."

Desperate, the girl went to her grandmother, Lettuce Harper.
Lettuce told Eva, "Why don't you listen at her when she tell you
something? I ain't never known her to lie." But Eva responded
angrily, "I *don't* believe it! I *don't* believe it! I *don't* belive it!"
Lettuce gave her daughter an exasperated look. "One day you is
gonna *believe* it!"

Lettuce had not confronted her husband about his extraordinarily cruel treatment of their son Marvin. Now Lettuce's daughter Eva would not confront Isaiah about his alleged sexual abuse of
Eva's daughter. Waters was on her own. The rapes continued.

She got pregnant and began to show. Eva asked her who the
father was. "I told who it was. Then she believed." She asked herself
why her mother had waited "until it was too late. She could've did
something about it before then."

Eva now confronted her husband. She told him, " 'Stead of you
trying to teach her things, telling her right from wrong, you were
making sex with her."

Waters never emotionally recovered. Forty-six years after the
rapes, "I sits down and think about it, you know. Even today. I sits
down and cry about it. It hurts real bad. I just keep it inside of me.
I talk to my children about it." The rapes produced a child, a boy.
Waters was only twelve years old when she went into labor on March
10, 1941, and delivered the baby in a room at the farmhouse.

With all her pain, there was no one for Waters to talk to. "My
mother, she was not a friend. Couldn't sit down and talk to my
mother. Never could sit down and talk to her. Never could. She

didn't like me. She just come right out and told me she didn't like me."

Sometime after Waters's first child was born, she finally learned that all her efforts to win her mother's love, all the pain she had endured in her mother's house, all had been for nothing. Her mother, an aunt, and Waters were weeding, or "thinning," cotton in a field together. Her mother began to yell at Waters, saying that she was not thinning the cotton correctly. Waters complained that she would do it right and it was not necessary for her mother to yell.

Eva responded with something that Waters had not expected, that was out of any context of what they were doing or what had been said. "Well, I don't love you no way. I love [your aunt] better than I do *you!*"

Crushed, tears welling in her eyes, Waters responded with a shrillness she had not known she had in her. "Well, if you didn't love me, why didn't you let me *die* before I was born?" Her mother did not answer. "She just walked off from there." The aunt "was very embarrassed." The aunt and Waters still talk about that scene today.

Two years after the birth of her first child, fourteen-year-old Waters married a twenty-two-year-old man she had met only three weeks before. "I didn't love him." She wanted to get away, escape from all the pain—her mother, Isaiah Hill, the memory of the rapes. The young man was desperate to marry to qualify for a sharecropping arrangement. Waters and her new husband, William Henry "Toochie" Manley, moved away, leaving her two-year-old son with her mother. The couple moved to a farm sixteen miles west of Kinston, near the town of La Grange, North Carolina.

No Escape

Waters soon realized that her marriage would not provide the solace she craved. Her husband, according to her, was "a terribly jealous" and insecure man who swept the dust in the front yard each morning before leaving for the fields. When he returned in the evening, "Toochie searched the dust to see if any man's footprints had crossed it while he was out."

Toochie told her he had seen other wives "cheat" on their husbands, and she was not going to get the chance to do the same to him. "Honest to God, that man was *mean.* That man beated me [during] breakfast, dinner, supper 'n' 'tween meals. He was just that *mean.*"

At the end of August 1943, Waters went into labor, "and he wasn't even home." She was a month past fifteen and frightened. She walked up to the farmer's house, notified the couple there, and walked back home. The farmer and his wife brought a very elderly midwife, who delivered Waters's first daughter, Lillian, on August 28, 1943. The midwife died before she made out Lillian's birth certificate, and Waters never bothered to get one. She wrote her daughter's birth date in her Bible years later.

Her husband was "crazy about Lillian," but Toochie's love for his daughter did not produce any peace in the couple's relationship.

Lillian was a year old when Waters, who was five months pregnant, overheard Toochie telling the farm owner how he kept his wife barefoot and pregnant. "Yeah, that's how I keep my wife. I keep her pregnant all the time and barefoot." Waters was furious. "I didn't have no shoes to put on my feet. *Oooooh,* that made me so mad. I went and I hit him on top of the head with my suitcase and cut at him the same time with the butcher knife. And I left." Toochie tried to stop her, but she told him, "I heard you talking to the white man about me. You ought to be 'shame of yourself talking to a white man 'bout your wife." All she had for her feet were a pair of sandals. "He purposely didn't give me no money and no shoes." Waters returned to her husband after a brief stay at her mother's house.

On December 9, 1944, their son, William Earl "Bill" Manley, was born in Portsmouth, Virginia, where Toochie had recently been employed as a factory boiler tender. They were living with Toochie's relatives. The beatings continued, in some ways worsened. On one occasion, Toochie was choking Waters so badly that his brother-in-law pried his fingers away from Waters's throat. Waters left soon after, leaving her children, including Lillian, with her husband. Her son Bill was not yet walking. She went back to her mother's farm. Unskilled, uneducated, penniless, she had no place else to go.

Waters's brother-in-law brought the children to her mother's house a month later. Toochie came to Kinston six months later, but stayed only a short while before returning to Portsmouth. Waters has not heard from him since.

At the age of sixteen, Waters found herself back at her mother's house caring for her three children and working in the tobacco fields. She had to share the space of the narrow house with her stepfather, a daily reminder of the rapes. It was not where she wanted to be.

Remembering: 1953

The years of hurt finally came to a climactic head between mother and daughter during a July tobacco harvest. As Waters sat in her living room in Baltimore, she remembered the incident and got angry all over again:

> *It was the summer of 1953. She was twenty-five. She was using thread to loop tobacco leaves onto sticks so they could be hung and dried. The thread kept breaking, so she doubled it for more strength. Her mother told her not to double the thread, that there wasn't enough thread, but Waters ignored her. Eva picked up a " 'bacca stick. Great big thick 'bacca stick" and broke it across Waters's back. "I kept right on looping," she said. "Yeah, it hurt. She was fixing to hit me again, so I snatched it out of her hand. You know what?" she told Eva. "You better thank God you my mother 'cause you weren't my mother I would break this stick over your* head!" *She threw the stick down and walked out of the tobacco barn. Her mother yelled, "Come back here! Come back here!" but she ignored her. "I went home. I packed my clothes. Washed up." She walked out of her mother's house, got a ride to Kinston, and did domestic work there for a year. She also abandoned her children once more.*

Lillian remembers the day, too. She still isn't sure what happened. She only knows that the pattern was repeated again, that her mother left, walked right past her without saying a word:

> *She was nine, standing on a corner of the porch at the wooden farmhouse. Suddenly she heard her grandmother loudly cursing at her mother. "The profanity that she used, I would not like to repeat it. Eva Bell was very rough. Every word come out her mouth, it was a cuss word. I was wondering what was going on." Her mother walked across the porch and out to Route 58, all the time ignoring Lillian's grandmother's loud cursing. Suitcase in hand, she got into a car. Lillian said she remembers thinking, "She isn't coming back!"*

The Years in Washington

Following the path of thousands of other sharecroppers, Waters arrived in Washington about a year later looking for work. She got a job as a room cleaner at a Silver Spring, Maryland, motel in the suburban outskirts of Washington.

Once again, she had left without taking her children—she had five by this time, the last two the result of brief affairs in 1947 and 1952. The first two, including Lillian, she left with her mother. The third, Bill, was taken in by her former husband's mother. The last two she had given to two married friends who were childless. Months later, a relative knocked on her door and told her some shocking news: Isaiah Hill, her stepfather, had tried to molest eleven-year-old Lillian.

Waters said the relative told her: "You know what happened to you, and didn't no one believe you. You go get your child before it is too late."

Waters headed for North Carolina, where she confronted Hill. She said they had this conversation:

Waters: "I hear you went to my daughter's bed and tried to bother her? Have sex with her?"

Hill: "You know I ain't done nothing like that."

Waters: "You did me the same way."

Hill: "Well, that was a mistake."

That was enough for Waters. She took Lillian and went back to Washington. She made no effort to retrieve her other four children. One of them, four-year-old Cherry, did come to live with Waters and Lillian a few years later; the others grew up without knowing their mother.

Inside a basement apartment near the Howard University campus, Lillian and her mother developed an uneasy relationship. Lillian had been glad to leave North Carolina, glad to escape the harsh, periodic beatings from her grandmother, glad to escape the sexual abuse, glad to get away from her step-grandfather. But she quickly learned that her mother could be just like grandmother Eva—quick-tempered, profane, ready to beat Lillian for small things.

Before she came to live with her mother, "I used to get whippings and things like that for things I didn't do." Her grandmother Eva beat all the children with ropes and extension cords until they bled.

Punishment included staying under a bed or under the house for hours.

Lillian can remember picking cotton as soon as she was tall enough to drag a shoulder bag hooked over her left shoulder and walk down the planted rows to reach the ripening cotton balls. At other times, she picked ripening cucumbers up off the ground.

She also remembered five families living together in her grandmother's house when she was a child. Grandmother Eva had eleven children with Isaiah Hill, three of Eva's unmarried daughters had eight children between them, and there was Lillian and her two brothers. Up until the time she left, Lillian did not recall her grandmother once complaining about her daughters' having children before marrying, and Lillian did not see these circumstances as anything but normal.

There was constant violence in the house between her grandmother and her step-grandfather. "They fought all the time. Isaiah would be raging" when he came home drunk. "He was a heavy drinker. Was often drunk. She didn't take nothing off him." Eva and Isaiah had fistfights. "Sometimes [they fought] with knives. One time she shot at him with a shotgun." He ran. "He was just shaking dust behind him. After then, Daddy didn't do much bothering her. If he love-ed her, he didn't show it."

It was the afternoon of March 21, 1985, when Lillian was interrupted at this juncture in her family's history. Her firstborn, Kenneth Earl Williams, twenty-three, walked into the living looking very dejected. He had been sent home again, the third time in as many days, from the construction site where he worked as a general laborer. "It seems like he doesn't want us to work every day," Earl told his mother. Since our meeting in September, this was Earl's sixth job, one that had held the promise of steady, full-time work. After Earl had gone back outside, Lillian turned to me and said, "Earl is very discouraged and depressed" about his inability to find a full-time job.

In June 1985 I visited Isaiah Hill in Lenoir County. From his front porch, Isaiah pointed out a tall clump of trees where he had hidden a whiskey still when he and Eva were married. He said making and drinking moonshine was one of his few pleasures when he was a younger man. He also denied another part of his stepdaughter's and step-granddaughter's recollections. He said he and Eva never fought.

Lillian said when she lived with Isaiah and her grandmother, Eva did not express any love for her. "I felt unloved. I felt nobody cared about me. I come from a family [in which] I felt like there was no love in the home. Even as a child right up until now, I feel like there is no love in my family."

After her move to Washington, Lillian learned how much her mother's wrath could be like that of her grandmother. Waters had put a pot of black-eyed peas on the stove over a low flame to simmer. She told Lillian to watch them while she was out and to turn the flame off when the peas were done. Lillian went outside to play and forgot all about the peas. When her mother returned, the peas were burnt, and an angry Waters accosted Lillian. "She love black-eyed peas. My mother cussed me, and she called me *all* kinds of names. I already felt bad because I already felt like she didn't want me!"

Lillian began looking elsewhere for comfort. "I used to run from man to man, looking for love. When I was young, I didn't get that love. I didn't get that attention. I didn't get no love at all," she said.

By the time she entered Banneker Junior High School in the mid-fifties, Lillian often did not bother to go to school. "I got out there and got wild. I played hooky." She dropped out in the seventh grade. When Lillian was fourteen, in 1957, she dated her first boyfriend, an eighteen-year-old youth she dubbed "Red Reggie" because of his light-colored skin.

At first, she did not like him because of his light complexion. "See, I had a color problem. I didn't like red people." When she started seeing him, Red Reggie tried to force her to have sex with him. "Red Reggie felt he could get any girl he wanted because he was light-skinned. It was different with me though. I've always like-ed dark people. Black people. I never had sex with him."

Lillian's next boyfriend was different. He was brown-skinned and in his twenties. "He was the first one. I was so in love with him I did *want* to have a child by him. Matter fact, I *did* have a child by him."

It did not occur to her, she said, that fourteen was too young to have a baby. In the sharecropping world she had grown up in, it was not uncommon for girls to have babies at even younger ages. Her mother and three of her aunts all had had children as teenagers; if they regretted it, they never talked about it around Lillian.

As soon as Lillian showed an interest in boys, her mother told her: "Be careful! You know if you have sex now, you know what's going to happen." Periodically, her mother would ask: "When's the last time you seen your monthly?" and threaten to evict her if she got pregnant. Her mother seemed to accept that Lillian would have sex, telling her only that she should make sure that her boyfriend used "protection."

Like many of the other women and girls of Washington Highlands today, Lillian's family sex-education instruction began and ended on these three points: *Do not get pregnant, you will be put out if you do, and use protection if you are sexually active.* Lillian ignored the advice about contraception for reasons that some teenagers in Washington Highlands do: "I didn't like [birth control]. It wasn't natural."

One day, when Waters asked about Lillian's "monthly," Lillian said it was two months late. Lillian had told her adult boyfriend already. He had reacted happily and asked her to marry him. She told him no, to wait a couple of years. "I just wasn't ready to get married. I didn't want to be tied up."

Her mother's reaction was very different. Waters was furious. Using a concoction of powdered mustard, she made her daughter have an abortion. "I hated my mother for that."

The boyfriend also was angered by the abortion and reacted in a manner identical to that of Willie Hood, who grew up a generation later in a separate but equally poverty-stricken community in Southeast Washington. Lillian's boyfriend "was so angry he threatened to kill me for getting rid of my baby." Lillian said he was serious, and she avoided him for several days until he had cooled down. Their relationship sputtered to an end after the abortion.

Lillian said she was in her late thirties before she was able to forgive her mother: "I felt abortion was wrong. That's murder. I still feel the same way today." When her second-oldest daughter talked of aborting her second pregnancy, Lillian talked her out of it. When an uncle tried to convince her third daughter to abort the girl's first pregnancy, Lillian angrily told him to mind his own business. As disappointed as Lillian was with the girl's pregnancy, she proclaimed, "There will be no abortions in *my* house."

Lillian met the father of her oldest child, a former farmer named Charlie Williams, Jr., during an early summer visit home to Kinston in 1959. They were sexually active without any contraception, but Lillian did not get pregnant.

Charlie's father had been "a thirder," a tenant farmer who had his own equipment and livestock and received two thirds of every crop he cultivated. Charlie's father was, therefore, better off financially than his neighboring sharecroppers, who only received half the crop after debts were paid off. But the life of the farmer was not going to be for him, Charlie decided early in life. "I never liked the farm. Never liked the work on the farm."

Charlie's mother had had one child by another man before she married his father, and Charlie was the firstborn of the seven children in his mother's marriage, he said.

The year after he met Lillian, Charlie was headed to New York City to look for work, traveling with one of Lillian's uncles. He had planned to make Washington just a stopover, but he ran into Lillian again. He found a job tying steel rods in building construction and stayed in Washington.

The couple resumed their relationship. Her first child was born on May 22, 1961. She was in love with Charlie and *consciously* desired to have *his* child, she said. She did not expect him to marry her. He just don't look like the marrying type, she told herself at the time.

Nonetheless, they did marry on July 3, 1961. Charlie was twenty-one; Lillian was seventeen. Her mother had objected to the marriage. "Oh, that boy," said Waters recalling her advice to Lillian not to marry Charlie, in spite of having a child by him. "He was a black boy. He was *real* coal black, and he thought he was the prettiest thing in the world. He wasn't the kind or type of person that could take care of a family, and I knew this." In her lifetime, Waters had seen similar marriages in rural North Carolina and felt her daughter's union would not work out. Waters also knew Charlie's family from Lenoir County.

Lillian remembered what her mother had to say: "He's not good for you. All he's gonna do is get you stuck with a lot of babies and leave you." Lillian said, "Looks like she was right about it. I wish I had listened to her. It seemed as though she knew what he would do."

By his own description, Charlie Williams followed a life-style that had been part of his childhood and suited him. He did not agree that he had shortchanged his household and growing family. "I gambled and I drank and I was mean. Well, I had a temper." His mother told Charlie that his temper came about by her "fighting my father" when she was pregnant with him. "I'm still that way today," he said in a June 1985 interview outside his Kinston home, where he lived with a second wife.

Lillian remembers him the same way. And the nickname he earned from his days-long gambling exploits. "Most people called him Big Time Charlie."

There was a lot of violence in the Williams house, according to Lillian, Charlie, Waters, and several family members. It was the same type of family violence they had all witnessed as children growing up in Lenoir County.

Once, Charlie went after Lillian with a knife; he was stopped by a female in-law who stabbed him in the throat, chipping a bone in the back of Charlie's neck. "I never will forget that. I had plastic surgery on" the long scar, he said.

Another time, Waters knocked Charlie across a room with a right-hand punch to the jaw. The conflict between Charlie and Lillian's mother evolved in this manner, family members agreed: Periodically, Charlie would not be seen for days during one of his gambling and heavy-drinking sprees. Lillian's brothers and Waters would often have to buy food for the Williams children. When Waters once fussed with Charlie about it, he told her that the food was "Lillian's problem" and demanded that his mother-in-law get out of his house.

Finally, Waters insisted to Lillian that she go on the welfare rolls, leave Charlie out of her life, and get an apartment for herself and her children. Waters came over from Baltimore to put some furniture in the apartment. "The first thing I saw was him propped up in her apartment. *Oooooh,* that burnt me up. I smelled blood." Waters challenged Charlie. "What in the world are you doing in here? I don't want you 'round here!"

Charlie told Waters he could come to see his children anytime he wanted. Waters did not accept that. "No, you can't. You can't do this." Waters remembers that she "hit that man so hard I knocked him slam 'cross the room." She was not finished. "I'll kill you, you black bastard! I want you out of here right *now*!"

Charlie said Waters hit him when he went to walk past her. "I really didn't think she had the heart to hit *me,* really. She's a tough cat."

He went out onto the sidewalk and loudly dared Waters to come out and fight him. Waters said she started to go, but two of her sons, who were there that day, stopped her. They went out in her place. There was a great deal of loud talking between the three angry men but no more fighting.

On another occasion, Charlie shot a gun at one of Lillian's brothers, Bill. Both men agree that the bullet grazed the man's forehead. Charlie said he was forced to do it. Bill had punched him in the face for "messing over my sister." To Charlie, shooting Bill in the face was the correct and manly response.

After five years of marriage, there were six children. Lillian had wanted to have a tubal ligation after her fifth child was born, but Charlie would not hear of it. "I told him I wanted to have my tubes tied. He said, 'That's what God put you here for, to have babies!' " In the fall of 1966, when their sixth child was three months old, Charlie and Lillian split up, and Charlie left for good.

They accuse each other of ruining the relationship. Lillian said, "My husband cut out on me first. And I said, 'Two can play this game.' I was running around, not realizing I was hurting myself."

Charlie sees it differently. "Her and I were both too young. We were growing up when we got married." But he believes they would have stayed together if Lillian's family had not interfered. "We was doing fine until [her] family got into it."

Charlie said he paid a lawyer two hundred fifty dollars for a divorce from Lillian sometime between 1970 and 1973. The divorce was granted by Washington's Superior Court, he added. A lengthy check of court records from 1961 to 1985 did not turn up any record of a divorce. Lillian said she had never received any notification of a divorce.

After they separated, Lillian had a brief romance with one of Charlie's friends, a relationship that resulted in her seventh child. "I was looking for love, but I didn't get it." Her lover was "real sneaky" and never bothered to tell Lillian that he was a friend of Charlie's.

"Before I got saved that was my biggest problem—men. It was like I was looking for something out of a man that a man couldn't give. I was just looking for someone to just *love* me!"

She did not feel very good about herself, and she wanted a man to make her feel good. She said: "Hey, if I love you, why can't you love me back? If I was carrying your child, you can't show me that you care? I was very easy to be hurt if I had a boyfriend and I really got stuck on him. Then he tells me, 'I love you.' And I would say, 'Tell me that you *love* me!' That's all I want to hear. Tell me that you won't do me wrong. Even by me bringing this out now, I feel like I'm gonna cry. I been done wrong *so many times!*"

Then, in 1969, she met Fred Lee Williams, who had been born twenty-eight years before in the same rural community as Lillian outside La Grange. Fred had come to Washington from Lenoir

County looking for work. He had sharecropped from the age of eight, when his father died of a stroke. Two of his parents' twelve children "were behind me," making Fred the eldest male in his mother's house. So he dropped out of the third grade and began farming. His mother worked tobacco, chopped cotton, and did general farm work for forty cents an hour. "I don't read any," said Fred, having forgotten what little he'd learned.

Fred said he moved away from Kinston after being cheated by a white farmer on sharecropping work. The farmer's brother and son-in-law had told him he was being cheated. In Washington, Fred got work "digging ditches and pulling concrete" slabs on building construction sites. He became Lillian's common-law husband and the father of three of her last four children. He had left his wife, he said, after he caught her with his younger brother.

For a short period, Lillian was content. "I knew Fred loved me. He was just like a husband to me." Fred helped her financially with her children. Lillian was pregnant in 1969 with the first of Fred's children when Charlie Williams showed up for a short visit. Charlie asked Lillian, "Do you know [Fred's] my cousin?" Lillian told him she had not. "It's too late now," she added. Fred said Lillian told him that she was married to his cousin after their child was born. Nevertheless, he asked Lillian to marry him. Somehow Lillian never got around to getting a divorce. "I'm against divorce," she said.

Although Fred and she lived together for thirteen years, Lillian said her desperate need for love led her to "run around." She had a secret affair for two years that resulted in her tenth child, born in 1972. First, she told Fred the baby was his, but he did not believe her. Later, she admitted the child was by someone else. Fred forgave her.

"I was a nagging woman," Lillian said of herself during these years. "I was afraid to receive love [from Fred] because I had been tricked so many times." She was so suspicious that she accused Fred of "running around with other women, even though he said he wasn't doing anything."

Lillian finally had a tubal ligation immediately after her eleventh child was born in 1974. Two years later she began to feel the spiritual pull of religion. She and Fred responded to a palm reader's tract they found on his car's windshield.

During several increasingly expensive trips to the woman, who called herself Sister Rose, Lillian told her that she was always under a great deal of stress and that she was seeking the Lord, but did not know how to find him. The palm reader sold Lillian an amulet to ward off the evil spirits, which Sister Rose said was the cause of the stress. She instructed Lillian to wear the charm every day. Lillian wore it under her bra. After the woman asked for six hundred dollars to help Fred and Lillian find the Lord, the couple decided to stop going. However, Lillian continued to wear the amulet.

Months afterward, she was watching the religious television ministry of Jim Bakker's *PTL Club* program. She does not remember if Bakker hosted the program that day, but she vividly recalls the preacher on the show speaking to her.

The man said, "There is a lady watching who is seeking the Lord, but you don't know how to go about it." According to Lillian, the preacher went on to describe the dress she was wearing and the blue amulet. The minister told her to take off the charm and burn it. And she did, in a trash can. "That's when the Lord came into my life. It wasn't like an instant thing. It took several years."

Her relationship continued with Fred, but in 1982, after Lillian became a born-again Christian, she decided that living with him was sinful and asked him to leave her house.

"It didn't look right for him to be living here and us not being married," she said.

Welfare Myth

Throughout these years, there was never enough money. Lillian's older children remember standing silently around their mother, her head down in her arms, as she cried on the kitchen table because she did not have enough food for them or had to separate them, sending them to different relatives' homes after they had been evicted from an apartment. Charlie's six children said they resent their father for not helping to support them.

Lillian has received welfare and food stamps ever since she split up with her husband in 1966. When her daughters became pregnant, they, too, became eligible for assistance but refused to apply because, they said, they saw it as an embarrassment. They finally registered after Lillian badgered them about it for months. Theresa, twenty-three, took herself off the rolls after six months because she found a job; another daughter, nineteen, received payments for a few months, was cut off for giving incomplete information, and then refused for twenty-one months to reapply.

At a point in the winter of 1985, Lillian was trying to feed herself, her younger sister, her eleven children, and five grandchildren all from her 350-dollar monthly welfare check, from which she also paid 117 dollars in rent. She never conceived any of her eleven children seeking to increase her welfare payments. She learned early, as all welfare-dependent families do, that the stipend is *never* enough to carry one child through an entire month, much less a large family.

None of Lillian's three oldest daughters had gotten pregnant to qualify or increase their welfare stipend, a below-subsistence payment the family saw as a shameful and embarrassing necessity. All three mothers deeply resented the questions of the application process and the required certification process every sixth month. Each of them went to great lengths to have their names removed from the rolls once they were employed.

Welfare payments were not a part of their thoughts when Lillian and each of her oldest three daughters got pregnant. Waters, annoyed that she had to come to Lillian's rescue every few months when her daughter and Charlie Williams were together, demanded that Lillian go on welfare after her sixth child was born. Not one of Lillian's three daughters thought of welfare payments as being able to support them in the manner in which they wanted to live. But they were caught in a web that they had not spun: little education, no skills, and a profound need to become women in the eyes of their peers and community.

Lillian and her three daughters were following patterns set long before they were born. Lillian and three of her daughters each got pregnant to meet some basic human needs—essential requirements that the adolescent children of the more affluent fulfill in other ways.

LILLIAN'S CHILDREN: THE PATTERNS, AGAIN

In interviews with the Williams children, one theme came through: The pregnancies were not accidents. The Williams children knew the consequences of sexual activity, and they knew about birth control, but they wanted children for a variety of reasons—to achieve something *tangible,* to prove something to their *peers,* to be considered an *adult,* to get their mother's *attention,* and to keep up with an older brother or sister.

It was not always easy for them to talk about their reasons. At delicate points in the interviews, every one of them would watch my eyes and listen intently to my questions. They were watching me to see if I would judge them. Only months after they had not seen condemnation in my eyes or heard a judgmental nuance in my voice did they begin to open up. Three of them reached a point where they felt comfortable enough to speak candidly.

Firstborn

Kenneth Earl Williams introduces himself as Earl, and that is what everyone in the Williams family calls him. An adult of twenty-three when I met him, Earl spoke with a smoldering, deep resentment toward his great-grandmother, Eva Bell Hill, whom he referred to as Evil Bell Hill. Eva left Isaiah Hill in North Carolina and moved to Washington in the 1960s. For a time, she lived with her granddaughter after Lillian and Charlie split up. The family lived in an apartment in Northwest Washington near Park Road and Seventeenth Street in those days.

About the age of ten, Earl was caught stealing a dime handball in the neighborhood drug store, and the store owner told Eva. Lillian was not at home, so Eva administered one of her infamous Lenoir County whippings. She made Earl strip off all his clothes and get into the bathtub. She tightened the base of the doubled-up electric extension cord around her beefy, powerful right hand, held onto Earl with her equally strong left hand, and whipped him.

Earl cried and screamed. He could not get away. The whipping seemed to go on and on. The memory poured out of Earl in a torrent of words. He had never forgiven his great-grandmother. "I was really hurt by it. I felt the sense of being wronged. I still feel I didn't really deserve to be whipped that way. I ain't never experienced something like that. It just gets me upset" even when he talked about it.

He also remembered what his mother said, an expression that told him how she saw her role in her children's lives. "I have to be the man and the woman in this house" Lillian would tell all her children. That was even before his parents separated in 1966. Earl recalled about his father that "I really wanted him to show us that he was gonna be there. Help us. Help me. I just wished that we had a father. Things might have turned out different. Seemed like we had problems really getting to be a family."

Earl hid under a bed with his mother the day his father came after Lillian with a knife. He remembers when a female relative stabbed his father in the throat, trying to keep Charlie from crawling under the bed after Lillian.

During his growing up in Northwest Washington, the family was evicted from about ten separate apartments for nonpayment of rent. In a one-bedroom apartment, Earl and nine of his brothers and sisters shared the bedroom, while Lillian and her common-law husband, Fred Williams, slept on a foldout couch in the living room.

No adult in his life had given him any instruction on how he should conduct his sexual life by the time he reached puberty at age twelve. His first formal instruction came during sex-education class in the seventh grade at Alice Deal Junior High School. A distant female cousin, nine, stayed over in the children's room one night. In the dark, she and Earl clung to each other and then went further. It was his first sexual experience. "As far as *real* kin, I don't think she is," he said.

Earl had started out with enthusiasm in elementary school. As he moved up the grade ladder, he unsuccessfully wrestled with mathematics and English without any help. School became an increasingly frustrating experience for Earl. He made it to the twelfth grade at Cardozo High School, but failed. He had already given up. "I would hang out in the hallways, smoke herb, and listen to music tapes while hooking classes." He repeated his senior year, but dropped out in the spring of 1981 when he was told he would fail again. "I felt I needed tutoring to really pass."

Tauscha Vaughn first introduced me to Earl on Condon Terrace SE one day in the early fall of 1984, even before I had met his sister, Boochie, and his mother, Lillian. Earl had just returned from job hunting. From that time until I finished interviewing the members of the Williams family in December 1985, Earl went through a succession of seven different jobs in the janitorial, security, and construction fields without finding one that delivered on the promise of full-time, forty-hour-a-week employment. He was always full of anger. I connected the anger to his inability to find a job that would pay him a living wage.

Second Born

Theresa Anne was born thirteen months after her brother Earl on June 18, 1962. She was shy but also the most candid of the Williams children. She still found it difficult to talk about her reasons for getting pregnant at nineteen. When we met, she was pregnant with her second child.

Theresa had been labeled in her early teens as a girl who did not like sex or boys. Even her older brother, Earl, teased her. When one of Earl's friends tried to "get fresh" with her one afternoon, Earl laughed and said, "Don't mess with her, she's a virgin!"

Theresa said she was embarrassed. "*God,* he was loud. The whole block could have heard him. I ain't want nobody to know all that stuff. It was nobody's business."

When girls got together and talked about their sex lives, which they often did in explicit detail, Theresa hung back. "I'd be the only one sitting there listening, not a thing to say," she said.

When she was eighteen, she sometimes found herself listening to much younger girls, many of whom already had one child. At one of these sessions, a fourteen-year-old cousin said to her—in front of several boys and girls—"Girl, you look like a virgin. I can tell you are." A sixteen-year-old cousin joined in, baiting Theresa by saying that she was obviously "barren" because she had not had a child by age sixteen.

Adolescent childbearing and the social stigma of infertility are two parts of Theresa's family's sharecropping origins that no longer serve an economic purpose but persist as measurements of one's self-worth. Girls and boys were expected to grow up early, to take on the responsibilities of adult life as soon as they thought they could. These expectations included not only cooking meals and doing a full day's labor in the fields by age eleven, but also engaging in sexual activity in early adolescence. With her understanding of how she was not measuring up to the family's criteria of womanhood, Theresa was deeply embarrassed by the girls' comments. She was older, but somehow less woman than they were. That she might be infertile created a nagging fear within her. That she might be stigmatized as "barren" deeply distressed her.

The humiliation Theresa felt that day would not leave her. All five of the other girls present were younger than she, and she was the only virgin. She had lost face and status when she was accused of being infertile. She had been laughed at for being a virgin. Before that day, she would occasionally lie to indicate that she was not a virgin, but no one believed her.

"They looked at a virgin as being something shameful. . . . They were the type of people who would always tell what happened if they made out with a boy or a boy made out with them. I was the only one they never heard from. They would say, 'You don't know what you're missing.' The more they talked, the more curious I got."

Theresa did not tell them why she was still a virgin. She did not tell them that she was hiding something, that she had a deep-seated fear of men that grew out of episodes of sexual abuse.

Theresa remembered the incidents clearly, and there are more of them than she wants to remember. When she was eight, a great-uncle forcibly touched her genitals. When she was ten, five neighborhood boys grabbed her one day outside her apartment building and touched her genitals. She broke free, got a knife, and attacked the boys, cutting three of them. But the most vivid memory is the years of being touched by a man who lived with her family.

In an interview, the same man denied ever touching Theresa. "Naw. Uh-uh. I don't know where she get all of that from." But Lillian said she knows her daughter is telling the truth, adding that the same man even lay on top of another daughter and backed off when that girl reacted with anger.

Even before the abuse, Theresa has disturbing memories of her father's drinking—periods when Charlie would curse and take out the gun he always carried. "He'd take it out of his pocket, swing it around, and I would see it." Theresa was five.

As she grew, her aversion to males remained; she picked up some additional negative thoughts about them, particularly after her breasts began to develop and boys began touching her against her will. Males became people to fear. She saw them as nasty, violent, cruel, doggish, unreliable, bossy, and unfaithful.

Still she would need to use one, she reasoned, after her day of humiliation. She needed a child; she needed to end the accusations of infertility; she needed to stop the taunting about her virginity. She wanted to find out what it was her girl friends told her she was missing.

She looked over her brothers' friends. She settled on a twenty-three-year-old man who had the reputation of being a womanizer among the girls and a successful playboy among her brothers. She figured she would not have to endure the painful suffering of the first time she had heard about if she began her sexual activity with such a man. "A lot of people knew him. He had a track record for girls." She made her interest in him known, and he invited her to his apartment. She turned him down. Days passed. They met at a neighborhood party, the same apartment building he lived in. He invited her to his apartment a second time. She said no again. He left and returned. She agreed to go to his apartment at his third invitation.

It was an easy beginning. There was none of the great difficulty other girls had told her about. But she was not impressed. She kept waiting for some overwhelming feeling. It never happened. "It was like my body must have been dead or something," Theresa said, giggling, " 'cause I wasn't even responding." Her mind wandered as she lay there. Two of her thoughts were, If I get pregnant, that would prove to them that I *can* have children! If I get pregnant that would show that I am *not* a virgin!

Theresa and her friend made love several times afterward. She was uncomfortable at times because she had flashbacks to the years of sexual abuse. Then her friend started coming around to see her at a relative's apartment where she was living "as if we had some kind of relationship or something. I didn't want him coming around. I wasn't really *that* interested in him. I liked him, but not as a boyfriend. I knew I didn't love him."

Theresa never told the father of her child that she was pregnant. After all, what business of his was her pregnancy? He was told by relatives of Theresa. He and Theresa ran into each other in his sister's building one day. He asked if she was pregnant. She was angered that he had been told, but told him the truth. He asked her to marry him; she told him she was not interested in marrying him and doubted if she ever would be. "He certainly wasn't right for me. He like to start fights. Carry guns. Every time you turn around, a girl was at his door. I wasn't jealous, but I just couldn't go with somebody that go with every Susie all over the place. I ain't want him to feel like he would have to marry me just 'cause he got me pregnant. He asked me a couple of times, but I just kept" turning him down.

Her pregnancy began to show after several months. She let the growing pregnancy announce that she was *not* barren, that she was *not* a virgin!

She smiled at the reaction of her female cousins and her girl friends. "They were shocked to see me pregnant. They didn't even believe it." They wanted to know if she enjoyed sex, to go into the sort of details they were accustomed to sharing among themselves. Theresa refused to tell them whether she had enjoyed sex—that was her private life, a part of her she did not even share with her sister Boochie.

Lillian was overjoyed when Theresa told her she was pregnant. "It's about time," Theresa remembered her mother shouting into the telephone. "She was laughing real loud." Theresa's child would be

Lillian's first grandchild. Lillian insisted that Theresa move back home, and she did. Her mother asked Theresa if she enjoyed sexual relations, and Theresa told her she did not, that it had been boring to her. Lillian responded that she would not enjoy sexual relations unless she was in love with the man. Theresa wondered about that because for a long time she had felt she could never love any man.

Lillian gave Theresa lots of attention during the pregnancy, and Theresa gave birth to a healthy Sherita Williams on August 1, 1982. In February 1984, Theresa spent one night with the father of her first child. On December 10, 1984, Theresa gave birth to their second child, a healthy boy, Jeremiah Williams.

We went over and over what she was thinking about on that visit, a cold and snowy night when the city's buses stopped running and she had been unable to get home to Washington Highlands from Northwest Washington. Why had she spent the night and made love to the father of her first child when she had relatives close by whom she could have turned to? Theresa insisted that she did not know why. She had nothing else to prove once the first child was born. "We made love once. I just did it, really. I guess because I was borrowing his apartment" as shelter from the snowstorm. "I don't know why I did it. I really don't."

Yet it is very important to her that both her children have the same father. "Because a lot of the girls I know get pregnant by these different men. I think if you want babies, you get pregnant by one man. It don't seem right to have all these fathers all over the place! If I had an urge for sex today, I would go to Sherita and Jeremiah's father. If I felt weak or something."

If Theresa visited the father of her children again, she would be taking a chance on a third pregnancy. She adamantly refuses to use any form of contraceptive. Some of her reasons, among many, are: "They're not 100 percent. They cause infections. They cause cancer. They can make you barren. You always hearing something is wrong with them after you done taken them and everything. I just don't trust no kind of birth control." The real underlying reason, Theresa admitted, is a deep fear she has about birth control. She does not know how the fear developed.

She had been "saved" in her mother's church before her one-night visit to the apartment of her children's father and felt that she had sinned. Her pastor told her she had "backslid," but he counseled against a worse sin, an act they both saw as murder—an abortion.

At the time of the interviews, Theresa was more interested in her church, the evangelical Christian Power Center, than in men. If she were ever to marry, the man would have to be someone who also is "born again." She could not abide living with a man who was as violent as most of the men she has known. "It's kind of hard for me because I don't like to be told what to do. You know how a woman has to do as [her] husband tells [her]. We're told that at church. Like women are not suppose to wear pants, either."

Third Born

Charlie III was born prematurely weighing four pounds on May 21, 1963. When I met him he was a very angry man of twenty-one —angry about most of his childhood. His earliest childhood memory was having a seizure at about age eight. But that was not a cause of his anger. He blamed his family for his anger.

"They made me like this. My brothers and sisters, they get on my nerves." The youngest ones "sass me, got no respect. They make me go evil, that's why I hardly stay home." His mother has always picked on him, he said, and he found it difficult to talk to her. She had accused him several times of stealing things in the house. At times, his things have been stolen or missing, but his mother did not care about his things, he said.

About his father, Charlie had nothing good to say. His father "was jive. Motherfucker ain't do *shit!* Still, I wanted a father to talk to sometimes."

Out of his ten brothers and sisters, Charlie only had warm feelings for his sister Theresa. "All of us hardly know each other. I hardly know none of them, really."

Charlie was seeing a woman who lived on Condon Terrace SE, around the corner from my basement apartment. The woman was in her late teens and pregnant with a child Charlie thought might be his. The woman smoked a lot of marijuana and drank vodka heavily. When I raised the subject of her habits endangering the unborn child, Charlie said she had given him gonorrhea since her pregnancy had begun. When I again raised the danger of the woman's life-style to the fetus, Charlie changed the subject. I raised it again. Charlie continued not to respond, began to talk about the type of beer he liked. I dropped the subject.

Charlie said he had been "burned" three times with gonorrhea since his first sexual experience at sixteen, yet he refused to ever use a condom because he felt it was not natural.

He was still furious with his mother because of an incident that took place when he was twelve. It was a period in Lillian's life when she was so unhappy with herself she said she would often shout angrily at her children, "You'll never be *nothing!*"

Charlie said he had just learned that he had passed the sixth grade and rushed home from school to tell his mother. But his sister, Theresa, had learned the same day that she had failed the sixth grade for the second time, and Charlie had to wait patiently while his mother consoled Theresa, who was in tears.

Instead of praising him, though, his mother said to Theresa, "Don't worry, Theresa. Charlie will fail, too."

Charlie's voice shook with anger as he told the story. "[A mother] supposed to treat her children the same. Don't put your son down. Your son got emotionals just like the daughter got emotionals."

Charlie said the incident killed his interest in school. He failed the seventh and eighth grades and dropped out of school when he was sixteen.

Fourth Born

Wesley Carl was born April 6, 1964, on the front steps of the Kinston, North Carolina, hospital. Lillian had moved back to North Carolina temporarily to live with her mother-in-law during a particularly difficult financial period for the family. She had gone into labor suddenly and had not been able to make it up the steps of the hospital before giving birth to Wesley.

Wesley has never had a birth certificate because of the circumstances of his birth, a factor that had caused him endless problems while growing up in Washington. At twenty, he was very resentful toward his mother because she had never made out a birth certificate for him. "I get kinda angry with Ma about it."

Wesley said he did not like going to school from the first day. He remembered being taunted in elementary school because his family was so poor. The other kids would point to the holes in his snow-dampened sneakers and whisper to each other, "They can't afford any shoes." They would laugh at him because he did not have a winter coat, just a thin windbreaker over layers of shirts.

Wesley said, "I used to hate that. I used to sit in the back in my little corner [of the classroom] and cry. I just wanted to walk out of the class and never come back."

After he entered the seventh grade, "[it] seemed like the work started getting harder. I stayed back twice. The work was like a mind-bender. I just got tired. I kept staying back, so I just came out" at fifteen. "It was a relief. I said, 'The depression is over!' "

Lillian said she had seen her world as hopeless and passed that view on to her children. Helping them with their school work was out of the question—Lillian had dropped out in the seventh grade, and Fred, who her children said was the only father they had ever known, was illiterate.

On December 11, 1984, Wesley and I went to see Theresa at D.C. General Hospital, Washington's main hospital for the indigent. Theresa had delivered her son, Jeremiah, the day before. While leaving the hospital, I began teasing Wesley about his being twenty years old and having not yet fathered a child.

"I have a child! I have a child!" responded Wesley defensively. His son had been born sometime after February 1981 after the family had been burnt out of a house they rented in Northwest Washington. A nineteen-year-old friend of the family had lived with the Williams family for a month several months before the fire. She was the first woman with whom Wesley, then seventeen, became sexually active. Wesley saw the woman regularly in a neighborhood church after she moved from their house. He noticed that she was pregnant and asked her if the baby was his. She refused to tell him.

After the fire, the city's public-housing department relocated the family to Washington Highlands. A family friend told Wesley months after they had moved that she had seen the woman's baby, a boy, and he looked just like Wesley. Wesley said it felt good to know that he had a child, but he had made no effort to see the boy. He had heard that the child had been taken away from his mother on charges of neglect, put into a foster home, and then returned to his mother's care.

Lillian laughed when I asked her about Wesley's son. "I have asked [the woman]. She called the young man's name who is the father. [Wesley] keeps thinking it's his child. He's trying to keep up with his brothers."

Fifth Born

Ronnie, born June 14, 1965, is the most introspective of Lillian's children. His description of his mother before Lillian was "saved" sounded like Lillian's description of her mother and her grandmother. "She was mean. I hated her ways. I didn't like the way she beat us. The way she talked to us. She used to cuss us out, use profanity." After she was "born again" she completely changed for the better.

Ronnie remembered hating himself as a child. Part of his self-hate grew out of being picked on by other children because "we were so poor." All of his brothers and sisters were made fun of. "They used to call us dirty. Charlie and Earl would fight. Wesley didn't like to fight too much. Boochie would fight. I took it badly. We didn't have much. We didn't have many clothes."

He has always felt he could never do anything right and would avoid doing it so he would not fail. He never felt comfortable in school. He still carried those feelings at nineteen, the age at which I interviewed him. "That's my problem. I think too much. And I got a lot of anger in me."

I interviewed Ronnie in January 1985 at the Harpers Ferry Job Corps Center in West Virginia. He had been there for almost eighteen months learning bricklaying and welding. In February, Ronnie returned to his mother's crowded Washington Highlands home hoping to get regular employment and move out into his own apartment. Ronnie looked for bricklaying or welding work in the Washington metropolitan area for seven months after his return. The construction companies that offered him employment were doing most of their building in southern Fairfax County in Virginia, many miles from where he lived. He needed a car to commute to the work sites, but could not afford to buy one, even secondhand.

Finally, Ronnie took a low-paying job on September 13 working alongside his brother Wesley at a Roy Rogers fast-food restaurant in Washington. Like his brother Earl, Ronnie was frustrated, depressed, and angry over his inability to find work at a decent wage. The one-and-a-half-year investment in the Jobs Corps had not paid off.

Ronnie had become a father at seventeen. He said he became sexually active with his son's mother when he was fifteen and the girl was twelve. The girl had told Ronnie that she was using "birth controls," the popular expression in Washington Highlands for birth-control pills. Before they became sexually active, Ronnie had demanded to see the pills, but it turned out that the pills she showed him were her mother's. According to Ronnie, "She was trying to grow up too quick." The girl's mother noticed that her thirteen-year-old daughter was pregnant and insisted that she have an abortion without telling Ronnie anything. She became pregnant with their child the following year.

This time, the fourteen-year-old girl's aunt came to the Williams's house to inform Lillian. Ronnie was playing basketball on a neighborhood court. It was spring of 1983. He had been told by a Friendship Educational Center teacher in the fall of 1981 that, at sixteen, he was too old to be in the ninth grade and was put out of school. Most of his time since then had been spent in idleness or playing sports until he went away to the Harpers Ferry Jobs Corps Center that winter.

His brother Charlie came to the basketball court and told him he was wanted at home. When he stepped into the living room, all of his brothers and sisters were there. His mother looked disappointed. Then he saw his girl friend's aunt and knew what this meeting was about.

He was scared. "Ronnie, you got [your girl friend] pregnant," her aunt said. His brothers and sisters "busted out laughing. I was embarrassed. She was in her fourth month."

Days later, the girl's mother visited Lillian. The mother told Lillian she had made the girl abort another pregnancy by Ronnie the year before. Lillian reacted angrily. "I came out boldly," Lillian remembered. "You know what?" she said to the girl's mother. "You gonna have to give account of that to God unless you repent. It's *murder!* You gonna have to pay for that!" The woman did not respond. "She just dropped her head."

Ronnie was not told about the abortion until after his son was born three months prematurely on April 1, 1983. Ronnie was very active and involved with his son and paid the mother child support whenever he was working. He was not interested in marrying her. "I don't think there is a woman on earth that is right for me. I just don't trust them. They're freaks. A freak is a girl all a guy has to do is just sing any type of love song to and they'll fall for it. Too easy to get them into bed. Most of them just like drugs. All you have to do is get a bag of herb. Get some beer or something. And you got them."

Ronnie's misogynistic views were racial, aimed at black women, a reflection of his self-hate. "I'd marry a white woman before a black woman. Ever since I was about eleven or twelve, I always thought of myself as marrying a white woman. I don't know why. Black women like to dog [abuse] people." He would not choose a light-skinned black woman either "because they think they too cute. The majority act stuck up. If I was going with one, I would not trust her. Light-skinned women are less trustworthy than dark-skinned women because most black males prefer light-skinned women. There're too many men after" light-skinned women.

Ronnie, like his older brother Charlie, turned up his nose at the mention of condoms, said he would never use one and felt withdrawal was a better form of birth control. "I just don't like them, period. They're unnatural." He said he would not use one even to protect himself against venereal disease.

Sixth Born

After our forty-five-minute interview in September 1984, Lottie Marie "Boochie" Williams declined to go through the five-interview process Lillian and her sister Theresa participated in. Boochie, who was born on July 18, 1966, said all the questions made her nervous and reminded her of the welfare-certification process she so resented and resisted.

Boochie's decision not to continue was a major disappointment to me. She was the most sullen and hostile of all of Lillian's children. Over the months I spent in the Williams household, Boochie gradually relaxed her guard with me. I felt that hidden behind her mask of anger and surliness was some very important information and insights, but I was never able to really reach her.

Her comments intimated that there was a lot going on with Boochie Williams under the surface. "Your questions make me nervous. I've been through *so* much!"

Boochie dropped out of Hart Junior High School when she was sixteen. Her first child, Quenshell, was born on July 25, 1983—a week after Boochie's seventeenth birthday. She did not know that much about birth control, she told me. She had not paid close attention during her sex-education course at Hart. "You know how teenagers are. They don't pay attention." Quenshell "was just something that happened."

Many months later, Theresa inadvertently told me Boochie had taken birth-control pills for two years before she became pregnant. Boochie had been competing with Theresa for their mother's attention and had loudly complained that Lillian favored Theresa over her. Lillian fussed over Theresa after she came home with the first grandchild in August 1982. Three months later, Boochie stopped taking birth-control pills. At dinner one July 1985 evening, Boochie acknowledged that she had intentionally become pregnant with her first child, but declined to give her reasons. It was eleven months after we had met, and she was a month away from delivering her second child. Boochie became pregnant with her second child the same month Theresa gave birth to her second child.

Seventh Born

Sixteen-year-old Melissa knew she was *a month* pregnant when I interviewed her on May 23, 1985, the day she told me she was still a virgin. She did have a twenty-year-old boyfriend with whom she "probably" would become sexually active, she told me. Four months after that interview, when her pregnancy was very obvious, we laughed together about what she had told me in the interview and what the reality was. Melissa's story illustrates how difficult it is to get people to tell you what really is going on with them.

Melissa had liked school when she began at Bancroft Elementary School in Northwest Washington. Her interest had begun to wane in the second grade after she was left back. The family moved, and she was transferred to Meyer Elementary School.

One of her most vivid memories from Meyer was a hallway fight she won against a male fourth-grade classmate and his girl friend. Melissa had attacked the boy after he persistently touched her buttocks and breasts against her wishes. His girl friend jumped into the fray on his side, and Melissa beat them both before a teacher arrived to stop the fight. She could still vividly recall her disgust with all boys, most of whom were fresh. "I didn't like boys at the time. Too nasty. Touching on me."

Now she was in the eighth grade at Hart Junior High School. "I belong in the eleventh." She had been left back in the seventh grade for "hooking" classes, had lost all interest in school, and spent her time much of the 1984–85 school year looking out of the window. Still she intended to be the first of her brothers and sisters to graduate from high school. "I don't wanna drop out." She wanted to be a hospital nurse.

Melissa was "saved" for a short period when she was fifteen, but hated going to church with her mother then. "I still acted as if I was saved to please her." Lillian told her to stay away from all boys after Melissa turned thirteen, that she did not want Melissa to become pregnant like Theresa and Boochie. And Melissa insisted that she had no desire to get pregnant, saying, "I don't want a baby now. It would only tie me down."

She was in love with her boyfriend, although Melissa said he had not "asked me for sex yet. I guess he get it, if he asks," she told me in the May 1985 interview. She had not thought about contraceptives and said she could remember only a little from her seventh-grade sex-education course.

Lillian had worked hard to keep Melissa, her third-oldest daughter, born July 21, 1968, from becoming pregnant. By 1985, Lillian preached every day against the sin of "fornication outside of marriage," trying in her own desperate way to make sure her third and fourth daughters did not become unwed teenage mothers. She forced both younger girls, including Melissa, to attend church with her.

Then one mid-July 1985 morning after Lillian awoke, she sat up in bed, and glanced across the bedroom:

> She saw Melissa lying flat on her back and noticed her stomach sticking up. The disappointment was acute. That girl just as pregnant as I'm sitting here on this bed, Lillian told herself. She forced herself out of bed, walked over to Melissa, and pushed down on her daughter's stomach. "And it felt real hard." Lillian shook Melissa awake and angrily confronted her. Melissa denied she was pregnant. "You might as well tell the truth 'cause what goes on in the dark comes out in the light," shouted Lillian. Melissa began to cry. "After all the talking I done. I talked to her long before she even got into that condition. I was kinda disappointed. It was like a shock." Melissa cried and cried. Lillian let up her wrath. "In spite of the mistake," she told Melissa gently, "I still love you."

Weeks later, Lillian said, Melissa's pregnancy "hurt me. It wasn't a deep, deep hurt. I made mistakes, too, before I got saved. I made mistakes."

Lillian's disappointment was more in not being able to break the pattern, a pattern she felt she had set. Lillian's eyes filled with tears as she told me she understood that she had turned to the church too late, that the paths her children were choosing were set by her before 1981. "I tell my kids, 'I don't want you to come up in the way I come up. Having a lot of kids. I don't want ya'll staying with me, having babies, bringing a lot of babies here on me. Pinning me down.' "

Lillian told Melissa that she did not have to marry if she did not want to. The father of Melissa's child asked her to marry him, but she turned him down. Lillian hoped that Melissa would marry someone else, someone "Godly," someone who was "born again," as Lillian was.

After Lillian discovered the pregnancy, one of Melissa's uncles tried on her seventeenth birthday to convince Melissa to have an abortion. An angry Lillian stopped him. "She knew what she was doing. She laid down, she got it, and she gonna have it," she said.

I took Melissa food shopping for the family at a Maryland supermarket one day in September. She had dropped out of school and had no intentions of returning. I asked her if the father of her child had ever raised the subject of birth control. Melissa said yes. Before they became sexually active in April, he harrassed her about getting the birth-control pills available free for her age group at the local health clinic. It was the same clinic she now attended for prenatal care, a two-block walk from her house.

I asked her why had she not taken his advice. "What!" Melissa said with the turned-up nose that reminded me of her brother Ronnie. "Mr. Leon, I wouldn't take those things. They're dangerous!" Her baby girl was born December 8, 1985.

Eighth Born

Janice, born September 15, 1969, was fifteen years old when I interviewed her in May 1985. She entered the tenth grade at Ballou High School that fall.

Lillian said she used to beat Janice severely when her daughter was a small child only because "Janice is red [light-skinned], and I didn't like red people." It happened before she was "saved," and when she thinks about it now, she cringes. "My own child. I was sick. I knew something had to change because I was terrible."

Since the age of twelve, Janice had attended the Christian Power Center several times a week with her mother. Janice did not consider herself a saved member of the church, however, because a person who is saved has "the Holy Ghost. I ain't got it 'cause I ain't accept it." Lillian has been trying to save Janice and all her brothers and sisters, she added.

Lillian had told Janice not to have sex until she married and added that Janice was too young to have a baby. Janice accepted only part of what her mother had told her. "I feel I am too young to have a baby, but I don't feel I'm too young to have sex." If she were to become sexually active, Janice said, she did not know whether she would use birth-control pills, the only type of contraceptive she said she was aware of.

Janice had a boyfriend who already attended Ballou. She had told him that she loved him and was anxious for school to begin to be able to see him every day. Her mother did not allow her boyfriend to visit her inside the home.

Ninth, Tenth, and Eleventh Born

During the school year of 1984–85, Anthony was suspended from Hart Junior High School three times "for walking the halls," Lillian explained. Anthony was born September 11, 1972. At the beginning of the 1985–86 school year, Anthony was thirteen and in the seventh grade, two grades below where he should have been.

Leon, who was born April 26, 1973, was in the fifth grade at Highlands Elementary School and two grades behind at the end of 1985.

Isaac, who was born on December 7, 1974, was in the fourth grade at Hendley Elementary School and three grades behind. Isaac's school counselor came to see Lillian on September 12, 1985, the beginning of the school year, in an effort to stop Isaac's hooking school.

WAITING FOR DELIVERANCE

Of Lillian's adult children, only Theresa said she was "saved" and was a born-again Christian. Yet Lillian was undeterred. She saw the church as the only salvation, the only way to break the patterns, the only way to heal the wounds left by the abuse and the violence that is her family legacy.

But she realized that the church had not changed her children's attitudes and that they continued to be sexually active and risked having more children rather than waiting for marriage to have sex.

She did not believe birth control was an answer. She had an emotional aversion, both religious and cultural, to it, an attitude shared by her children and by other teenagers interviewed in Washington Highlands.

So she retreated to her Bible, spent part of each day by the window, underlining passages that she used in preaching to her children. "I'm living a life without having a man. I feel great. I only have one man. That's Christ.

"There's many times when you have been here and I have been without food. I wouldn't open my mouth and say, 'Mr. Leon, could you help me?' No, God wouldn't allow me to do that. Even by me talking about it now, I feel like I just want to *cry!* God, he always has took care of me, my family, from day to day. It's not always having a whole 'frigerator full of food. He take care of us from day to day."

In the midst of her Bible study, Lillian occasionally sang a gospel song, as she did one day as I watched.

Her eyes closed, she rocked back and forth, singing, "In Times Like These We Need a Savior." For now, she said afterward, she had put her faith totally in God.

Daily journalism is a fragile enterprise. The very nature of its immediacy, the rush to meet hourly deadlines, leaves questions unasked, thoughts unvoiced, and motivations unknown. Reporters have the patience only for the present. Rarely are they afforded the opportunity to brush aside the veils that hide the true motivations for the choices people make; rarely can they search back well beyond just yesterday to look for the links to the past that govern our behavior in the present; rarely do they give it a thought except to hurriedly choose an expert to provide any one-sentence explanation of any particular behavior.

I was lucky to have had the time. I was luckier still to have met Lillian Williams and have her open up to me. Her story and the story of her family provided the closest illustration of how so much of the present is linked to the past. I had gone to Washington Highlands to look at teenage pregnancy among the black urban poor. I found much more as the lives of the members of the Williams family gradually unfolded before me. I could actually see how so much of the deprivation, isolation, and brutality of black sharecropping life still held them; how the past had limited and affected the needs and choices of Lillian Williams's eleven children—limited them not just in matters of sex, but in all areas of their lives. The Williams family explained so much to me about some of the underlying causes of teenage childbearing.

At least two people cried on January 28, 1986, the day my story of Lillian Williams and her family's many struggles appeared in *The Washington Post.* It was the third of six parts.

When I awoke that January morning, I was tired and exhilarated. I stayed at *The Post* late each night to check the first edition for the headlines on the pieces. I had been blindsided by an especially insensitive headline on the last piece on a six-part series I had done on heroin addiction in 1976. I was determined that I would not be blindsided again on this more delicate issue of sex, race, and class (if not caste) by another unthinking night copy editor. The copy editors are the people who write the headlines for the stories after the reporters have finished and gone home.

So as each part of the teenage pregnancy series ran, I was up early and, after reading that day's story, went downtown to *The Post.* In the office, I closeted myself with the editor on the series, Steve Luxenberg, to make last-minute changes (or argue over them) on the next day's story. Then it was grab a quick evening meal and, finally, walk over to the copy editor's desk to aggressively participate in the writing of the headlines with Steve. Steve and I collaborated on each headline on each column of each piece. He would then race for the last evening commuter's train to Baltimore, where he lived with his pregnant wife and young son. I would wait to read the first edition of the newspaper after it came up to the newsroom at about 10:30 P.M. Check the headlines and then home to bed.

I was very happy I did it that way because several suggested headlines were bitingly judgmental and we rejected them immediately.

On the morning that Lillian's story appeared, I read the paper in bed and cried suddenly after I reached the end. It came almost as a burst for all the sorrow I knew the Williamses had suffered for generations.

Steve, who had become familiar with the material, nevertheless read the story once again on the morning commuter train from Baltimore to Washington. We met in the office and together began making the changes in the next day's story. We were outwardly two hard-bitten journalists treating today's story as history and preparing the next day's story for publication.

"I cried this morning on the train when I got to the end of Lillian's story," said Steve.

"So did I," I said. "It just sort of burst from me."

Steve nodded his understanding. We never said another word about it.

CHAPTER FIVE

THE TRUTH BEGAN to tumble from Tauscha Vaughn as if a dam had broken. Sometimes, it came through her lips in short, painful bursts. At other times, her story flowed out with a steady cadence. I looked at her in amazement. I had completely misunderstood and misread the sweet-sixteen teenager I had met four months before. Tauscha Vaughn effectively masked her true thoughts and feelings at that first meeting. She felt that I had grown close enough now for her finally to reveal to me something of the reality of her life and thoughts.

It happened on a bright but bitterly cold day in mid-December 1984. Tauscha Vaughn told me she had been trying to get pregnant since September. I already knew about her efforts from two of her confidantes. Still, it astonished me that she started trying to get pregnant just days after I met her. She had been so clear and direct in saying that she did not want a child then. She had decided she wanted a child four days after our conversation. After our first conversation, I was mistakenly convinced that Tauscha would be the example in my series of a girl who was coming through her adolescence in Washington Highlands without wanting a child. I was disappointed.

I thought back to our original conversation: She had appeared so strong. She had said she was certain she did not want a child. She had told me why other teenagers wanted children and, in the telling, led me to believe she would not fall into the same trap. Yet, she had!

Why? How? What the hell is going on here? I thought. It doesn't make any sense, was my immediate reaction.

It did make sense. Tauscha did not know me the day I first interviewed her. She did not feel she should share her secrets with me. She was in emotional pain, but she wore a mask that hid the pain from me. She harbored deep fears about her sexuality, but she only had shared those fears with her boyfriend. She felt God would deliver her from her rough adolescent passage with a baby, but she communed with God in private prayer. Several times she thought God answered her prayers with a pregnancy, but she only shared that information with two female confidantes and her boyfriend. Now, she opened up to me.

Tauscha Vaughn remembered waking up on the morning of June 21, 1984—her sixteenth birthday—feeling both excited and uncertain. Behind the thrill of being "sweet sixteen" there was a nagging sense of foreboding. She was looking forward to seeing her boyfriend, sixteen-year-old Reggie Wiley, but she was doubtful about how her family would celebrate her birthday. Her stepfather had recently been laid off, and her mother was on sick leave from her job.

That day her foreboding would be replaced by pain, followed by anger, then by love. She would feel appreciated after feeling rejected; she would feel that someone cared about her after feeling that her family did not. Her feelings would push her across one of life's thresholds that night.

On that morning she remembered the disappointment of her fifteenth birthday, she said, when her family told her they had no extra money to give her a present. But only a few months later, her brother got a radio for his seventeenth birthday, she said.

As she got out of bed, her stepfather, Earmon Smith, kissed her on the cheek and said, "Happy birthday." She went into her parents' bedroom to find a comb and saw her mother, Melba Smith, who said, "Happy birthday. That's about the only thing I can give you." Her mother hugged her, and Tauscha remembered covering up the pain by saying, "I understand."

She went into her room and looked at her face in the bureau's mirror. She asked herself adult questions: What have you learned in the past year? Have you grown any? But the pain persisted; she could not put it aside that easily: It persisted.

"Why is there always an excuse when Tauscha's birthday comes around?" she whispered to herself. She needed something to do. She began ironing her clothes. She pretended to be cheerful.

Her boyfriend, Reggie, called about 1:30 P.M. Reggie knew from the false gaiety of her voice that something was wrong. Tauscha denied that there was anything wrong, but Reggie knew her too well, knew too much of the family's history, knew that Tauscha felt she was treated as a stepchild. It did not matter that she was not. That was how she felt.

Reggie's first guess hit the mark. "Your momma ain't give you nothing for you birthday *again*! I *bet* you understood again, didn't you? Just like a dummy! You just took it. That's why they gonna keep on doing the same thing over and over to you." The hurt she felt began to choke her. Tauscha could not muster the strength to deny Reggie's accusations. It would not be necessary. Reggie said he would be right over.

Reggie arrived twenty minutes later. He announced that he wanted to take Tauscha for a birthday dinner at the Chesapeake Bay Seafood House in Camp Springs, Maryland. He was her knight. This birthday would be special after all. They needed a ride, however, and Tauscha's mother said she would call around to find someone to drive them. When her first few attempts failed, Tauscha got angry. She began to lose control. "Forget it!" she shouted at her mother. She became insulting, her voice taking on the nastiest tone she could muster. "We'll go to McDonald's!" She remembered the way she felt. "I was mad."

An argument ensued. Her mother told her if her attitude did not change, she would not be going out. Instead of Tauscha backing down, she provoked a deeper confrontation. "Well, it won't be the first time!" she yelled. "I didn't hold nothing back after she pissed me off!" Her mother threatened to slap her. Tauscha would not let it rest. "Well, it won't be the first time for that, either! You can't hurt me no worser than you hurt me every birthday!"

She stormed out of her parents' room to the dining room and sat at the table. The pain would not leave her. "The first thing I did was hold it in for a while. I was just looking into thin air. Tears just started falling!" She kept her face averted from Reggie's. She did not want him to see her cry. She ran into her room, lay across her bed, and let the tears flow. "I was already prepared that there wasn't gonna be too much. That's just the way I program myself."

A few minutes later, her mother came into her bedroom and said that a neighbor would take them to the restaurant.

The argument behind them, Tasucha and Reggie went to the

restaurant. Reggie was slightly nervous. He didn't have much money —he was in school and did not have a job—so he asked Tauscha to limit her order to twelve dollars. Then Reggie lightened the mood with an imitation of Tauscha's mother. Tauscha laughed. He asked her to close her eyes, and he placed a small red box in front of her. When she opened the box, she found a silver-plated necklace and ring inside.

Reggie gave her a speech about loving her. He took her hand and squeezed it tight, all the time staring into her eyes. Tauscha told him that she loved him. The couple joked and laughed until the food came. The same neighbor came back to the Maryland restaurant to pick them up.

At about 11:30 P.M., they returned to Tauscha's apartment, a three-story building on Condon Terrace SE owned by the Paramount Baptist Church that her family attended. Tauscha was in a light, happy mood. As Tauscha climbed the steps of her building, she passed her stepfather on his way out. She greeted him, but he stared straight ahead and did not say a word.

Concerned now, Tauscha climbed the rest of the stairs. Reggie remained behind on the steps, talking with friends among the evening crowd which had gathered. It was cooler on the steps than in the building's apartments.

Inside the apartment, Tauscha's mother was sitting alone in the living room. She told Tauscha that the family was being evicted the next morning because of unpaid rent.

Numbed, Tauscha left the apartment and went outside. Reggie was still sitting on the front steps of the building. "I ain't feel nothing," she remembered. She prayed for ten minutes. The Lord is gonna handle what's up, she said to herself at the end of the prayer. The crowd on the front steps continued their summertime routine, chatting, gossiping, listening to music, and break dancing. She and Reggie shared a bottle of beer. Sometime after midnight, she and Reggie walked the seven blocks to his house.

Reggie's mother and stepfather were out, and the two teenagers began petting on the living-room couch. She found his kisses especially stimulating this night. What happened next she had never done before. "I took my clothes off right in front of this man. I guess I ain't never been body shy." Reggie was surprised. "Why are you doing this?" he asked. "Because I want to," Tauscha replied.

"I really wanted to express my feelings to somebody at that

point," she remembered in an interview. "I wanted to hold him. Just feel like I belong somewhere. Be appreciated. I ain't have no doubts in my head about whether or not I wanted to do it. I didn't hesitate. So I turned out the light. Reggie was body shy. He finally took off his clothes." They went to his room. It was the first time for them both.

Tauscha said she did not think about the possibility of getting pregnant. "It just didn't cross my mind. I just didn't think about it," she said.

"When I got up, I didn't feel shame or anything. I was peaceful. 'Now that he done this, is he gonna leave [me]?' was not in my head."

When she got home early the next morning to face the eviction, she learned that friends of her family had pooled enough money to pay the rent. The family would not have to leave.

THE FIRST INTERVIEW

I met Tauscha two and a half months after the June night of her sixteenth birthday. Estelle Harvey, the head of Paramount Baptist Church's youth committee, had given me Tauscha's name and that of another girl. Harvey felt that both girls were ambitious and would not be interested in having children at this point in their lives. The two girls, Harvey said, were interested in graduating from nearby Ballou High School.

I approached the other girl first. She was seventeen, a B student, and a senior at Ballou High School. In late August, Harvey, the girl, and I attended a planning session for an upcoming March retreat for Baptist youths of the Washington metropolitan area. The girl was disappointed with the planning session. The adults controlling the meeting rejected the topics of teenage pregnancy and drug use as topics not befitting discussion at the youth retreat. Instead, they insisted on such subjects as Bible study and how to apply lessons in the Bible to everyday life.

"They're not dealing with the real world of teenagers!" the girl said.

I interviewed her once in her parents' single-family home not far from Paramount. I was curious about how her life—outside the home, in the home, in the church, in the school—differed from the lives of the many other teenagers who were not doing as well. After a brief interview with her at the family dining-room table, I talked to her father. He was so hostile and suspicious about the project that I decided not to pursue her story, hoping the family of the second girl whose name I had been given would prove to be more receptive.

They were. Tauscha and her family were open to what I was doing. I was able to interview Tauscha, the older of her two brothers, Adrian, and her parents, Earmon and Melba Smith. Tauscha also introduced me to twenty-nine-year-old Charmaine Ford, who had gotten pregnant with her first child at sixteen, and eighteen-year-old Boochie Williams, who had become a mother at sixteen.

My initial interview with Tauscha was on September 7, 1984 It went well. She told me explicitly that she did not want to get pregnant and why.

"I don't want a child because there is so much that I want to give my child," she said. "So much love. So much attention. I'm not financially fit. I don't really have an education. I can't get out of my mother's house. To me that's like bringing a child into a world that all he's going to see is a lot of pain."

She also told me why teenagers in Washington Highlands are getting pregnant.

"People need to learn what's going on inside people's *homes* these days," she said. "When girls get pregnant, it's either because they want something to hold on to, because of circumstances at home, or because they don't really have [anyone] to go to. And some of them do it because they resent their parents.

"None of that is an accident," she went on. "Every teenage girl knows about birth-control pills. Even when they twelve, they know what it is."

Tauscha said she was very surprised when one of her fourteen-year-old girl friends became pregnant. The girl had been very close to her mother. "Real close, like sisters, really." Tauscha had presumed that the girl's close relationship with her mother would keep her from becoming pregnant, that the girl was the recipient of more than enough parental affection. Her mother was deeply hurt when the girl told her she was pregnant.

Tauscha, however, was upset about the reaction of the girl's Baptist congregation to her pregnancy. "What shocked me about her being pregnant was her church like declined her from everything. It was like rejection. They wouldn't let her sing in the choir any more. They wouldn't let her do anything in the church." Tauscha told me that she said to herself, " 'What is this? That's not suppose to happen. They suppose to be Christians, and Christians are suppose to help Christians, you know.' And they were just making her feel worse, as if God didn't appreciate what she did, either. He may have not, but at least all she had to do was pray and ask Him to forgive her."

I asked if she thought that this girl's pregnancy, at least, had been accidental. Tauscha laughed. "I'm put it this way. I don't think it was an accident, because when you don't use protection, it's no accident. But when you do, then that's an accident." The girl had been very aware of contraception and had chosen not to use any, Tauscha said.

We continued to talk for several hours, and Tauscha revealed a little about each of the different parts of herself in that first interview —her childhood in Washington Highlands, her experiences at Ballou, her attitude toward Paramount Church and her religious outlook, and her family life.

She had done well in her studies, she said, up until her sophomore year at Ballou the year before. Her mother had been sick often during that year. Tauscha said during her mother's illness the circumstances at home wore her down.

The task of running the household for her stepfather and two brothers had fallen onto her slim fifteen-year-old shoulders. "I was going through a lot myself last year at home. Everything was piled on [me] already, and I wasn't even sixteen yet. I was trying to be the person that everyone wanted me to be. I got tired of everybody, 'Tauscha this' and 'Tauscha that.' "

She felt that she forgot who she was; she felt lost. "By the end of the school year, I found myself." By that time, school was no longer as important as it had been. "Every time I would go into the classroom it's like nobody's listening. The teachers were really not teaching you what you expected to hear, or they were not teaching you as well as you want them to. And [I was] just bored to death trying to learn something."

She found her teachers at Ballou to be weak, lacking in self-confidence, and easily intimidated by the aggressive students. "I don't think the teachers are able to cope or deal with" the belligerent students.

Moving up a grade had not changed the atmosphere at Ballou. She had just begun, with very little enthusiasm, her junior year at Ballou and was expecting more of the same. "It is very hard to learn anything in school because of the disturbances that you have. The children are acting up. Both the boys and the girls. It is not necessarily those students who are doing poorly in their schoolwork, either. I think it is a need for attention or either they have problems, and that is the way they deal with it, by outbursting. There are a lot of disruptions during the day, right in the classroom. The teachers have to cut their lessons and ask the person to leave the room. You can't learn *anything!*"

She had begun to cut classes. "If you go [to school], it's OK. If you don't, it's fine, too. You want to know the truth? The majority of teachers cut class." Her classmates were smoking a lot of "loveboat," the drug phencyclidine. "Most of the time, when they wanted to smoke some, they go out to the football [field] area." Students offered to share their drugs with classmates, always asking, "Hey, do you want to hit [smoke] this? Do you want to hit that?"

Many of the teenagers wanted to be considered hip, to be in what they felt was the *in* crowd. "If you don't smoke, you're not hip. And so many want to be in groups. Just want to belong somewhere because they might have problems at home. Their parents are not home, or they [parents] smoke loveboat and marijuana and they drink. So the kids figure it's fine."

On August 23, one of her sixteen-year-old girl friends passed out after smoking some loveboat on the front steps of Tauscha's apartment building. The girl had been given permission to smoke by her mother, Tauscha said. "She fell out! It scared me when I saw her like that. We had to carry her upstairs to a friend's apartment. She was unconscious. She wouldn't move. She wouldn't say nothing."

Despite numerous warnings in school and public-service admonitions detailing the dangers of smoking PCP, most of her friends ignored the possible harm they could suffer by using the drug, said Tauscha. "People really don't know exactly what the stuff will do to them. They got a lack of information about that. If they knew, maybe they wouldn't do it. But maybe they would."

Tauscha had tried marijuana but added that she had not tried PCP. She was emphatic on her reaction to marijuana. "I didn't like it. I mean, it didn't do nothing to me. I was like asking myself, What are they getting out of this?" She occasionally drank a bottle of beer.

"I get high off of Jesus Christ, and that's the only thing I need to get high off of. He plays a major role" in her life. Tauscha started attending Paramount Baptist Church at five and joined the church when she was eleven. "I was so happy" the day she joined Paramount. "My mother never seen me so happy as I was that day. Ever since then, I have been a follower of God. And that has a lot to do with me being strong, understanding my mistakes."

Her willingness to admit her mistakes to God and Jesus Christ in prayer, she continued, had kept her out of any serious trouble, such as pregnancy or becoming a habitual smoker of loveboat. Many of her friends, boys and girls, had not been as lucky, nor were they as religious, she said. "When I know something is wrong and I do it anyway, then I have to be strong enough to say, 'OK, I was wrong and I know I was wrong, but please forgive me and I promise not to do it again.' And you have to be a strong person to admit your faults to God." One gains the strength not to follow the wrong path a second time after admitting the wrong to God or Jesus Christ, she added.

Tauscha said she had been disappointed by what she had seen in her church and in other churches in terms of the religious leaders' interaction with adolescents. "I think [the churches] play a very poor role. I figure the church is suppose to at least have a ceremony where they just talk to the children. In the Bible, there are a lot of places where we [children] are suppose to be playing major roles. And we're not playing them because we don't know where they are and we don't know what we suppose to be doing. The preachers aren't telling us, either. So what are we suppose to do?"

At Paramount, "they aren't doing much of anything. They fail to ask the children what they want to do." Tauscha was the first teenager to serve on Paramount's Youth Committee, but had never been called to attend any of the committee's meetings, she pointed out.

There was no gray area on the subject of abortion for Tauscha. "I'm against it because I don't feel that's a Christian thing to do. Also, you was responsible enough to lay down and enjoy yourself, as you might put it, and you knew if you didn't take no kind of responsibility to prevent it, then you were gonna wind up pregnant either way you go. You may. You may not. So it's not the baby's fault that you did what you did. So, why kill it? Even if you bringing it into the world, it's still a headache. For it, not just you. You still cheating it" if you are an unprepared adolescent. "But I'd rather cheat it than to kill it. 'Cause you never know what that child might wind up to be."

She also knew that many teenage girls have a second child within two years of giving birth to their first. "I seen it. You limit yourself when you have your first child, but when you have a second child, you just hang yourself, point-blank, period." A girl fifteen, sixteen with two children, "What can she do for them? What can she do for herself?"

A friend of hers had fallen into the trap. "I call this a triple dose of responsibility. She got pregnant when she was fifteen. She had a second child at seventeen and got married. She only been married about three months now. She didn't finish school. She doesn't have no type of skills. Her husband works. He's got a good job and everything, but now she has two kids. Her attention is gonna have to be focused on the two kids, and her husband gonna be left alone. And he might feel he's not getting enough attention from her, then he's probably gonna go find it somewhere else, have an affair, and they wind up breaking up. Then what's she gonna do? She doesn't have no skills. She can't do anything for herself. The only thing she likely gonna do is go on welfare."

I was excited when I left Tauscha's family's apartment that evening. Tauscha had appeared to be mature and perceptive. She certainly had begun to open my eyes to the notion that a number of girls were getting pregnant intentionally. Many thoughts raced through my mind, some of which were:

> *Here is a truly strong and savvy girl. She has seen a lot, figured out that it does not apply to her, and will probably avoid the pitfalls she has so clearly identified. Great! Tauscha Vaughn is going to be my success story and my interpreter of this world. She is the most perceptive young adult that I have ever interviewed—ever met, for that matter. She talks like she is going to make it out of Washington Highlands without becoming a teenage parent. She is not doing too well in school, but at least she knows she does not want to have a child. She offers no rationalizations about accidental pregnancies. She will not become pregnant unless she wants to. And she doesn't want to!*
>
> *Perhaps her family life, her religious attachment to her church, or both were the elements that had saved Tauscha. I will follow her progress in the coming months. I will have an unambiguous example of a girl who chose not to become a teenage mother. Over time, I will probably learn what has made her different from so many of the other youths of Washington Highlands.*
>
> *You're on a roll! This is almost too good to be true. You could*

not have come up with a better example of someone who can broken-field run their way through this maze called Washington Highlands!

Tauscha's thoughts were very helpful in interviewing other teenagers, particularly those who professed strong religious beliefs. By October, however, I was picking up very different signals from Tauscha and two of her confidantes. Tauscha was pregnant, I was told by her friends. I was disappointed. It was becoming clear that some of the things Tauscha had told me about the girls she knew also applied to her. I realized that any one of the motivations she described could have been her own motivation for wanting to have a child.

Within four days of our interview, she told me months later, she tried to get pregnant. It did not bother me that she had misled me in that first interview. Everyone I interviewed did the same. What struck me about Tauscha was how articulate she had been about not wanting to become an adolescent mother. But, as it was revealed later, she was another Washington Highlands teenager who wanted to have a child.

She appeared to be so self-confident in September, so clear on not wanting a child until she was an adult, until she had the income to raise her child in the best possible way, until she had a husband with whom to share the responsibility.

The pregnancy I was told about turned out to be a false pregnancy, but the knowledge that she might have been pregnant triggered a family and personal crisis for Tauscha at the end of November, the period when her parents found out she thought she was pregnant. At the height of the crisis, I could see from her actions and attitudes that she did not want to talk about it. So I watched from the sidelines. Her friends kept me up to date with the almost daily confrontations and explosions Tauscha was embroiled in with her family and her boyfriend, Reggie. I waited until she had settled down. Then one afternoon in December I called and gently asked if I could do the second interview.

She knew that I had heard from two of her closest friends a lot about what she had been going through. We had often bumped into each other in her friends' apartment in the same building she lived in. I would lock on to her eyes for a sign that she was ready to talk. Through October, November, and early December, her eyes had said, No. I'm not ready to talk to you, yet. We had run into each other again in the same apartment the day before I called her. Her eyes had said, Yes! I'm ready to talk.

And she talked for hours over days from December 1984 until January 1986. It was a story of her secret fear of infertility. It was a story of her inner rage. It was a story of her religious mysticism. Tauscha was an adolescent girl who craved a child, in part, as a sign from God that he loved her; that he had his hands on her. A child, she thought, would deliver her from the pain of an imperfect world; a child, she thought, would be her spiritual salvation.

THE FAMILY

Tauscha's mother, Melba Smith, forty-one, was born and grew up in the small North Carolina town of Troy. She was the eldest of three sisters and one brother. Her parents had been strict but loving, she said. After she graduated from high school, Melba attended college for two years before marrying her first husband in May 1965.

The couple's first child, Adrian, was born October 25, 1966, and Tauscha was born on June 21, 1967. After several years of an unhappy marriage, the couple split up in Pittsburgh in early 1968. Tauscha was so young she had not begun to walk.

Melba moved to Washington, intent on being independent of her parents, but she had a difficult time finding work. When her resources ran out, she swallowed her pride and called her parents in Troy. Her father told her to bring the two children to Troy. Two of Melba's younger sisters were at home to help with their care. Melba's mother was very sick, however, slowly dying of cancer. Melba's mother died in 1971. Melba's father sent Adrian and Tauscha back to her in Washington.

After several years of domestic work, Melba became a lab assistant in a Silver Spring, Maryland, medical laboratory in 1973. She and Earmon "Smitty" Smith married in 1977. When I met the family in 1984, Melba was on sick leave from her medical laboratory job.

Melba said Tauscha had always been independent, more mature than her older brother, Adrian. "I believe my daughter was just born with something special," she said. When Melba and Smitty were dating, a seven-year-old Tauscha asked Smitty a series of questions about his future intentions. Smitty responded that he was going to be Tauscha's father. Melba said Tauscha replied, "You're not my father. I don't want a father." Smitty asked why he could not be her father. "Because they're so *dangerous!*" Tauscha answered.

Smitty, thirty-seven, was born and grew up in Washington, the oldest child in a family of two girls and two boys. His parents were very strict with his two sisters but gave their two boys more leeway in their social activity. He, too, attended two years of college but dropped out in 1968 when his mother became sick with cancer. She died in 1969. Smitty married a year later, and a son was born in October 1971. His marriage soured, and the couple broke up in 1974.

Smitty ended a ten-year stint of working for the Post Office in 1978, a year after he and Melba married, because of "family hassles with my first wife. Going back and forth to court. Messing with the job." When I met him, he had been laid off for five months from his job as a bonded courier. He was doing work around the apartment building, which the Paramount Church had bought in early 1984.

Smitty said Melba sometimes asked him in connection with their strained finances, "Aren't you worried?" Smitty would answer, "Honey, the only thing I'm worried about sometimes is dying 'cause I'm not ready to go."

Tauscha always had been outspoken, said Smitty. "She is very aware of being a teenager. Is sixteen going on thirty-three." Tauscha came to him for answers about sexuality. He had always been very direct with her. (Melba had gone to her father when she was the same age as Tauscha because her mother had been too embarrassed to discuss aspects of sexuality with her.) Among the subjects Smitty discussed with Tauscha was pregnancy, which he warned her against. "You've got your education ahead of you, and I ain't doing no baby-sitting," Smitty told her.

Adrian Vaughn's earliest childhood memory is seeing his sickly grandmother walking through his grandparents' home in Troy. He remembers playing with Tauscha. "I didn't see much of my grandfather. He was always working."

Adrian would have preferred to stay at his grandparents' home but moved to Washington to live with his mother after his grandmother died. He stayed to himself after the move. "The other children thought I was strange."

Melba remembered that Adrian had difficulty adjusting. "An apartment was a very strange thing for him."

He did fairly well in school until the fourth grade. "I was gener-

ally unhappy and dropped the effort to study." Adrian repeated the
fourth grade at Highlands Elementary School. He remembered also
that he had begun to resent his future stepfather, who had been
dating Melba about this time. Adrian and Tauscha went to Spartanburg, South Carolina, in the summer of 1980 to meet their father for
the first time.

He stayed in Spartanburg and attended junior high school. When
he entered the eighth grade, Tauscha joined him and did her seventh
school year in Spartanburg. She missed her mother, so she returned
to Washington the following summer. Adrian stayed until he completed the first half of the ninth grade, and then he, too, returned to
Washington.

At Washington's Hart Junior High School, Adrian was not able
to keep up with his classmates. He became frustrated. "They went
so fast and I was trying to tell them to slow down. I just can't respond
that quick. So what I did was I just didn't go to classes and whatnot."

Adrian entered Eastern High School but again could not adjust.
"The students cussed teachers out and got away with it. When I
talked about it, some of [the students] threatened me." He began
cutting classes again. Unlike what he knew would have happened if
he cut classes in Spartanburg, his mother and stepfather were never
notified that he was cutting his classes.

Adrian cut classes and was left back. When I met him, eighteen-
year-old Adrian had just started again at Ballou as a sophomore—
a year behind his sister—and I didn't think it would be long before
he dropped out. He did in October.

When he was fourteen Adrian began dating a neighborhood girl
who was a year older. Their relationship lasted for two years. She had
asked Adrian to give her a baby. Adrian, on Tauscha's advice, had
refused. "She was actually trying to get pregnant. She didn't tell me
why, but the way I look at it, it's like she wanted a lot of attention
and plus, I guess, some freedom from her mother. Every time you
turn around they were fighting. I guess [his girl friend] was trying
to get back at her mother and trying to hurt her. She never did finish
school. She kept asking me to try and get her pregnant. I said, 'I can't
accept that.' This was when I was in the ninth grade at Hart" Junior
High School.

At sixteen, Adrian visited Spartanburg for the summer and dated
a fifteen-year-old girl. Late one night, the girl's thirty-one-year-old
mother invited Adrian to spend the night, saying, "If you want to
spend the night, you go ahead and spend the night." Adrian said he

was shocked. He did not stay over that first night but did on subsequent nights.

He made love with his girl friend without using any contraception. "She used the word 'love.' I'm a sucker for that stuff. It made me feel good. I felt that she really did care for me!" His girl friend "and her mother had a relationship like anything that would happen just happens, and you just gonna accept it. I told the mother that if [the girl friend] ever got pregnant, 'Hey, I'll come back.' "

When he returned to Washington from his summer vacation, a letter was waiting for him from his girl friend. She was entering her sophomore year in high school and was pregnant. Adrian said to himself, "If she is, I don't want my mother to know." Melba had told him many times, "If I ever get a girl pregnant, she'd *kill* me."

Sexual relations with girls had presented Adrian with a dilemma. If he began petting and stopped, "girls looked at me as if to say, What seems to be the problem?" Then his masculinity would be challenged and he would become defensive. "Why you want to do that to me? Put my back up against the wall? I'd be forced into doing it to prove myself to her. To prove I was not afraid to do it." He had had an extensive course in human reproduction and birth-control methods in a Spartanburg junior high school. He knew full well the chance he was taking.

But he was not unhappy that his Spartanburg girl friend was pregnant. He began making plans to move to Spartanburg in order to marry his girl friend and be a father to their child.

He called her house, and her mother answered the phone. The mother blurted out, "[She] lost the baby!" His girl friend had been slammed into a pole at school and had a miscarriage. "I *cried*! I was really looking forward to being a father and enjoying the responsibility. I was *looking forward* to it. I called her at the hospital. We talked." Adrian was still planning to move to be with his girl friend, but she did not respond when he told her so. She became "snappy" whenever he called. Their relationship ended.

REGGIE AND TAUSCHA: GROWING UP

When Tauscha and Reggie were together, they tended to attract attention. Reggie's body was muscular and seemed custom-made for the T-shirts he liked to wear. He often kept his feelings to himself, hiding behind a poker face that made him seem aloof. Tauscha was the opposite; she admitted to having a temper and found it hard to disguise her unhappiness or anger.

Of the two, Reggie was more experienced in sexual matters. His sexual lessons began early, although he does not remember at what age. He was a student at Abram Simon Elementary School, located just on the outside of the Oxon Run Park border of Washington Highlands. A teenage baby-sitter was his first instructor. He recalled the scene:

> It is the early 1970's. The baby-sitter is standing in front of the television in his parents' apartment. She encourages him to watch her as she undresses. Pointing, she asks him, "Do you know what this is?" When Reggie answers he does not, she tells him, "My vagina." Pointing again, the girl asks, "Do you know what these are?" Reggie knows them as "titties," a word the girl is familiar with, but she corrects him. "They're breasts," she says. She asks him, "Have you ever done it before?" He knows what she is asking him and tells her he has not.
>
> "And I black out right then," said Reggie. "I can't remember what happened [from] that point."

Reggie's memory had triggered one of my own. I, too, had had a teenage baby-sitter undress in front of me when I was in elementary school. I cannot remember how old I was, but I can remember her name and the things she said.

She was a girl whom my mother had befriended when working as a nurse at Harlem's P.S. 136 Junior High School for girls on 135th Street. The girl looked after me on several occasions when my parents had gone out for the evening.

On one particular night, she came into my room and turned on a lamp. I was still awake. She undressed. "I know you've seen naked girls before," she said. I told her I had not. I remember that she lifted the covers and crawled into the bed beside me. After that, my mind blacks out, too.

Reggie said he did not know if his experience with the baby-sitter had had any effect on his sexuality. I don't know if my experience did either.

* * *

Reggie remembered his first sexual expression, something he thought he picked up from older boys. It was aggressive and disrespectful to girls, something he did in the hallways of his elementary school, something he would not do today. "When I was young, I always had a thing for smacking girls on the butt. Every pretty girl I'd see, I'd smack them on the butt."

At age eleven, Reggie looked up male and female anatomy and development in his mother's medical books. He felt he had to be surreptitious. His mother appeared to be embarrassed about his sexual queries. As he grew older, his mother and stepfather told him to keep his "thing" in his pants because they did not want any children around the house. "I didn't like talking to my mother and [stepfather] about [sex] because they always said, 'You shouldn't do this' and 'You could hurt the girl if you don't know what you doing,' and some more stuff."

An aunt carried Reggie's formal sexual education further when he was thirteen. While watching a movie on Home Box Office with his aunt, she told him to cover his eyes when a sexual scene came on in the movie they were watching. Reggie peeked through his fingers as his aunt described the scene to him. "The man is kissing the female and he is rubbing her body. These are the things that happen as you go along to sexual intercourse," she explained. After the movie, his aunt expanded on the lesson. "First, you should know what you're doing before you do it," the aunt said.

"She was real seventh-grade level about it. She came down to my level and told me about it. I was embarrassed" by her explicitness. She told him, "Your penis will reach the female vagina and insert. And excitement will build up within you, and you will ejaculate a fluid which is sperm. [It] will travel through the vagina and hit the egg and fertilize it." For the first time, Reggie remembered, "I really understood" what sexual intercourse actually was.

Months later, when visiting with the same aunt, he saw she had "a nasty reel," or pornographic videocassette. Reggie knew how to operate her videocassette recorder. He waited until after midnight, when the aunt had gone to sleep, and played the cassette. "My face was glued to the picture that whole night. I played it at least three times. I thought the oral sex part was common. I never was interested in that part."

Their relationship always had been open and frank, so Reggie told his aunt later the same day that he had watched the pornographic cassette. His aunt was not upset. She asked, "Well, did you understand what you saw?" Reggie was truthful and told her he had understood parts of what he had seen.

She sat him down. She had explained the physical act of intercourse to him, and now it was time to discuss the emotional basis of a relationship, the important part, which should come before the sexual aspect. From her bedroom, she brought out a book on male-female love and how a loving relationship ideally should be conducted. She read him a chapter at a time and then explained "in detail" what she had read. She talked to him about pregnancy.

In the eighth grade the following fall, fourteen-year-old Reggie took a detailed sex-education course, which addressed human reproduction, male-female anatomy, and every type of available contraception. The boys in his class did most of the giggling during the lessons. "The girls giggled at the shape of the penis," he said.

When he was fifteen, Reggie went out for a year with a seventeen-year-old girl. She lived across the street from his apartment and was sexually advanced. Reggie ended the relationship just after her first attempt to initiate sexual intercourse with him, after he discovered she had plotted to use him to protect a male relative who had gotten her pregnant. Reggie and the girl were alone in her parents' apartment. "She was real romantic. She took off all her clothes and took off my clothes. Then she pulled off her underwear. I pulled off mine. We both were under the covers. She wanted me to go and I chickened out. I told her I wasn't ready. Since she was two years older I felt inferior to her 'cause she would always say, 'One more year. I'll be a grown woman!' At eighteen. I knew I had to go all the way to twenty-one to be a grown man."

His girl friend was angered by his refusal. She sullenly said they would try it again some other time. The next day, the girl's brother told Reggie that she was pregnant and that his father was looking for Reggie. "Her father was on a rampage." Reggie realized the girl had been seeing someone else and had hoped to blame him for her pregnancy. He told her brother that he never had sexual intercourse with his sister. The girl's brother ran into the house and told his father. The father confronted his daughter and demanded to know who the father of her child was. She confessed. On his way out of the apartment building to see the nineteen-year-old relative the girl had named, the girl's father apologized to a very nervous Reggie for thinking he had gotten his daughter pregnant. Shortly afterward, the girl's father beat up—"very badly"—the adolescent relative who was the father of her child.

The same year, Reggie said, he became involved with a twenty-seven-year-old woman who made it clear that she wanted to have sex with him. Reggie was less interested in having sex with the woman than in riding in her white Chevrolet Camaro with black trim.

The day he met her, Reggie was wearing tight jeans. The woman looked directly at where the jeans stretched across his groin and said, "You have a bulk bigger than some of these [other] fifteen-, sixteen-year-olds out here. There! In front of your pants." Reggie said he was embarrassed. The next time he saw her, Reggie looked at her driver's license and discovered she was twenty-seven. They began seeing each other every day. "She taught me how to be a gentleman." The woman showed him how to open doors for her and how to order in restaurants. He felt like he was growing up.

Three months went by. The woman invited him to her apartment. They ended up in her bedroom. Reggie undressed under the covers. She pulled him toward her. He penetrated. He was frightened—afraid of being "drowned" by an older, experienced woman. His body stiffened. He did not want to be humiliated. He jerked back. Even with the seventeen-year-old girl, Reggie had held back from sexual intercourse out of a fear of "drowning." His fear had grown out of boyish folklore. His friends had warned him the seventeen-year-old girl "would drown me," that he was still too young to handle an older girl or a woman. He feared "that my penis would not be big enough. That's what is meant by drowning."

The woman did not know what caused his fear. She did not know that her age and experience frightened him. So she salvaged his ego and gently told him she understood that he was not ready. She also told him she needed someone who could fulfill her sexual needs, so they had to end their relationship. Reggie was relieved.

Tauscha, too, had resisted the urge to become sexually active, even in the face of teasing from her friends. Tauscha had been a tomboy in her early years, enjoying roughhousing with neighborhood boys and her older brother's friends. By the fourth grade, she became acutely aware of the difference between herself and the boys with whom she was accustomed to playing. The same boys began patting her on her buttocks in the hallways at Highlands Elementary School.

Two years later, eleven-year-old Tauscha made her first passage toward womanhood with the onset of her menses, an event that excited her mother. Melba wrapped her in a blanket and brought her hot tea. Tauscha was flabbergasted. She felt fine. Her mother was happy because Tauscha had become "a young woman." Melba announced the news to every woman who lived in their apartment building, said Tauscha, but her mother did not issue the warning that is common among the mothers of the girls I met in Washington Highlands. Melba did not tell her that she could get pregnant now if she engaged in sexual intercourse. Even so, such a warning to the very savvy Tauscha was unnecessary. "I already knew I could get pregnant from a film we were shown in the sixth grade."

After Tauscha's twelfth birthday, she and Adrian went to Spartanburg for the first time and met their father. Tauscha attended a Spartanburg junior high school for her seventh-grade year and was given an extensive course in human sexuality and contraception.

In Spartanburg that year Tauscha began to suffer from very painful menstrual cramps and an irregular cycle. When she returned to Washington, a doctor recommended to her mother that Tauscha's cycle be regulated by birth-control pills. Her mother reluctantly agreed.

"One of her ovaries is overactive," said Melba, but when the gynecologist suggested contraceptive pills "to regulate her, I was kind of skeptical. It wasn't that I was afraid of her using them as a crutch to be permissive. It's that I had a bad experience with birth-control pills. You don't know what the complications will be!"

Tauscha took "the mildest kind" for two months "even though they didn't make her feel so well," continued Melba. The pills did help reduce Tauscha's suffering and regulate her cycle, but they did not eliminate the problem. "I really worry about her in that area," her mother said.

Tauscha worried also. The worry became a fear—a fear that she might be infertile, a fear that pushed her to make a choice. The fear grew until Tauscha became engaged in a desperate effort to have a child—one sent from God.

Before the fear took root, her girl friends' sexual activity almost pushed Tauscha into following them, if for no other reason but to end their name-calling because she was still a virgin at twelve.

Tauscha went to a girl friend's pajama party. She listened in amazement as her twelve-year-old girl friends described in explicit detail their sexual involvements with their fifteen- and sixteen-year-old boyfriends. One girl said she and her boyfriend had gone to a popular Washington park, gotten under a blanket, and "we just got down." Tauscha asked what she meant by "got down." The girl responded, "We had sex." Tauscha was startled and surprised. She said, "*Girl,* you doing that all early and junk." Her friend, offended by Tauscha's reproach, replied angrily, "It's not too early for me!"

Another girl at the party also talked about "getting down" with her boyfriend after the two of them had gotten high on marijuana. "She went through the motions of what they did and how they did it. '[The girl's boyfriend] taught me this position. [He] gave me this position. He did this to me. He kissed me here.'"

A third girl went through another graphic description before they all turned their attention on Tauscha, the only virgin among the four of them. They ridiculed her because she was a virgin, Tauscha said, insulting her with the nickname "Miss Goody Two Shoes 'cause I wasn't into sex!"

Sometime later, on a night when Tauscha's parents were away from the apartment, her thirteen-year-old boyfriend was visiting and suggested they have sex. Tauscha remembered his line, "I'm a man, and I need my needs fulfilled." Tauscha told him she was not impressed with his needs and not interested in fulfilling them. "I ain't want to hear that junk." Her boyfriend was not put off, however. He continued to ask her.

She felt her resolve weakening because she did not feel good about herself. "I felt like I was an ugly duckling. Like I didn't have it all or something was missing."

Two other thoughts bounced around in her head as she listened to her boyfriend's insistent requests: If I do it, they won't be calling me Goody Two Shoes anymore. She no longer felt comfortable around her girl friends "because I knew what the subject would be. I knew that I would be the one out of the crowd that they would choose to pick on. I used to get upset because I figured like I was doing something wrong or I wasn't attractive."

The other thought was, Do not go ahead! "I didn't feel right because my mother had told me something beautiful is suppose to happen. You're suppose to feel these sparkles, and you're not suppose to have any doubts, and I didn't love him."

She finally told him that she would do it. "But I was scared." Her boyfriend tried to begin. "I thought *it* was the ugliest thing. I *felt* ugly! It didn't hurt, but I said it hurt because I didn't want him to do it." She told him, "I'm not ready for this." He stopped.

After a few minutes, he began to urge her to try again. Tauscha reached back into her tomboy days to give herself an out. "I don't care if you go back and you tell your friends that you did something. You can tell them. I'll go along with you, if you want me to." Tauscha said by hanging around boys, she knew what they talked about and knew what was important to them. Being sexually active with a neighborhood girl gave a boy status. "I just wanted him off me!"

Later that night, the boy's sister came to see Tauscha. "Did you give it to him?" the sister asked.

Tauscha was startled. She wondered what the girl had been told and realized her boyfriend and his sister had collaborated. "No!" she said emphatically.

"See, I told you. Miss Goody Two Shoes!" the girl said.

A year later, a close adult family friend confided to Tauscha that her former husband had given her syphilis, and the disease had made her sterile. "She told me that she wished she had gotten pregnant early. She was twenty-four. She said, 'I wish when I was seventeen or eighteen I would've gotten pregnant. At least, I would have a child of my own.' She loves children. I was thirteen when she told me this," in her eighth-grade year at Washington's Jefferson Junior High School.

Soon after that conversation, Tauscha developed a desire to have a baby. "I wanted something of my own. 'Cause every time I love somebody or something I get hurt someway, somehow, some form or fashion." She felt she did not get the love she needed from her mother and stepfather. The desire to have a baby passed, but in its place came a gnawing worry. She was still irregular in her menstrual cycles. She began to fret that she, too, might be infertile.

On a school trip to a New Jersey amusement park near Trenton, Tauscha met an eighteen-year-old boy who had his own car. She was fourteen and no longer felt ugly. People often told her she was cute, but she felt that her looks were "just OK." After the school trip, the boy drove down to Washington to visit her. Tauscha was very excited. Not only did he have his own car, but he was a high school graduate and had a job. He was a rare find compared to boys of the same age Tauscha knew in Washington Highlands. They had to walk or take the bus, had rarely finished junior high school, and were unemployed, if not selling illegal drugs.

The boy from New Jersey also impressed her mother. In fact, Melba thought he was "too fly," meaning too handsome and too fast.

Melba felt he could too easily turn Tauscha's head. She told him to write to Tauscha and give her a chance to grow up before he visited again.

Tauscha blew up and said some things that day that strained her relationship with her mother for years afterward.

Tauscha remembers how she felt. "It was the first time I got something that looked halfway decent. Got a job. Got a car and doing good for himself. Got his [high school] diploma." Nevertheless, Tauscha said her mother told the boy to "say bye forever 'cause you can't see her anymore" for at least two years.

Tauscha erupted, saying, "Why is it every time that I find a boyfriend, you always trying to break us up?" She demanded to know if her mother wanted her to become a lesbian. Her mother replied, "I don't want you to become a lesbian! It's just that it's a certain way that you go about getting a boyfriend." Tauscha lost control of herself and said, "Damn! Every time I get one it seems like you say the same motherfucking thing. Over and over again. I'm starting to hate you, *bitch*!" She ran out of the house crying. "I walked in the rain so I could get my head straight." The boy from New Jersey was still waiting for her when she returned a half hour later. He tried to console her. It was the last time they saw each other.

Melba did not speak to Tauscha for a month. "I hurt her and I could feel it. It hurts me now to think about what I said to her, but I apologized so many times," Tauscha recalled. When they finally talked, her mother told her she would not forgive her, Tauscha said. Her mother periodically brought up that incident years after it had happened.

In the summer of 1983, Tauscha won Washington's citywide junior mayor contest and was given a summer job in the mayor's youth office. She became interested in a twenty-one-year-old Democratic party politico who worked in the same office. They dated. At fifteen, she thought of herself as old enough to date a man, but he insisted that they keep their relationship a secret. Their relationship might have a negative impact on his long-term political ambitions because of her age, he told her.

Tauscha was asked by a woman coworker if there was anything between her and the man. She thought the woman would keep the answer to herself so she told her that she was seeing him. The women went to him and congratulated him on having a girlfriend so young.

The aspiring politician was furious with Tauscha. He later became bored with their relationship when she told him on two occasions that she was not ready to make love with him. He stopped calling her. Tauscha was carrying the hurt from the breakup when she met Reggie Wiley one day at Ballou High School. It was February 1984.

THE CRISIS

From Tauscha's point of view, her parents fought too much and demanded too much of her. "It's not the family you would write about in a family-life book. It got to be a hellhole. Me always trying to be the peacemaker."

She felt she couldn't rely on her family. When her relationship with Reggie Wiley began to flourish, she said she turned to him as her "anchor."

Tauscha had felt, even before she met Reggie, that she was going to become sexually active by her midteens. "I just felt that my body was taking over. I felt I was going to sooner or later. I could feel it. One day, I just got on my knees and prayed, 'Lord, it seems like this excitement of my body is about to happen, but I hope you let me have this [sexual] relationship with not just anybody.' I just knew I was changing and boys were starting to look real different to me. So I did ask God that he pick the guy that I do it with."

Tauscha's relationship with Reggie grew until they became sexually active the night of her sixteenth birthday. They had not discussed contraception. Their lovemaking that night was not something either had planned. Reggie said he thought about using a condom, "but I didn't ask her what she thought about it." Instead, he withdrew just at the point of ejaculation. In the weeks that followed, he used a condom.

Eventually, Tauscha asked him to stop using one. "I did not like it. I just wanted to do it [another] way for a change," she said.

Reggie readily agreed. "It didn't feel comfortable, and I didn't enjoy it either," Reggie said, "so I kept taking my chances on withdrawal."

Then something changed. Tauscha decided she wanted a child. Both Tauscha and Reggie remembered when interviewed that on September 11, 1984, Tauscha held Reggie to keep him from withdrawing. "She assumed that she would become pregnant. I asked her why she held me down. She said she didn't care about the possibility of pregnancy," Reggie said.

During that incident, she told Reggie when he was about to withdraw that she was at the point of orgasm and he was about "to blow it. She said, 'I want my orgasm!'" Reggie asked her if a pregnancy was worth the risk of an orgasm. Tauscha told him she would not mind having a baby and that she liked babies and wanted to have his baby. Reggie argued that neither of them was prepared to raise a baby. Tauscha agreed and promised not to hold him again.

But she held him anyway, several times during the rest of September. According to Tauscha, she did this "because during that period, I wanted to get pregnant, and to me it would have been a blessing. I just wanted a child by him, point-blank, period! I always imagined a little Reggie running around. I want five children, if I can have children."

Tauscha's nagging worry that she could not have children had grown into a deep fear since her days in the eighth grade at Jefferson Junior High School. "It's just a feeling. But I always ask God, 'Just give me one child. Just one!' And if I do get that one, I promise that he will always follow the word of Christ."

In October, her menstrual period was a week late. In November, it did not come at all. At the end of November, Tauscha told her parents she thought she might be pregnant. The reaction was not what Tauscha had hoped it would be. Her brother said self-righteously, "I told you so!" Her stepfather took the news calmly. Her mother was furious and threatened to send Tauscha to South Carolina to live with her father. Her mother "couldn't just show me how much she loved me. To her, what I did was wrong, and that just turned me off!"

Tauscha's mother told her that she should be ashamed to be interviewed by me, that I was probably still thinking of Tauscha as a girl who would get out of Washington Highlands without becoming a teenage mother. "I ain't gonna feel no shame. *Shoot!* Everybody out here does it. Make love. She wanted me to stay a virgin till I was married. She try to be Miss Goody Two Shoes. I love her, but she's a trip."

As it turned out, Tauscha hadn't been pregnant. A cyst on her ovary had interrupted her cycle, she was told by the doctor who examined her. Had she been pregnant, she would have told her mother she had planned it. "I wouldn't let my mother think that it was an accident. Any reason that I would give her wouldn't be good enough, so why not just tell her the truth."

But the false alarm triggered a deeper crisis: For the next six months, almost no one—not even Reggie—could control a raging, angry Tauscha. She began regularly to skip her classes at Ballou High School "because I didn't like it." Studying and attending school seemed "like it was not worth it." Both her parents had gone as far as college, "and they just barely making it." She asked herself, Am I gonna be like this? Is there some type of future for me? Is going to Ballou worth the hassle?

I told her she even looked unkempt during her crisis. "I didn't feel attractive, so I didn't look it. I was so moody. You look at me wrong, and I'd say, 'What the fuck are you looking at?' I was just nasty. I didn't care. I was like a devil. I could be just as nasty as I wanted to be just because of all the hostility in me. I would curse Reggie out. I would fight Reggie. I would hit him. There were times when I wanted to hurt me. I wanted to commit suicide a couple of times."

She fought with her stepfather, with her brother, with Reggie, the quarrels sometimes climaxing in physical struggles. At different times, she ended up with a black eye, a fat lip, finger marks on her face, and countless bruises and scratches.

She felt that her family had deserted and rejected her when they thought she was pregnant. So she told them to stay out of her life. "Ya'll ain't want to handle my problem when I really had a big problem, so just leave me alone," she would say to them.

In December, she again decided she wanted to have a baby. She thought the baby would be a signal from God. If she could conceive, if she could actually bring a child into the world, then maybe that would be God's way of bringing her out of her emotional crisis—a deliverance. She manipulated her Baptist religious upbringing to meet her needs. There was nothing in her religious instruction that justified having sex outside of marriage or having a child outside of marriage, but she called on God to give her a child to free her from her torment.

Surprisingly, Tauscha stopped attending services at Paramount Church during the same period. The majority of the parishioners at Paramount had grown up in Washington Highlands but had moved up the economic ladder and now lived in the surrounding Maryland suburbs. They had house mortgages and cars and only came back into Washington Highlands to attend weeknight or Sunday church services.

Tauscha felt the class cleavage the suburban parishioners represented. Her parents' income was below that of most of the people who attended Paramount. She explained her reason for no longer attending services: "If you don't have the right clothes and you can't do this and you can't do that, then you just out. You have to dress to a certain standard, which mean bourgeois. They have an attitude. If you don't have any money or you don't have a car or you don't drive a car or anything, then you out. I'd rather have the temple inside my heart and pray on my own."

During an April 1985 conversation, Tauscha said she was convinced that she was infertile. She had been trying to get pregnant for five months. "I'm not gonna be able to have kids, you watch! It's a feeling inside. A doctor told me I was gonna be able to have kids, but I don't think so. If I can, God bless me, because I do want eleven, twelve children."

After that conversation, Tauscha missed her period again. This time, she had no doubt she was pregnant, she told me on May 2. She felt she had achieved the pregnancy through seeking contact with Reggie's soul and through prayer. She would try to make their two souls meet by looking deeply into his eyes. "You try to make them become one. If that don't work, what you do is you think of Christ. You think of your partner as the man that He has sent for you to conceive this child with. It'll be all right."

God also had given her a sign that she was pregnant, she believed. "I always ask God, if I would get pregnant, to give me the urge to to pick up the Bible and read it constantly. I pick up the Bible now. I just noticed it last night, what I was doing. It seems like I just can't put it down for some reason." Reggie wanted a girl. Tauscha wanted a boy.

When they both thought Tauscha was pregnant during the winter pregnancy crisis, they decided they wanted to have a child. "I saw how Reggie really wanted one. No matter what had happened or what was said." Reggie's attitude was, "This [child] is mine! Nobody's gonna harm you or the child." Reggie could have run out on her, but instead he faced up to her parents. "He took all the abuse from my mother, from my father. They cussed him out. Well, my mother did. Reggie didn't disrespect her."

Reggie responded to her parents, "Well, if she's pregnant, she's pregnant. I'm do my best to take care of it. I have to find a job. I have to do something. There's no burden that will be put on you all."

"That was amazing to me!" Tauscha recalled.

Later in May, after she was certain she was pregnant, that God had given her the sign by her increased interest in Bible study, Tauscha was told that hers was a tubal pregnancy. The fertilized egg had become lodged in one of her fallopian tubes, a condition that is life-threatening to the mother and requires an operation to remove the egg.

I saw her after the operation. She seemed relieved, calmer, more like the self-assured girl I had met in our first interview. For now, she said, she had lost her interest in having a baby. She had decided to wait until she and Reggie had better job prospects.

"When I'm around [Reggie], I'm happy," she said. "Even when I'm fussing at him, I'm happy. . . . I'm determined to make my relationship with Reggie work."

JANUARY 1986

When they met in 1984, Tauscha had lost interest in school. Reggie was repeating the eleventh grade and also had lost interest. They dropped out of Ballou High School in 1985 and did not return. They worked on and off. Tauscha went to work in the summer of 1985 at a McDonald's restaurant in downtown Washington. In mid-January 1986, she quit. Reggie was laid off from a construction job in October 1985 and then got a job at the same McDonald's in December.

In late January 1986, during an interview, Tauscha expressed doubts about the future. She and Reggie had been planning to marry on June 21—her eighteenth birthday—but wondered whether she was "maturing a little too fast for him." She had become interested in a twenty-three-year-old man she met at work, someone who "is one of those type of guys that wants to help you so much. Just be supportive. Like he wants me to go to college."

At seventeen, she was already looking back on her life. She was straightforward about it, almost matter-of-fact. She said she made a mistake by dropping out of school but added, "I don't think it was a *big* mistake. I see girls and guys who finished school, and they still can't find a job. That mistake has brought me to learn no matter what decisions you make out of life, whether they good or bad, you going to have to live with that."

When Reggie read the newspaper article and found out Tauscha had been thinking about dropping him, he angrily refused to talk to Tauscha for days, she told me in the spring of 1986. They patched up that quarrel, however, and together rented an apartment in Northeast Washington. Twice I called Tauscha and had two long conversations with her. They had decided to live together for an indefinite period before marrying.

I called Tauscha again in July 1987. Their telephone number had been disconnected, a recording informed me. There was no new telephone number. I did not hear from her again. I missed her!

CHAPTER SIX

Joye Jackson's fervor struck me first. She was the last teenage mother to speak to the Mayor's Blue Ribbon Panel on Teenage Pregnancy Prevention on October 30, 1984. Joye obviously had not been scheduled to speak. The other adolescent mothers were dressed up and had elaborate hairstyles to match their outfits. They read their prepared speeches with a studied dryness.

Joye, on the other hand, wore a pair of faded pedal-pusher-style jeans and a plain white blouse. Her hair was swept back into a bun. Her speech was extemporaneous and stirring.

The clothes Joye wore that day were not representative of the way she normally dressed. Joye was materialistic. She often dressed for a day of classes at Ballou as if she were in a fashion show. The Ballou High School nurse impulsively invited Joye to speak at the last minute. Joye grabbed the chance.

Because Joye had given birth to two girls by the age of fifteen, Ballou's nurse felt the loquacious teenager would have something dramatic to say about adolescent childbearing. She did.

Joye said parents were remiss in not telling their teenage children about the pitfalls of sexual passion. Desire is what had gotten her pregnant with both her children, she told the panel and audience of eight hundred students.

"I don't care what you think, when passion hits you, you're going to do it," Joye shouted.

After the hearing ended, I introduced myself to Joye and asked if I could interview her for the project I was working on. She agreed and I went to her house the next week. Six months later, Joye told me a very different story from the one she had given at Ballou. Joye's story of the beginning of her sexuality was something I never could have imagined.

When Joye Jackson and Tony Smith met on a balmy spring day in 1982, Joye was fourteen years old and considered herself a "player"—a term used among her friends for someone who secretly has several boyfriends. She was conscious of her appearance. She wore clothes that showed off her slim body, and she frequently experimented with elaborate hairstyles.

To Joye, dating was a game and boys were something to be conquered. She said she couldn't wait to have her first sexual experience so she could brag about her exploits to her girl friends. She wasn't interested in long-term relationships or in getting pregnant.

"I was one of those girls who said I don't want none of those brats!" she said, her voice taking on a hard edge. She was mostly interested in maintaining her popularity, dressing stylishly and keeping up her image as a player. She expected her boyfriends to give her money, jewelry, and clothing, and they did. If they did not, Joye quickly ended the relationship.

Tony Smith also considered himself to be a player. He was fifteen, a ninth grader at a junior high school outside of Washington in the Maryland suburb of Suitland. He was dating six girls simultaneously and had been sexually active since he was thirteen. On that spring afternoon in 1982, he and his older brother took their stepfather's black Fleetwood Cadillac and drove over to the Tolliver Court apartments in Capitol Heights, Maryland, where Joye was living at the time. Tony said he and his brother smoked marijuana and did some girl-watching.

As they sat in the car, Joye was standing in front of her apartment building, talking to a boy whom Tony assumed was her boyfriend. Tony said he was immediately attracted to her. She was wearing tight jeans that showed off her "Popeye" legs. "Popeye" is slang for a girl who has slim thighs and muscular calves, features that some adolescent boys find appealing.

The conversation between Joye and the boy ended, and Tony shouted to Joye. "The car caught my eye," said Joye. "Tony didn't catch my eye." He was not prepared for what happened next. Joye hurried over to the car and furtively slipped him a piece of paper with her phone number on it, then ran back to the front of the building. She's trying to be slick, thought Tony. He was more than interested now.

That night, he called her. They talked for five hours. They talked many times over the next three weeks, and after hours of conversation, they decided to get together.

From the outset, their relationship was a conscious game of trying to control and outdo each other. If Joye saw boys, Tony started seeing other girls. If Joye showed up with a "passion mark" on her neck, Tony went out of his way to get one on his.

Joye said, "I was just boy crazy. Can't have one, take them all. . . . I ain't care if their heart was broken or nothing. I used to be over at Tony's house and call somebody to come pick me up."

Joye's impact on people was very important to her. She needed some to respect and admire her; she needed others whom she could manipulate and collect gifts from; she needed both admirers and flunkies to do things for her. Joye's exercise of power over others made her feel good about herself, and she exercised that power every chance she got, even, at times, to the point of cruelty.

Tony said, "She was trying to play a lot of boys, and I was trying to play a lot of girls. Joye was more or less a challenge. Trying to get her to stop messing with all these boys. I was trying to slow her down 'cause she was as fast [as I was]."

By the time Joye appeared before the panel on teenage pregnancy prevention at Ballou, she had moved with her mother into the city's Washington Highlands community. The panel Joye addressed was chaired by the well-known sociologist and author Joyce A. Ladner. Joye told Ladner, the other members of the panel, several television camera crews recording her testimony, and eight hundred classmates who filled Ballou's auditorium how she became pregnant. It was a story of being so overwhelmed by sexual passion that she had become a mother of two girls by the young age of fifteen.

"The first time I laid down I got pregnant," she told them. "[He] didn't have to say he loved me to make me have sex with him. It just happened. If passion hit you, you're gonna do it."

Many months later, after a series of lengthy interviews, it became clear that passion was not what motivated Joye when she and Tony made love the first time. Passion had had nothing to do with that first time, she explained. She wanted to conquer him, to *overwhelm* him. She needed to keep pace with her girl friends; girls who engaged in a female game of sexual dominance called "drowning"; girls who purposely went after the "macho" boys known as players.

For those reasons, Joye did not tell Tony it was her first time. "No, I had an image to hold," she said. "I told him I was experienced. I was a player! I was raw! I was awesome! Had to hold my image. Let him know he was messing with *fire*!"

In the intervening weeks before Tony came to see her, Joye had challenged him several times on the telephone, saying, "I can't wait to get you in the bed. I'ma tear you up!" Tony, always cool and tough, said, "Yeah, we'll see."

On the Friday afternoon Tony came to see her, Joye had gone swimming after school and her legs were still ashy. She intentionally wore shorts to emphasize her muscular "Popeye" calves. She said she wanted to be sure she aroused Tony, to ensure that he would make a move toward her. Tony walked through the door high and red-eyed from smoking marijuana. The scene for the contest was set. Joye played the role of the awesome woman, goading Tony's macho exterior to get him to respond. Tony did not realize his strings were being pulled.

In Joye's bedroom, she closed the blinds. "I started pulling off my clothes. I said, 'What's taking you so long to get undressed?' I got in the bed, then he got in there. I said, 'Shorty, you gonna be drowning. You gonna need a lifeboat.' " Tony, unable to match Joye's verbal thrusts, said, "Naw, naw. You gonna need a raft."

Joye was ready. "My girl friends taught me everything." She had been going to an X-rated Maryland drive-in to watch pornographic movies since she was twelve. "That's how I got all my positions." Joye had been fascinated by everything in the movies except the oral sex, a practice she and most of her friends found disgusting. From her girl friends' instructions and the movies she had seen, Joye already knew what she was going to do to humble player Tony, to let him know he had gotten into bed and "messed with *fire*!" She was determined that she would emerge from this liaison as the top player.

"I was the second girl he ever made love to," Joye said. Not so, said Tony. "Well, it seemed like I was 'cause he ain't know what he was doing," added Joye.

Even as she and Tony made love, she said, "I was thinking about, Let's get this over with so I can go brag about it."

But before she had the opportunity to brag, Joye needed to go the next step in the game. She attacked him where her girl friends said he would be most vulnerable—his ego. "Is that all?" she asked Tony. "I didn't even feel it."

She told Tony that he had been drowned. "She said she drowned me, right? I was like, 'How do you figure you did that?' She know better than that. I don't know what she was trying to prove," he said.

Both of them were very sophisticated about birth control from sex-education courses in school, yet neither one of them raised the subject of contraception. Since Joye had told Tony she was experienced, she was not going to lose face and ask him how they were going to prevent her from becoming pregnant. "I thought normally he would pull it out when he getting ready" to climax. "That's what my girl friends said. Their boyfriends just pull it out when they getting ready to shoot." Since Joye told Tony she was experienced, he put the burden of contraception entirely on her. He assumed she was taking birth-control pills.

She was confused, however, because she did not experience what her girl friends had told her to expect. "I was expecting it to hurt or feel good or whatever. All my friends were doing it, and I wanted to do it, too. My friends were talking about it was this and it was that; it's so good. There wasn't none of that. I *really* didn't feel it!"

Immediately after Tony left that day in May 1982, she got on the telephone and called her best girl friend. "I *drowned* him," she said, using the term she had heard her other girl friends use in describing their sexual conquests. "And I bragged and I bragged! I said, 'He was swimming.' I was so happy that day."

She even outdid her girl friends and called the boy who thought he was her boyfriend. "I told him I just made love to Tony. He cried and cried. He came over and he cried and he cried and he cried. I was just laughing. I was just selfish 'cause I didn't love [him]. He was just there. Just somebody to have fun with."

Tony called her back later the same day. They talked for a short time. Joye was bored and told him she would call him back. She called him a week later. Then a month passed before she called him again. "It was just one of those things. We'd done it. It was over. No strings attached."

In plotting her sexual conquest of Tony, Joye decided not to accept her mother's recent offer to obtain birth-control pills for her. "I felt funny. Fourteen years old. 'Momma, I want some birth control.'" She believed that her mother, despite her offer, would have been upset because of Joye's age. "Could you go to your father, Mr.

Dash, and ask him for some condoms at fourteen?" I admitted to her that I would not have done so. "I didn't want to tell my mother I was ready to make love. I wish I had now!"

GROWING UP

Joye's father was a Vietnam army veteran whom Joye's mother said she married when she was eighteen. "My mother said he used to shake me a whole lot. When she leave to go to work, I wouldn't move [from the chair] till she got back home. I didn't like him. I don't know what it was." She sat in the chair, although her father did not make her do it. Joye was two years old when her parents separated.

School had never been very important to Joye. "I was never on my reading level from the first through the sixth grades. I was just one of them bad students that liked to play a lot, joke, be the class clown."

At age eleven, Joye's menses began while she was playing football with a group of boys. She ran into her apartment to tell her mother. Her mother told her what hygienic procedures to follow and told her she could now get pregnant. "And that's all, really," said Joye.

When Joye was twelve, her mother became a "saved" woman, a born-again Christian. Whenever I called Joye's home, her mother answered the telephone with "Praise the Lord!" before she asked who was calling. Her mother gave me permission to interview Joye, but declined to be interviewed herself.

Joye reacted to her mother's conversion with mixed feelings. Her mother stopped cursing, smoking, drinking, and going out to parties after she was saved. She also became strict and closely monitored Joye's activities. "When she wasn't saved, I would do anything. Or if she was drinking, I could get anything I wanted. She'd go to parties just about every weekend. Her and her friends. They'd go out all the time. I preferred her when she was a sinner."

By the sixth grade, Joye noticed boys' interest in her legs. "They liked me because of my legs. The muscles in my legs, big calves." She learned to show them off, glorying in the sexually suggestive comments she overheard the boys make about her "Popeye" legs.

It also was in the sixth grade, with her mother's permission, that Joye took sex education. "I already knew about making love, but I didn't know what to do or nothing like that." The course covered human reproductive organs, menstruation, and all forms of birth control.

Joye used her increased sophistication to pry money out of boys who were interested in her but whom she was not interested in dating. She would tell a boy that "if he wants to make love" he'd have to give her twelve dollars every two weeks so she could buy birth-control pills. She claimed to have strung one boy out for seven months with this gambit. After she became sexually active, Joye told several boys she was pregnant and needed two hundred fifty dollars for an abortion, "and he has to pay half." They never knew that Joye is against abortion and would never have had one if she was pregnant. "It's murder."

She said she also got a lot of pleasure out of getting boys to fall for her and then dumping them.

In June 1982, a month after her first sexual encounter with Tony, Joye met another boy. He was eighteen, three years older than Tony and four years older than Joye. "He was bowlegged, nice skin, had pretty wavy-curly hair. He could dress. He drove a Camaro" sports car. "He opened [the car door] for me. I ain't never had anyone do that. He had a good job. He had his own apartment. And he was a high school graduate." This time around, it was Joyce who fell in love.

She made love with him at the end of June. "I got really turned on. I felt I was making love with a man. He was experienced." She was not interested in drowning him, and he always used a condom. They dated through the month of July. He bought her designer clothes. The labels were more important to Joye than the items. "He bought me Jordache, some Calvin Kleins. He bought me a gold watch."

Her boyfriend joined the Marine Corps, and she did not hear from him during August. "I was hurt," Joye recalled. "I felt like I was used and I was hurt."

All of her life, her mother had told her that men are untrustworthy and would always "mess up on you" by running around with other women. Even when her mother became a born-again Christian, she repeated this instruction to Joye. She now understood what her mother had meant. "This makes me mean to them. Seems like when you mean to boys they like that. They fall in love with you quick. One out of ten men [is] straight, trustworthy. Most are no good!"

Still sad, still missing the Marine Corps boyfriend, Joye entered the eighth grade in September 1982. Her friends asked her if she was pregnant. Her maternal grandmother asked her if she was pregnant. Her stomach was big for such a slim girl. But Joye insisted that she was not pregnant.

Tony got word about her condition and called. He told her that he knew she was pregnant and that he was the father.

"Boy, you sound like a fool," Joye remembered telling Tony.

"Well, I shot it in you, and was you on anything?" Tony continued.

"No."

"Well, then you pregnant."

"If I am, you're not the father. [The Marine] is the father," Joye responded.

Joye did not want Tony to be the father of her child. She wanted the Marine she so badly missed to be the father. "So I went to my sixth-grade teacher," the man who had taught her sex education. She asked her former teacher, "When a boy uses a condom, can you be pregnant?" The teacher told her yes, if the condom breaks during intercourse or if it has a hole in it.

The Marine called her shortly afterward. She told him she was pregnant and that he was the father. He did not believe her.

Finally, Joye's mother asked her if she had become sexually active. "No," Joye told her. "I'm a virgin." Joye's mother took her for a medical examination. Joye repeated she was still a virgin as the doctor examined her and her mother watched. The doctor looked up at her mother and said, "She looks to be about six months pregnant." Joye said, "And my mother stood up there and she cried."

Joye told her mother that her Marine Corps boyfriend was the father of her child. Her mother called the Marine's mother, who said her son was in Texas and she could not get in touch with him.

Her father called her for the first time in years—the first time since she was eleven, when she waited for him a day and a night for a shopping trip that never materialized.

He asked her, "What you doing pregnant? Why don't you wanna have no abortion?" Joye exploded. "Who are you to judge? You ain't been around all these years. What's on your mind? Don't ever call again and try to raise me! Are you crazy?"

In her eighth month, Joye and her mother moved from Maryland into Washington Highlands. Joye dropped out of school. "All [my mother] ever said is she think I ain't gonna finish school. She always thinking the worse of me. I'm just gonna have twenty babies, she says."

Her mother told Joye that she was following in the footsteps of an older relative who had had her first of four children at seventeen. The relative goes "to clubs and do those nasty dances, you know, striptease." Her mother had told Joye that Joye's "blood ain't right."

Tony sensed he was the father of her child, but stayed away from Joye. "Tony wasn't very interested in me then. I was going after Tony 'cause I began to like him," said Joye. "I wanted to believe that [the Marine] was the father so I would always pray to God that the baby came out looking like him. When I got in my ninth month, I kind of knew Tony was the father."

Just before the baby was due, Joye said, she finally told Tony the truth. They began to see each other again. "Tony started getting closer to me," Joye said. "That's when he starts telling me he love me and all this and that. He was going to see me through the baby, make sure everything all right."

Their first daughter, Taisha Tamar Jackson, was born on January 9, 1983. Tony remembers Joye calling him and crying on the telephone that night. Joye remembers it differently. "Me? Cry?" she said laughingly. "Lose my image? Ain't no way I cry to no boy! Never, never in front of him or any other boy! No, no, no. Got to be macho to live in this world! That way, you heart never get broken. If you cry in front of them, they learn that they can manipulate you!" The one time she was hurt by the Marine, Joye insisted, "it was my pride, *not* my heart!"

For the first time, Joye revealed the identity of Taisha's father to her mother and former boyfriend. "I told my mother that Tony was the father, and that made her mad. I told [the Marine] that he wasn't the father, and that made [him] mad. Tony never told his mother, so I called her and told her. I told her she had a three-month-old granddaughter named Taisha Tamar Jackson."

Over the next few months, Joye and Tony continued to see each other. To prevent another pregnancy, Joye said, she decided in April to take birth-control pills. But she apparently started taking them too late; she learned in mid-May that she was one month pregnant. "I started crying then. I was just a young kid. Fifteen and I'm pregnant with my second child!" Her mother asked her if she wanted to have it, and Joye said she would not have an abortion.

Throughout her second pregnancy, Joye said, she was "booking boys," her phrase for lining up frequent dates. She came home one day with a passion mark on her neck. "So [Tony] went and got a hickey on his neck." Meanwhile, her relationship with Tony foundered. Then, after their second daughter, Rochelle Nicole Jackson, was born January 8, 1984, they began talking seriously about marriage.

Joye was reluctant. She was still very young, still an adolescent. "I got tired of Tony, got tired of looking at him. I didn't want to be held down," she said. "Too many cuties out there to be held down to one boy. I asked him why he stayed with me. He just said we were so much alike."

Her mother would not let any other boy visit Joye. Her mother told her, Joye said, "Look girl, you got these two babies, and you hot. You hot in the drawers." Joye said she did not see how she had done anything wrong. "What's that got to do with being hot because you got two babies. OK, most of the girls I know got babies. If they don't want to be with their baby's father, fine! They don't have to be with the baby's father. She don't let me see nobody but Tony. That don't mean y'all married just 'cause y'all got babies!"

For the next year Joye and Tony went through hard times. One day Joye would tell him that she loved him only to change her mind the following day and say the opposite. Tony did the same.

During their ups and downs, Tony and Joye managed to stay in school, Joye at Ballou and Tony at Croom Vocational High School in Upper Marlboro in Maryland.

She began secretly to date another boy in early 1985 while seeing Tony. He was a classmate at Ballou who bought her a pair of designer jeans, a watch, and a diamond engagement ring. "I don't know were he gets the money to buy me these things. Maybe his people have money." She kept the ring and watch overnight, but felt uncomfortable about accepting gifts of a high value, and she returned them the next day. "He cried." They continued to see each other, until a boy nicknamed Boo-Boo decided to interfere. Boo-Boo had dated Joye and wanted her to go back with him.

To break up Joye's relationship, Boo-Boo told her boyfriend that he and Joye had engaged in oral sex, a taboo among the youths of Washington Highlands. (A girl who had sex with a boy other than the one she was dating was called a "freak," a term synonymous with whore. A girl who engaged in oral sex was called "kinky," a term that translates into weird. Both freaks and kinky girls were ostracized by both sexes.)

Joye's boyfriend confronted her. She angrily denied Boo-Boo's story and said she had not even made love to Boo-Boo. She caught

Police block a section of Condon Terrace SE that they say is a drug center. Charmaine Ford, who lives nearby, refused to let her nine-year-old twin sons go to or from school alone.

An apartment stoop is a magnet for summertime socializing.

Chesapeake Drugs is a popular spot among neighborhood students.

Joye Jackson and Tony Smith on their wedding day, with daughters Taisha, left, and Rochelle

Rochelle, two, and Tony share one tricycle; Joye and three-year-old Taisha, another.

Sheila Matthews testifies before the mayor's Blue Ribbon Panel on Teenage Pregnancy Prevention.

Petey with his father, Mario. Both parents provide Petey with affection, and Sheila is about to begin night school.

Sheila takes Petey for a visit at the clinic. Before becoming a mother at sixteen, Sheila was an above-average student and hoped to become a pediatrician.

Charmaine Ford with her sons Charles, front, thirteen, who has cerebral palsy, and twins Lawrence, left, and Lionel, nine

Allie Downie and author Leon Dash in front of a deserted sharecropper's house

Irene Winston Taylor

Catherine Mitz

Joe "Bubba" Green, Jr., stands under an old bell that landowners rang to call the sharecroppers out of the fields at midday and evening.

up with Boo-Boo in a school hallway during the changing of classes. Joye could not have picked a better time or place for her revenge. She had dozens of witnesses to her outrage. She loudly and publicly cursed Boo-Boo out in front of the many students who gathered around them. Boo-Boo was branded a liar. Her boyfriend subsequently believed her, but the insulted Joye would have nothing further to do with him. He should not have believed Boo-Boo in the first place.

February 25 to March 1, 1985, was Teenage Pregnancy Week at Ballou. Joye attended one of the auditorium programs. "I didn't like it. Really none of the teenage mothers liked it. They tried to make it look like teenagers can't take care of babies. If you put your mind to it, you can do anything. They saying teenagers can't find baby-sitters. Welfare can pay for baby-sitters, or they can get a night job and still stay in school," said Joye. "Maybe I am one of the lucky ones. My grandmother keeps the babies" during the day while Joye was in classes.

Throughout this period, Tony and Joye were constantly breaking up and getting back together. Sometimes they argued with words, sometimes by hitting each other, they said. Somehow, the relationship survived. Finally, they decided to get married.

Tony had begun to settle down, something Joye viewed as a mixed blessing. "Tony is a good supporter and father. Always there when I need him. I want to marry him, probably because of his children. I think that's what's keeping us together. But I don't feel like I used to for him. It dies off."

Joye was still thrilled when boys would "crack on her" as she walked through the halls of Ballou High School. The expression means telling a girl how good she looks in preparation for asking her out on a date. "It feels good," Joye said. "They always tell me that I've got two children and that most girls, after two or three children, don't dress up as good, but I'm keeping myself up."

After they decided to marry, Tony remained "scared he's going to lose me. Every time he comes close to losing me, he cries. He used to be macho. Tony used to smoke pot, go to dances, everywhere. He used to be wild."

He was now trying to rein her in, Joye complained. "He don't want me to wear bikinis. He don't want me wearing short shorts or just shorts. He don't want me seeing anyone else. I told him, 'We ain't married, yet!'"

On June 8, 1985, three years after they met, Joye Jenise Jackson, seventeen, and Anthony David Smith, eighteen, were married in a church ceremony. Sitting in the front pews were their families and their two children, two-and-half-year-old Taisha and eighteen-month-old Rochelle.

After the marriage, Joye and Tony moved with their two daughters to an apartment in Capitol Heights, Maryland. Tony worked at a clothing and furniture store and Joye attended night school at Spingarn High School, studying for a high school diploma.

Their plans revolved around Joye graduating from high school and, possibly, going on to college. If they could, they wanted to save money to buy a house in five or six years.

Tony said during an interview at their apartment in January 1986 that they had children too early. "There's a lot of things I think I'd rather have done [first]," he said.

Joye, who had not wanted children at all, said she would try to prevent her daughters from becoming teenage mothers. "I'ma be a strict parent," she laughed.

Joye called me in December 1987. She graduated from high school and was working as a clerk. She and Tony had a third daughter and then separated. Tony kept the two oldest girls, and the youngest child was living with Joye in her Suitland, Maryland, apartment.

We made a date to have dinner on a Saturday night, but as often was the case when I was interviewing her, Joye was not at home when I called prior to going to pick her up.

CHAPTER SEVEN

SHEILA MATTHEWS WAS THE third girl I met in the Ballou High School auditorium during the October 1984 testimony on teenage pregnancy. Fifteen-year-old Sheila was the youngest girl and the only mother-to-be who testified. Her unborn baby was six months along and showing. Sheila wore a white maternity blouse over a black skirt. A titter rippled over the eight-hundred-odd juvenile students in the audience as the obviously pregnant Sheila rose to speak.

She was not embarrassed by her pregnancy, Sheila told the panel and the students. After all, it was God who had created this life inside of her, and there was no reason for her to be self-conscious about anything that is God-given. Abortion was out of the question. "If you can't make a life, why take a life?" continued Sheila. "If I could breathe into dirt like God does and make a life, than I feel I have the authority to take a life."

Sheila stood out to me because of the slight girl's reliance on her religious upbringing to shore up her self-esteem. I wanted to know how Sheila could possibly use religion to justify her condition.

Sheila lived with both her parents. My first interview with her was in the family's living room in front of her mother and father. I did not foresee that this situation would lead to a confrontation between mother and daughter. Sheila's mother cut right through her daughter's religious rationalizations and told me that Sheila had *wanted* to get pregnant.

Sheila said that was not true.

Her mother cut in and said in a loud, angry voice, "Then why did you swear that you were not intimately involved?"

Sheila, equally angry and rising from her chair, countered, "Well, why am I going to tell you that I was involved!"

Jumping up from the couch to stand between them, I exclaimed, "Wait a minute! I don't want to be in the middle of a mother-daughter fight!"

Sheila's father reared back in his rocking chair laughing at my discomfiture.

Sheila's mother said to me, "She has two girl friends who have babies. Sheila wanted to get pregnant. She wanted a baby of her own, like her girl friends."

Sheila responded, "That's how you feel!"

Sheila's mother said, "Yes, and it's true!"

Otis Mario Jones, known as Mario, remembered how the conversation began: He was standing next to Sheila in her parents' apartment in Southeast Washington in February 1984. She was washing the dinner dishes when she suddenly whispered to him in a voice that only he could hear, "Mario, I want a baby."

The startled Mario did not trust what he thought he had heard. "What?" he asked.

"I want a baby," Sheila whispered a second time.

Mario said he looked at her, trying to decide whether she was serious. At first, "I just laughed" at the absurdity of what she was proposing. He was eighteen, a high school graduate working for four dollars an hour as a security guard at the Iverson Mall in suburban Maryland and dreaming of running his own business some day. His girl friend, Sheila Matthews, had just turned fifteen and was in the ninth grade, an above-average student with ambitions of becoming a pediatrician. As far as Mario was concerned, this was no time to talk about having a baby.

Besides, Sheila's statement flew in the face of plans they had already made. First, they had agreed to wait until Sheila graduated from high school, which was more than three years off. Then they would live together for a year before getting married. Once they were married and settled, they would attempt to have children.

But when it came to sex, they acted as if they had no plans. Birth control was a sporadic practice: Sometimes, Mario said, he used a condom. Sometimes Sheila kept track of her menstrual cycle so they could avoid having intercourse when she was ovulating. Sometimes they used no birth control at all. In the heat of the moment, Mario said, "Sometimes you just want to take that dangerous chance."

Sheila raised the subject twice again in the following days. Each time, Mario's response was the same. "I'd still put her down every time."

None of that mattered to Sheila, according to Mario. A few weeks later, she told him: "Well, I'ma have me a baby. . . . You're gonna give me my baby." Mario laughed at her. "Yeah. Right. That's what you think."

The conversations did not change the couple's sexual habits. They still had sex frequently, sometimes at a local motel, and they still used birth control haphazardly. One day in early June 1984, Sheila told Mario that she was pregnant, that she had conceived sometime in late April. She was scared and confused. Mario knew what he wanted; it was still early enough so he insisted on an immediate abortion. He would pay for it. Sheila, a practicing Baptist, said she couldn't go through with one, that she didn't have the right to "take away" the unborn baby's life.

The couple's relationship began to unravel, slowly in the beginning, in the almost predictable pattern that has destroyed other father-mother bonds.

Sheila was content with her pregnancy: Mario was furious. He threatened to end their relationship if she did not get an abortion. Sheila responded that their relationship would have to come to an end if that was the way he felt. Mario's anger deepened. "To me, it was underhanded. It's better to have a baby when you've both planned it. That way, you can give the baby all your love. When you plan it, it seems like things work out for the better. But when one person tries to do something underhanded—at least you feel that she did—it kinda makes you hold back a little bit. Even if you try to show as much love as you can, inside there's a little bit held back."

Mario finally agreed to deal with his new role as best he could, but a smoldering resentment remained. From June until their child was born in January and for months thereafter, Mario and Sheila went through periods dominated with a fury of one for the other or of rarely seeing each other at all.

On January 14, 1985, Mario Pierre "Petey" Matthews was born. If his birth had not been planned, that no longer mattered. Perhaps in the end all their plans—Sheila's graduation and hopes of becoming a pediatrician, Mario's desire to own his own business—amounted to nothing more than a kind of teenage fantasy, easy to believe in but hard to achieve.

Now the questions were: How would they take care of their newborn baby? And would they do it together?

SHEILA: GROWING UP

Sheila always was in advanced, "enriched" classes from the day she was tested for the first grade. She was reading on the seventh-grade level in her fourth year of elementary school. Her teachers favored, pampered, and spoiled her, pointing to her and praying that she would be one of their charges who made it out of this dismal corner of Washington. Sheila, they said, would not be one of their school dropouts. Sheila, they said, would not be one of their teenage mothers.

By the fifth grade, Sheila announced that she would like to be a pediatrician. Her teachers approved. They were beside themselves with joy. Sheila, they knew, had the ability to be anything her education could make possible; nothing could be denied her. She also was encouraged at school to use her beautiful voice.

She was the solo lead of the choir of her Atlantic Street Baptist Church. Her mother said Sheila had been singing in church since she was three and a half years old, when she sang "The Lord Is Blessing Me" at the Good News Baptist Church.

But Sheila's accomplishments in school and church did not provide her with the status she felt she needed among her friends, most of whom were school dropouts, or close to it, and had passed out of adolescence into adulthood by having children.

Sheila began trying to outdo her friends at eleven, when she found that her best friend, also eleven, was drawing the attention of the boys. "I saw that she was more developed than I. She had very large breasts, and I had none. Boys would drool over her," Sheila recalled. Sheila was envious and upset, so much so that her mother bought her a padded bra and bikini underwear. "I felt good about that," Sheila said.

Sheila and her best friend competed in nearly everything, and most of the time the other girl led the way—by getting a boyfriend first, by menstruating first, becoming sexually active first, and getting birth-control pills first.

When she reached fourteen, Sheila decided it was time for her to become sexually active as well, but with whom? "I figured all the guys around [Washington Highlands] were jerks," school dropouts who used or sold drugs and eventually ended up in prison. She had dated two neighborhood "jerks" for brief periods.

Sheila was only twelve when she dated a seventeen-year-old community bully, "a knucklehead" jobless school dropout. Sheila "went with him" for two months only to defy her oldest brother's demand that she not go out with the boy at all. The bully liked to grab her, pin her arms to her sides, and suck on her neck until she had a purple passion mark. She would bite his arm in return. "I liked passion marks, but I just didn't want one from him. [Passion marks] show ownership. Possession. That's one sign to show another guy that you're taken. You're not going to have a passion mark from just anybody."

One day her mother noticed the passion mark and angrily accused Sheila of letting the boy touch her. Sheila denied that that had happened, angrily thinking to herself, "Let her think what she wants." The bully lost interest after Sheila's mother let him know she was only twelve. Sheila had told him she was fourteen.

Soon after, she became the girl friend of "a slow" sixteen-year-old boy from Hart Junior High School. "I was in junior high school, and when you're in junior high school you get a junior high school boyfriend." The brown-skinned Sheila did not like him when they first met at a party. "He wasn't my type. He was dark-skinned. He was just too dark." Her best girl friend had a boyfriend who worked in a shoe store and had money to take her out and buy her nice things. Sheila felt she needed someone to do the same for her, so she agreed to be the boy's girl friend.

They often argued. Sheila wanted him to take her out and to buy her things. He told her he did not have any money. "Then in August [1981], I demanded that he take me over to the carnival in the Eastover [Maryland] Shopping Center." He said he did not have any money. Sheila countered that he had money enough to buy marijuana and beer to get high on. Angered, he told her that he was tired of her demands that he spend money on her and she told him to "get lost!" He did.

She wanted a boyfriend from the nearby Maryland suburbs, someone who had more money to spend on her, someone who had graduated from high school, someone who could take her out of Washington Highlands. The boys from Maryland "had class." They came from families who were better off than the families of Washington Highlands: families that had cars and homes and strove toward such mainstream American goals as college. They were middle-class and, therefore, "had a better attitude towards girls because boys [in Washington Highlands] like beating girls to show their manship. Guys over in Maryland believe in treating a lady like a lady."

The next boyfriend, however, was a youth from Franklin, Virginia, who was enrolled in a bricklaying course at a Job Corps center near Washington Highlands. He was sixteen. "I liked him because he took me out. He bought me potato chips and pop. He recognized my birthday [with a gift] and Valentine's Day [with card and gift]. He gave me a silver [plated] cigarette lighter because I was trying out smoking." For her fourteenth birthday in February 1983, he gave her thirty dollars. Sheila and two of her girl friends "got messing drunk" on beer she bought with the money.

The boyfriend found them drunk; he threatened to beat Sheila. "That was the first and last time he ever thought about hitting me." She told him, "Look, I'm fourteen years old. I'm *grown* and you don't tell me what to do."

It was during that summer that Sheila's best girl friend became sexually active and was given birth-control pills by her mother. Sheila was right behind her. She twice tried to have sexual intercourse, the first time on the Fourth of July, with the boyfriend from Franklin, but he was unable to penetrate. He used a condom on both attempts without her urging.

Sheila began having a recurring dream that summer. She said in her dream appeared a tall silhouette, a man who made love to her and treated her "like a lady." She said to herself, "This man loves me, whoever he is." The dreams continued even after she and her boyfriend broke up at the end of July and he moved back to Franklin.

She told her mother about the dreams. Her mother said, "It is telling you something. Anytime you dream a dream more than once, it's telling you something."

After she met Otis Mario Jones on September 22, 1983, she came to believe that he was the silhouette in her dreams. Mario was tall and lanky, with a dark brown complexion and dark eyes, closely cropped hair, and at times, a thin wisp of a moustache and goatee. He spoke bluntly about himself and others. I met him after Sheila had delivered their child, a time when he alternated between being furious with Sheila and being deeply in love with her.

In Sheila's social circle—both at school and in the area around

Washington's Barnaby Road SE where she lived—Mario represented something else: Mario gave Sheila prestige.

He was, she said, "one of those guys from Maryland," someone who grew up outside of the poor Washington Highlands community where Sheila lived. He was older and a graduate of Oxon Hill High School. At the time she met him through a friend, he was a student in business at Prince George's Community College. He had a car, a 1971 Plymouth Fury, and a job—and, Sheila told her girl friends, he treated her with respect.

That was enough to impress her girl friends, but she really drew their envy when Mario took her out for dinner by candlelight at a Tysons Corner suburban Virginia restaurant: None of their boyfriends could afford such an expensive meal.

A month before she met Mario, Sheila had decided she was going to get birth-control pills.

She said she went to a local doctor, who agreed to write the prescription needed to obtain the pills. She put the prescription in her bureau drawer, but before she filled it, her mother found it. As Sheila protested, her mother tore the prescription into small strips. Angry, Sheila told her mother that she wanted to take the pills because her best friend was taking them. "Monkey see, monkey do," her mother said as she threw the strips into the kitchen trash can.

After she met Mario, Sheila said, she tried again. One day in October 1983, the couple got into Mario's car and drove to the Union Medical Center in Northwest Washington, where Sheila's family was eligible for free medical care because her father belonged to the construction laborers' union. She saw a doctor, who called her mother—without telling Sheila, as was the doctor's prerogative in dealing with a minor—and found out that her mother objected. The doctor then refused to prescribe the pills.

Sheila said she tried to get the pills secretly because she knew her mother would disapprove. She said her mother also once told her, "If you get pregnant, you better not come home."

For one thing, her mother knew the family could not afford to care for another child. The family's only income came from Sheila's father's job as a laborer, and that money had to cover the cost of feeding and housing Sheila, her two older brothers, and her younger sister. The six of them lived in a small, two-bedroom apartment in privately owned Jeffrey Gardens, a run-down, partly boarded-up complex just inside the city's border with Maryland.

Sheila's mother had lived on the edge of poverty for most of her life. She grew up in the tobacco country of North Carolina, the youngest of thirteen girls and one boy in a sharecropping family. There was a lot of distrust and violence within her family. Her mother and father fought a lot, and all members of the family drank prodigious amounts of homemade corn whiskey. Her father had not liked his only son. Sheila's mother met her husband in 1960, and they had lived together most of that time. She wanted a better life for her two sons and two daughters.

Sheila's father did not want to be interviewed. Her mother talked freely about the trials of the family's daily life—how financial problems led her to take a part-time job as a domestic worker, how they worried about paying the rent each month—but declined to discuss her past in detail.

Sheila said she decided at an early age that she did not want to live the way her parents had. She said she still felt that way when she met Mario Jones.

MARIO: GROWING UP

Mario Jones said he never expected to fall in love with Sheila Matthews.

It started out as a lark, a foray into the Washington Highlands neighborhood, where girls had the reputation for being "fast," someone a boy could have sex without the ties of a relationship. One night in September 1983, one of Mario's friends wanted to see his girl friend in Washington Highlands, and he asked Mario to drive him there. He told Mario he would introduce him to a girl named Sheila.

"At first," Mario said, "I wasn't looking for a relationship. I was mainly looking for something fast. But Sheila seemed like a whole different person from what I was expecting."

She was anything but fast. They did not kiss for weeks, he said, and she was clearly inexperienced when it came to sex—far less experienced than Mario. Still, he said, he was strongly attracted to her. Although she was just fourteen, she had a quality that set her apart from his other girl friends.

Sheila is diminutive, barely five feet tall, with a broad, expressive face and round cheeks. She appears shy at first, but that shyness gives way to a kind of combativeness, especially in her relationships with her mother and Mario. She is religious and regularly attended services at the Atlantic Street Baptist Church near her home.

Mario had been involved with other girls before meeting Sheila, and he had an active sex life. Some girls insisted he use a condom, while others did not seem to care; Mario said he rarely brought up the issue himself. Some girls insisted that their lovemaking only go so far; despite those good intentions, Mario was not always careful.

Mario was born in Southeast Washington and moved with his family to Oxon Hill, Maryland, when he was ten; his informal sex education began with that event. Mario and his older brother found a "big stack of dirty magazines" left by the previous owner in the garage of the new home. The boys hid the magazines and, periodically for the next two years, they would pull them out for secret perusal in the garage with their neighborhood friends. "Those were the first pictures I saw that clearly showed sexual intercourse." They eventually grew bored with the magazines and threw them away.

Four years later, Mario and a friend were sexually initiated in that same garage. It was a spontaneous occurrence, something neither he nor the others who participated had planned. Mario and a seventeen-year-old male friend were visiting the older youth's girl friend, who also was seventeen. Besides Mario and his friend, just the girl and her fifteen-year-old brother were home. All four youths drank whiskey that day, more out of idle curiosity than from habit.

The older youth and his girl friend teased Mario and her brother because they were "virgins." Suddenly, the girl's boyfriend suggested that she give the two younger boys their first sexual experience. She agreed. The four trooped over to Mario's garage. "She was a little tipsy, but she wasn't that much. She jumped up on the car and then told us just what to do and how to do it." Her brother went first and Mario followed. Whenever she gave either of the two boys instructions, the two standing on the side watching, including her boyfriend, would laugh. "She was on the Pill." The incestuous part of that ritual was never discussed among the four of them. "After that, we just let it go."

Shortly afterward, Mario began a sexual relationship with the thirteen-year-old younger sister of another male friend. They planned the day they became sexually active: They "hooked school" together and spent the day at the girl's home after her parents had left for work. Although it was her first time, before they began the girl made Mario promise that he would withdraw before he climaxed. He did withdraw that first time. They engaged in sexual intercourse regularly, pretending to her brother and her parents that there was nothing special between them.

The girl often worried about Mario: He did not withdraw every time. Mario was not frightened by the possibility of pregnancy. "I knew that she could get pregnant, but I had that type of feeling like it wasn't gonna happen." He also felt that he was ahead of himself. "I felt I shouldn't be doing this till later on, till I was older, but I was doing it early. I was feeling that maybe I couldn't really produce a child. I knew I could!"

The first time he failed to withdraw "she didn't like it," Mario remembered. "She got into a depressed mood because it was going through her head like what would she do if she had got pregnant. How could she face her mother, her father. Fun is fun, but when you come down to reality, you know, that's when you start facing the facts of what could really happen." After Mario failed to withdraw several additional times, "that's when she first wanted me to start using condoms." So he did.

The pair did not think of themselves as a couple, just as friends and suburban Maryland neighbors who had a special sexual relationship. The yearlong sexual intimacy ended when Mario met and became infatuated with a thirteen-year-old pregnant girl from Washington in the summer of 1980. "She was pregnant when I first noticed her," just weeks short of delivery, at an Alexandria, Virginia, roller-skating rink. The girl also had noticed Mario.

A short time after she had her baby, the girl sent a boy over to Mario at the same rink one Saturday in the fall of 1980 "to check out if I would put her down because she had had a child. Her friend said she was interested in me, but did not want to be put down. I told him I wouldn't." The boy introduced the two of them.

The young mother told Mario she lived on T Street SE two blocks down from Good Hope Road in Washington's Anacostia community. Anacostia is near Washington Highlands. Both areas of the city were considered by Mario and his Oxon Hill peers to be neighborhoods where they could find "fast" girls. Mario already felt this girl was fast. She was thirteen, already had a child, and had been the one to approach him. He had concluded that sex would be a part of their relationship. She was bold, direct, and aggressive. Mario was intrigued.

Sexual relations between the pair started the first time they were alone, but for the first time, Mario did not feel entirely good about what they had to do to see one another. "My sexual relationship with [her] felt sneaky" because they had to cut classes at school and meet at her house. That first time they had sex, he used a condom. She agreed thereafter that he did not have to use one if he promised to withdraw. "But sometimes you just want to take that dangerous chance. Sometimes you just feel so good you don't want" to withdraw. When he did not, as happened occasionally, the girl "would cuss me out. It wasn't no bad cussin' out. She'd call me a name. Get on me a little bit." It happened more than once, but they felt they "were in love with one another. We really loved each other." Their feelings for one another lasted until the following spring when they gradually drifted apart. They remained friends.

Through his junior and senior high school years, Mario did not date anyone special. He had a number of sexual liaisons with a number of girls. Sometimes he would use a condom. When he did not, the girls he was seeing did not seem to be worried and did not raise the subject of contraception. After graduating from Oxon Hill High School, he entered Prince George's Community College in August. The next month he met Sheila.

Minutes into that first meeting on September 22, 1983, Mario asked Sheila whether she was a virgin. He did not consider his question to be too bold. "No. Not for me! It's something that's not personal. It's just another question out of conversation." Sheila was not insulted or put off by the question, he said. "She said that she was" a virgin. "She didn't want to tell me, though. I saw it in her face. If she tells me, maybe I'll lose interest in her or something. It was something that she ain't want to let nobody know. It seemed like something that she should be able to say that she's not. She didn't want to lie, and she didn't want to tell me. She was looking for an experience, but she was still scared."

Sheila also remembered the day a girl friend introduced her to Mario. "He had the funniest approach. I wanted to curse him out." Ten minutes after they met, Mario asked her, "Can I hold you?" Sheila told him no, "You don't even know me! How could you possibly want to hold me?" He explained that was his approach with women. "Try again!" Sheila told him. They continued to talk. Something he said really interested her. "I found out that for once I was talking to someone who was in school." He also was working part-time at a department store and "had money to take me out sometime."

Sheila told her mother that Mario was sixteen. Her mother asked

Mario if she could see his driver's license. Mario's birth date indicated that he was eighteen. Her mother said nothing at the time, but when Mario called the next day, she told him he could not see Sheila anymore. "She thought he was too old for me," said Sheila. "She was looking at his car, that he was working and was in college. He appeared to be too much of an adult."

Mario remembered the conversation with Sheila's mother. "We don't want you calling here no more," he said she told him. Then the mother put Sheila's father on the telephone, and he gave Mario the same message. Sheila called him at home the same night, and Mario told her what her parents had said to him.

"I told him to ignore what my parents had said," said Sheila. They arranged to see each other secretly. The girl friend who introduced them would call on Sheila so she could get out of the house. Sheila was growing anxious. She knew her girl friend was interested in Mario. The girl friend's boyfriend had a job, but he did not have a car. Sheila was relieved when Mario continued to focus all his attention on her. He took her to the movies, a roller-skating rink, and, very importantly, out to dinner.

But Sheila's mother knew her daughter and was not fooled. In late October, Mario's male friend came to the apartment and asked Sheila if she could step outside for a moment to talk. Sheila's mother had had enough. "Tell Mario to come inside and stop playing me stupid," Sheila said her mother told the friend. "Then Mario began bringing things to the house. He brought me candy. He brought my mother candy. After that, it was no problem" for the pair openly to date.

After the first time they made love Sheila was convinced that Mario had been the silhouette in her dream. It was late November, near to the Thanksgiving holiday. They went to his parents Oxon Hill home with the intention of making love. "Mario told me not to be scared." Sheila responded, "Me? Scared? If anything, you should be scared," she added.

"She was scared," Mario said. "I told her I would be as gentle as I possibly could."

Mario remembers that he withdrew that first time. "I didn't want to get her pregnant." Sheila thinks he used a condom. They do agree that they felt they were in love. Mario was eighteen; Sheila was fourteen.

Sheila felt very different from how she had during the unpleasant experience with the boy from Franklin. "The first time he made love to me, he did everything to me that I fantasized in the dream. He was the silhouette. No doubt about it. I liked it. I didn't feel dirty and low. I felt more like a *woman,* you know, like I'm not a little girl anymore."

Sexual intercourse with a condom became a regular part of their relationship. "One night, we decided not to try the condom because I wanted to see what it felt like without the condom. Curiosity. We followed this thing called the rhythm cycle."

Sheila felt that she determined when they would have sex. She would signal her willingness to him. "I'd blow in his ear." In February 1984, Mario turned nineteen and Sheila turned fifteen. Sheila told Mario she wanted a baby. Mario said not at this time.

In late April, Mario and Sheila made love twice at a nearby motel without any reference to the rhythm method, without the use of any contraception or contraceptive method. Sheila's mother realized her daughter was pregnant in early June "because she noticed I wasn't going through the box of Tampax. I was going to the box, but I wasn't using them. I was hiding them in the bathroom. After she went to bed, I'd take the same one and put it back in the box. The next day, I'd go and hide the same one. My mother also started to see that my nose was spreading and I was feeling sick in the morning."

Sheila and her mother were lying on beds opposite one another one afternoon. "You're pregnant," her mother suddenly said to Sheila. "Are you kidding?" Sheila tried to bluff. "I knew that I was." If her mother was hurt, "she hid it remarkably. See, I expected her to cry. Maybe hit me. Or not say anything to me at all. She told me she was against abortion. She said because if you can't make a life, why take one?"

It was a sentence she had heard from her mother's mouth several times before—before she became sexually active, before she told Mario she wanted a baby. Sheila repeated her mother's antiabortion position almost word for word when Mario demanded that she have an abortion.

Sheila cried and cried throughout that summer. She asked herself, Will Mario still love me when I get fat? Then she noticed that he was gradually changing. "He didn't want me to sit next to him. He told me he couldn't drive like that. I'd been doing it for eleven months, and all of a sudden he couldn't drive like that. Our relationship got on the rocks."

In Mario's middle-class circle of friends, fatherhood meant responsibility. Even before their son was born, Mario said he felt pressure—from himself and from Sheila—to help care for Sheila and his child, mostly by providing money. During the pregnancy, the pressure became so intense that he tried to pull away from Sheila, he said.

"I really tried to block her out," he said. "I tried to block her out completely out of my mind. She wasn't listening to what I had to say and was thinking that everything was going to be cotton candy. I told her, 'There's gonna be financial problems. It's gonna restrict you from what you want to do.' She just looked at the whole thing like it wasn't gonna be a problem. . . . All she was thinking about was just"—and his voice got louder—*"having the baby!"*

UNDER PRESSURE

On the night of October 30, 1984, Veda Usilton was at home watching the television news when something caught her eye. The news story concerned a hearing on teenage pregnancy held that day at Ballou High School—an issue of some concern to Usilton, who counseled junior high school students at Friendship Educational Center in Washington Highlands. But it was not the subject that drew her attention. It was the appearance on the screen of fifteen-year-old Sheila Matthews, testifying about how she got pregnant six months earlier.

Usilton, who is not easily surprised after years of counseling teenage girls, was shocked. She had known Sheila for several years and had been her counselor in seventh and ninth grades at Friendship, a city elementary-junior high school. She thought of Sheila as a cut above most students—bright, alert, able to hold her own. Many of her students have come to her with questions about sex, but Sheila never did, she said.

Usilton had given up trying to stop ninth-grade girls from becoming sexually active. Young girls in Washington Highlands saw sex as a natural part of their lives, she said. "It's stupid to teach abstinence, so I preach birth control," Usilton said. But many girls pretended to themselves that they couldn't get pregnant and that birth control was unnecessary because they were "not doing that much," she said.

To make her students confront reality, Usilton would occasionally hold "rap sessions," which have shown her that students feel tremendous peer pressure to have sex. She summed up their feelings this way: "It's not cool to be an A student. It's not cool to be a virgin. It's not cool to say you're a virgin. You shouldn't be on birth control."

A week after Sheila's testimony at Ballou, I visited the pregnant girl for the first time at her family's apartment. Sheila's mother and father sat in on my first interview with her. Her mother warned me not to let Sheila mislead me that her pregnancy was an accident. "She wanted to get pregnant," her mother said.

"The reason I said I believe she wanted to be pregnant," added Sheila's mother, "is she has two [eighteen-year-old] friends. They're pregnant. Sheila's fond of babies, and she wanted to be pregnant."

"I don't blame myself nor [Mario], but I couldn't have an abortion," said Sheila.

Sheila felt the peer pressure that school counselor Usilton described, according to her mother and Mario. "She noticed that all her friends were getting pregnant," Mario said.

Shortly after Petey was born, Sheila began teasing Mario, in front of her mother, about her desire to have a second child, according to Mario. He was taken aback. He remembered the conversation this way:

"Not by *me* you won't," he said.

"Yes I will, too," Sheila said.

"You only wanted this one because all your friends had one," Mario said.

"I *did* not," Sheila shot back.

Suddenly, her mother interrupted, looking directly at Sheila.

"He's telling the truth," her mother said.

MAKING NEW PLANS

On a cold, sunny Sunday in February 1985, about a month after Petey was born, Sheila bundled the baby to protect him from the thirty-eight-degree temperature and went to sing in the choir at the Atlantic Street Baptist Church as she had done so many Sundays before he was born.

She donned the green-and-beige robe, cradled Petey in her arms, and took her place before the congregation. She felt secure in the church—the pastor, the Reverend Milton Wilcher, had told her after she got pregnant that she was still welcome—but the rest of her life was in turmoil.

Her mother made clear that Sheila's father's earnings as a laborer were not enough to feed the family and Petey, too. Sheila was missing classes at Ballou High School, where she was in the tenth grade, because she did not have money for a baby-sitter and her mother had refused to take care of Petey every day. In April, she dropped out of school.

Mario's life, too, was in turmoil. He was fired from his $150-a-week job as a warehouse clerk three days after Petey was born and had no money to pay for Petey's disposable diapers and milk. He was living with his grandparents after a bad fight with his stepfather. He was arguing with Sheila constantly about money for Petey and seeing her sporadically because he was dating another girl.

He finally broke up with that girl in April 1985, the same month he and Sheila scuffled and, finally, reconciled.

Mario was broke, and "Sheila was playing head games," he said. Their son was ill and needed a prescription filled, the slip for which Sheila had put in his car's ashtray without telling him, Mario said, on their way home from a medical examination by Petey's pediatrician. On the telephone the next day, Sheila told Mario where the prescription was and asked him to have it filled and bring the medicine to her house. Mario showed up a short time later with the unfilled prescription.

Mario came into Sheila's apartment, handed her the prescription slip, and walked back out. She slammed the door behind him. "I just kept going."

Sheila came running out of the building behind him. "I hope you got a good look at Petey!"

"What's that suppose to mean?" Mario asked.

"From now on you gonna need visiting rights," she added.

"If you feel that way, I will no longer be sending milk and [diaper] money over here for him. Evidently, you can take care of him by yourself," he said.

What followed was an ugly outpouring of anger from both of them in front of the neighbors of Sheila's three-story apartment building. "She called me a whole lot of dirty names. She said that she was tired of her feelings being fucked over. It got so bad we were both out there hollering at the tops of our lungs. Calling each other every kind of name. We ain't mean all that but it's just the way it got."

Their screaming degenerated into a hurtful description of their private sexual practices and preferences. I visited the home the day after the argument. Sheila's mother was deeply embarrassed by what had been said and told me all that had occurred and all that had been shouted.

At the conclusion of the shouting, Mario stormed back into the apartment to take back Petey's car seat and swing that he had borrowed from a relative. "I went to get his car seat, and Sheila picks it up and throws it at me. So, I pushed her and her mother grabbed Sheila."

Sheila's mother held on to her struggling daughter and yelled at Mario, "Just get out!"

Two weeks passed. Mario called Sheila. They agreed to meet on a street away from her house. Her two brothers and her father would pounce on him if he came to the house, she explained. They met. Sheila brought Petey. Their son giggled and drooled. They laughed. Sheila apologized. Mario apologized. Soon, Mario was able to visit at the Matthews home again.

Mario and Sheila said she was unhappy in her home, living in her parents' crowded two-bedroom apartment. "Sheila doesn't like living there," said Mario shortly after their reconciliation. "She wants to get out, and she wants to get out with me. She wants to be with me. That's what she's been looking for, her way out!"

Their relationship grew closer, but they still had many rocky moments.

A month after their fight, Mario got a job at a messenger-service firm and then a job as a security guard at a suburban Virginia Crystal City office building, making $130 a week after taxes. By January 1986, he earned enough to give Sheila a little money for one-year-old Petey, but he needed $197 for his monthly car payment and $100 a month for rent at his grandparents' home.

After months of just trying to cope, he and Sheila were making plans again. They were talking about getting their own apartment and living together for a while before deciding about marriage. Meanwhile, Sheila had enrolled in night school. She turned seventeen on February 16, 1986, and Mario turned twenty-one on February 17.

At the time, they had put off any long-term plans. Mario said he still wanted to run his own business and to earn enough money to be financially independent, but he hadn't decided what kind of business or how he would find seed money to get started. "See, I don't really care what the business is. I just want my own business because that's how I know I'm going to make it," he said.

He said he wanted Sheila to finish school and get some sort of vocational training, "just in case she has to get a job." But Sheila said that if Mario's dreams came true, if he made it as a businessman, she wanted to stay at home and run the household.

Sheila knew one thing for certain: She wanted to move out of Washington Highlands. The neighborhood, she felt, was treacherous.

"You have to look both ways" when leaving her apartment building, she said. "I'm looking for drug addicts. I'm looking for the police. I'm looking for gunshots. I'm looking for people stampeding over my baby."

If things were to go their way, Mario said, they could predict a "good life" for Petey. "What I don't want," Sheila said, "is to be living from paycheck to paycheck."

Sheila graduated from high school near the top of her class in May 1987. Her relationship with Mario fell apart before then, although Mario continued his financial support and his relationship with their son, Petey.

A friend of Sheila's mother's called me at *The Post* in October. The friend told me Sheila's mother was very upset because Sheila had won a scholarship to a vocational training school but refused to go. Instead, Sheila was working as a cashier at a drugstore.

I called Sheila's mother, and she confirmed her friend's story. Then I asked her to put Sheila on the telephone. Sheila said she did not want to speak about her decision while members of her family were in the apartment with her. We made a date to go out to dinner to a seafood restaurant, one of Sheila's favorite places to eat during the project. Sheila made one stipulation regarding the dinner conversation. "No lectures from you!" I agreed.

We took Petey, then two years and nine months old, with us to dinner. I listened to Sheila's rationalizations about not taking the ten-month medical-assistant course. She was tired of school (this from an eighteen-year-old girl?). She needed time to rest. The cashier job was not so bad. And on and on, in that vein.

I spoke in my softest voice (trying to sound like I was not giving the lecture I was about to give). I talked about her dreams, the things I knew she wanted for herself and Petey in the future. I talked for an hour.

I said her relationship with Mario was dead. She had a new boyfriend, but God only knew where that would end up. I told her she would earn twice as much immediately at the end of the medical assistant's training as she was making as a drugstore cashier and that she had to begin to think of providing for herself and Petey. She was not going to do that on a drugstore cashier's salary. Ever! I went back to her dreams. She could forget all of her dreams—the suburban house, white picket fence, prestige car, and a good school for Petey. A drugstore cashier's salary would not even bring her close to realizing them. Forget them!

We were both exhausted when we left the restaurant that night. Only Petey was full of energy. Sheila told me she would think about what I had told her. I held my breath. She called me at work about a week later. She had decided to go to the school. She had made a November 2 interview appointment with an official at the school. Would I take her to the appointment and sit through it with her? I did.

Sheila started school the week after the appointment and soon after rose to the top of the class!

CHAPTER EIGHT

THERE WAS LITTLE EXTRAVAGANCE in Charmaine Ford's life when we met in 1984. The twenty-nine-year-old woman wore little or no makeup. Her clothes were simple and inexpensive, mostly jeans and blouses. Her three-bedroom basement apartment was small and spare, and she shared it with her mother and her three sons. Charles was twelve. Lawrence and Lionel were eight-year-old twins who were the result of a planned pregnancy in a relationship that broke apart a month before they were born. Within a year of our meeting, her grandmother and a nephew also moved in with Charmaine.

There also was little extravagance in Charmaine's demeanor. She had a beautiful smile—a wide, exuberant smile—but rarely showed it. She tried to hide her anxieties, but her stomach gave her away: Whenever she got upset, her ulcer would become irritated, and she would soothe it by drinking directly from a bottle of liquid antacid.

Charmaine and her family lived in a fourteen-unit apartment building on Condon Terrace SE, one of two notorious drug-traffic streets in Washington Highlands. Tauscha Vaughn lived in the same building and introduced me to Charmaine. Charmaine was like an older sister to the sixteen-year-old Tauscha. Charmaine often set her own life in front of Tauscha as a forewarning to the young girl not to have a child as an adolescent.

Charmaine's life had taught her to be guarded in her relationships, especially those with men. After many months and hours of interviews, she still made a point of insisting that all our conversations take place in her home or in public places such as restaurants.

"Oh, I trust you, Leon," she told me. "But after all, you *are* a man."

There were several relationships in the years after her first son was born, but she had never been in love, although she believed that she could find the right man some day. She said she felt there was "something missing in my life. I can't place it, but it just feel like something is missing. It could be because I have never been married. I don't know."

There are eight rooms above the nightclub on the edge of Prince Georges County, Maryland, just a few blocks away from the border with Washington, and they rent for twenty-one dollars a night. On Friday and Saturday nights, when the club gets crowded and the drinks begin to flow, there's a lot of traffic between the dance floor and the rooms upstairs.

Charmaine Ford had not been to the nightclub for a long time, but for several months in 1971 she went there often to escape her mother's tight control over her social life. She was sixteen, living in the poor Southwest Washington community known as Buzzard Point, an isolated neighborhood between Washington's Southwest Freeway and the South Capitol Street Bridge. She was eager to grow up and angry at her mother for restricting her activities. "I wasn't allowed to go to parties. I wasn't allowed to have a boyfriend. If I went out on a date, I had to have a chaperone," she said.

Mother and daughter fought bitterly until, finally, Charmaine became defiant and refused to obey her mother's orders. "Me and my mother fought like cats and dogs. One time she said, 'You can't go out!' I said, 'I'm going anyway.' She hit me and I hit her back. Slapped her across her face. She started crying. I just walked off and out of the house." Charmaine began going to the nightclub with her twenty-one-year-old boyfriend, where they drank a little and frequently ended up in one of the inn's upstairs rooms. One night in May 1971, Charmaine got pregnant.

Charmaine did not care. She thought that a child might free her, once and for all, from her mother's grip. "I got pregnant out of spite. I told my mother the same thing. I told her that we might not be in the position we're in today if she had let me have some freedom. She had me on a choke chain," she said.

The pregnancy changed her life, but not in the way Charmaine hoped it would. In September 1971, five months pregnant by her boyfriend and clearly showing it, she was turned away from the eleventh grade at Western High School. She was turned away, and not told that the school system had a special school for pregnant students. Charmaine stayed home and earned money by ironing clothes and doing hairdressing for her neighbors. Her boyfriend helped out by giving her seventy-five dollars every two weeks during the pregnancy.

Her boyfriend wanted to get married, but Charmaine said she turned him down because a marriage license meant "a man had papers on you." She felt he might act as if he owned her by beating her or ordering her around. She also thought the father of her child already ran around with other women. "I could picture him as my boyfriend, even as the father of my child, but not as a husband," she said.

The night after their son was born in February 1972—Charmaine named the baby Charles, for his father—she went to a night club with her boyfriend's sisters and was stunned to see him walk in with two women, one on each arm.

(The boyfriend, who stopped seeing Charmaine years before I met her, did not respond to several telephone messages and a letter asking him for an interview. He did contact Charmaine's mother, Rosalee, and said he had received the letter.)

Charmaine's account of what happened next is this:

Her boyfriend saw her on the dance floor, she said, and demanded to know why she wasn't home with their newborn son; Charmaine told him it wasn't his concern. The confrontation ended there, but later in the parking lot, she discovered him in his car, kissing one of the two women. When he saw Charmaine, he climbed out of the car and began cursing at her. Charmaine turned to leave, but he kicked her buttocks. She cursed at him, and he grabbed her, spun her around, and slammed her against the late-model Cadillac's door handle. The knob of the handle hit Charmaine in the small of her back. She was blinded momentarily by the sharp pain. In the seconds it took for Charmaine to recover, she decided that her boyfriend was going to pay dearly for the affront to her dignity and the injury she had just suffered.

Hidden under the right sleeve of Charmaine's blouse was a straight razor. She said she had carried the weapon on and off for four years because several sexual assaults had occurred in her neighborhood. As her boyfriend moved toward her again, she slipped the razor out into her right hand. "I ought to smack the shit outta you," he said as he raised a hand to slap her. Charmaine opened the straight razor in one motion and cut him across the throat.

"I let him have it. Right across the throat," she said. "I started from one side and worked my way right on around." He began yelling that he could die. "I looked him dead in the face and said, 'At this point, I do not care!' "

The incident was never reported to police. The man lived, although he needed stitches to close the wound.

After she cut his throat Charmaine went back home to Buzzard Point. Her white blouse and blue skirt were soaked in her boyfriend's blood. Her mother was up when Charmaine came in. "Girl, what happened to you? Where did all that blood come from?" Rosalee asked. "Charles," Charmaine answered and walked back to her room. Rosalee followed her. "He pushed me to the limit, Ma!" Charmaine said. "He pushed me to the limit!"

Rosalee took the straight razor away from her. After all, this was still her house, where she made the rules, and freedom was something to be negotiated. "My mother would say, 'You living in my house. You eating my food. You go by my rules. When it get to the point you don't want to listen to what I say, get out! Get your own place!' "

Charmaine saw her former boyfriend only occasionally when I met her in 1984, and he rarely provided any child support for their son. About two months after Charles was born, he came to see the baby for the first time. The incompletely healed razor wound was visible as a red line across his neck. The infant started crying at one point, and the man yelled at him, "Shut up! Shut up!" Charmaine told him, "You just trying to get back at me. Don't be hollering at my child. You holler at me. I'm the one who cut you."

"I let you get away with cutting my throat," the man told her "I won't let you do it again."

"I see you starting up with a whole lot of mess," Charmaine answered. "I'm telling you right now, *get out of my house!*"

"I ain't going nowhere," he continued.

"You getting out of here," she insisted.

"No I ain't, and you can't make me."

Charmaine had anticipated this meeting with her former boyfriend and knew him well enough to know that his wounded pride would cause him to provoke another confrontation. She had recently spent $250 on a .38-caliber revolver, purchased from one of her

Buzzard Point neighbors. She walked away from the father of her son and went to her bedroom to retrieve the handgun. She returned to the living room with the gun hidden behind her back.

"You went in there and got an ole knife," he said. "A knife ain't gonna do you no good 'cause I ain't gonna let you get that close this time. I ought to take it from you and whip your ass."

"What's stopping you?" Charmaine asked.

He moved toward her, and she whipped the gun around with the barrel pointed into his face.

"Now, you open your mouth," she said, her anger rising. "I'll blow your motherfucking head off in here! Back up! I'm tired of you. I'm sick of you and I hate you. Get away from me!"

For the first time in the several years that they had dated, Charmaine began to cry in front of her boyfriend, and when she cried, her hand shook with the gun in it. The father of her son backed up quickly to the door and opened it. "Girl, you are crazy. You ain't right," he said as he closed the door.

Alone now, Charmaine quickly learned that a baby was far more confining than a strict mother. Then, just before Charles's first birthday, she learned the full consequences of her having become a mother.

One morning eleven months after his birth, Charles, who was normally a vigorous, active crawler, stopped moving. Charmaine thought he was sick and went to comfort him. She hugged him, but he just lay there, so quiet, so still that she became terrified and rushed him to Children's Hospital.

There, after a month of tests, the doctors told her that Charles had cerebral palsy, an irreversible condition that results from brain damage and affects the central nervous system. They also told her that he would not develop normally, that he would require special care every day of his life, and that he would probably die before the age of twenty-five. When I met them, Charmaine and Charles slept in the same bedroom, their beds just inches apart.

Doctors were never able to explain exactly what happened to Charles; he appeared healthy at birth, weighing six pounds six and a half ounces, and seemed to grow normally during his first eleven months. But sometime before he was born, or perhaps during his birth, something caused some brain damage that, inexplicably, did not show up until he was eleven months old.

Charles's condition was severe. At age twelve, he had to be fed from a bottle, wore a diaper, and had grown only slightly since that day he stopped crawling. He was between two feet and three feet tall and suffered from an untreatable dislocated hip that periodically caused him severe pain. When he was uncomfortable, he told Charmaine by making guttural sounds that only she, her mother, or his twin brothers understood. He spent much of his day in a baby's car seat, propped up so he could watch television or sit with the family at the dinner table. He seemed mesmerized by what he saw on the TV screen.

After Charles's condition was diagnosed, Charmaine said, social workers "wanted me to talk to some counselors and welfare people about putting him in a home for kids like him, but I told them no. I decided to take care of him at home myself." She had done it, but only with great struggle and the help of her fifty-seven-year-old mother, Rosalee.

Charmaine and Rosalee began to get along well, and their past disagreements faded. Their relationship began to change when Charmaine established her independence at age twenty-five by moving into an apartment she shared with a boyfriend. The new place was just down the street from Rosalee's house in Buzzard Point, and Charmaine depended on Rosalee to care for Charles while she was working. Then, in 1981, Charmaine decided to leave Buzzard Point altogether and move to Condon Terrace. Rosalee asked if she could come with her, and Charmaine agreed.

Together, the two women kept the household functioning. Rosalee even became the manager of the building. The family's income came from four sources: Charmaine's irregular work as a visiting nurse, caring for elderly patients in their own homes; a monthly social security stipend she received for Charles's care; her food-stamp allotment; and Rosalee's medical-disability check. Their monthly income ranged from $600 to $1,150, depending on how much Charmaine was working.

Whenever things seemed bad, Charmaine said, she found that Charles was a major source of comfort. "Matter of fact, practically my whole life is him. It seems like when I'm upset or I have a problem, he cheers me up. When I'm around him, he can sense when something is wrong with me. If I'm sick, he'll just lay there. He'll take my hand and run it over my face. When I'm OK, seems like he's OK. He's happy as long as I'm happy. He is just a wonderful child. He is my heart."

Charles's twin brothers, Lawrence and Lionel, would talk to him.

"They really don't fully understand why he don't answer them back. They'll go to him and say, 'Charles this is a ball. Charles this is a truck.' And he'll smile as if he really understands what they're saying. They'll dance to the music on the radio, and they'll hold his hand and dance with him while he's sitting in his chair. He enjoys that."

The twins know when Charles wants them. "If they're near him, he will touch them with his foot or touch them with his hand. If he's laying in bed, he'll want their company. He'll make a certain sound, and they'll go [into the bedroom] and say, 'What is it, Charles? You want me to lay on the bed with you?' And he'll smile at them, and they'll get up there and lay down with him. He'll be so happy!"

THE FAMILY'S HISTORY

Charmaine was not the first teenage mother in her family, and she was not the first child who was kept on a "choke chain." Her grandmother was just thirteen years old when she gave birth to Charmaine's mother, Rosalee, in 1929. As a result, Rosalee was raised mostly by her grandparents while her mother worked in Washington as an elevator operator. Her grandparents lived in the countryside near the Maryland town of Indian Head. They took extraordinary steps to make sure that Rosalee did not become a teenage mother, too. In effect, Rosalee was kept on a "choke chain."

Rosalee's grandfather worked tarring and repairing the state roads around Indian Head. Her grandmother took in washing and ironing "of the different white peoples around Indian Head," said Rosalee. She attended a segregated school up to the seventh grade, then dropped out to take a job scrubbing floors. The small amount of money Rosalee earned made a big improvement in the way she and her grandparents lived. "We were so poor my grandfather walked around with holes in his shoes," remembered Rosalee.

Growing up in rural Charles County, Rosalee was not allowed to date. If she wanted to see a boy, she had to meet him in public view—a talk over the fence in the front yard was considered proper —or have a chaperone present. "I didn't even know what a boy was when I was eighteen years old," said Rosalee. It was a time when a number of her girl friends already had two children.

A boy named Andrew respectfully approached Rosalee's grandparents one day and asked the couple if he could "keep company" with Rosalee. Her grandfather said no. Even at eighteen, he insisted, "Lee is not ready to date." Rosalee was deeply angered by her grandparents' tight control. Her grandparents did not consider her a grown-up woman because she was still living "under their roof," she said. She gave her grandparents a fictitious story of going to visit some girl friends and "stole out" one night with Andrew. It was the first time she made love. It was also a night, for another reason, she will never forget.

When she returned home about 11:30 P.M., Rosalee was surprised to find her mother, down from Washington, waiting up for her. Her mother was furious and fearful, afraid that Rosalee's actions that night would bring an unwelcome pregnancy. Her mother's fears pushed her into a frenzy. "My mother had been through so much when she had me and did not want me to go through the same thing. She beat me *so* bad. My mother liked to kill me that night. I had whelps all over my back and my legs" from the thick leather belt her mother swung against Rosalee's body again and again. "My grandfather jumped up out of bed and asked her was she crazy. He told her if she put her hands on me again what he would do to her. That was my last whipping." Not surprisingly, she did not see much of Andrew after that night.

Rosalee did not become a teenage mother. In her early twenties, she married William Ford, the son of a neighboring family. William was a construction laborer who dug ditches and poured concrete. "I was sorry I ever got married. That was the hardest damn bed I ever laid down in in my life." Her son, Donald, was born on July 2, 1953. Charmaine was born January 7, 1955. Her husband began to spend his time in a local beer garden and with other women, one of whom had been Rosalee's best friend. When Rosalee asked him where he was going at night, "he punched me in my face with his fist. He was just nasty. He was hateful." The beatings continued over several years.

Part of Charmaine's distrust of men goes back to those beatings and her father's rejection of her from birth. She was born with lighter skin than that of her parents, and William Ford refused to believe that Charmaine was his child. Rosalee explained to her husband that her father and all of her father's family were light-skinned, which accounted for Charmaine's lighter complexion, but he stuck to his belief and accused his wife of having an affair. As Charmaine became older, she learned of his feelings.

"It really got to me," she said, her voice cracking. "He would never actually acknowledge that I was his. I mean, he actually had me thinking that I was not his child. . . . What makes it so bad is that I'm the spitting image of my father. Even up to the time I took care of him till the time he passed away, he would never say, 'That's my daughter.' As I was coming up, he never gave me love. In a way, I kind of hated him for it because I figured I was really missing out on something. Missing out on love."

William Ford hit Rosalee often enough finally to break up their marriage. Charmaine and Rosalee both remember the last beating, the most brutal of them all: It was one night in late 1960, when Charmaine was five years old.

William Ford had been seeing Rosalee's best friend. Ford came in late this night, slamming the door behind him. Charmaine and her brother were awakened by the door slamming. He'd been drinking heavily. Soon the two children could hear their parents arguing in their bedroom.

Ford was accusing Rosalee of having had a male visitor that same night. "He knew he was doing dirty, and he was trying to make it look like she was doing dirty. He tried to do dirt for dirt," said Charmaine. Charmaine remembered that she and her brother ran into their parents' bedroom and yelled, "Stop it! Stop it." She said, "I just couldn't take [the arguing] anymore."

But Charmaine's father ignored the children and hit Rosalee hard enough to knock her down. When she tried to get up, he began kicking her with his heavy, square-toed work shoes. She covered her face, leaving the rest of her body exposed; at one point, Rosalee said, he kicked her in the genitals. "He throwed his foot right into me," said Rosalee.

Charmaine and seven-year-old Donald tried to stop him. They grabbed soda bottles and hit him repeatedly across the kneecaps, shouting at him. The two small children stood there, swinging the bottles again and again, until Donald, frustrated by his inability to stop his father, screamed at the man, "You fucker! You fucker!" Their father turned on Donald and chased him out into the Maryland countryside.

The noise had attracted the attention of one of Charmaine's great-uncles, who lived next door. The uncle knew that William Ford had a violent temper, so he grabbed a double-barreled shotgun and telephoned Rosalee's father, who lived around the corner. "Ford is over here beating up Lee again," the uncle told Rosalee's father. The uncle went outside and Donald ran into him. William Ford was right behind Donald and reached for his son. The children's uncle leveled his shotgun. "If you put your hands on that child, I'll kill you!" the uncle said. Ford backed off. Moments later, Rosalee's father arrived. The two older men, their guns leveled at Ford, walked Ford and Donald back to the house, where Rosalee still lay on the floor, writhing in pain.

When Donald and her father had run out of the house, Charmaine had tried to help her mother get up off the floor. "She couldn't get up. She was hurting. She was moaning and groaning," she said.

"[My father] was just raising hell. He was telling them that they didn't have nothing to do with it, that it was between him and his wife," Charmaine said. But Charmaine's grandfather told her father, "If you lift that foot to kick Lee again, we will take that foot off." The two men lifted Rosalee and carried her out of the house.

Charmaine was only five, but she remembered her reaction. She was following the men carrying her mother when she stopped. "I turned around and I looked at my father. And I hated him. He was just walking around and talking to himself," she said. She said she shouted, with all the venom she could muster, "I could kill you!"

A short time later, Rosalee left her husband. She was grateful her father had rescued her that night. She always had known her father cared about her. The fact that he and her mother had never married mattered little to Rosalee as long as she had a relationship with him. When she was recovering from the beating, her father told her, "If you ever go back to [William Ford], don't speak to me as long as I live." That was the final word on her marriage, as far as Rosalee was concerned. She took Charmaine and Donald and moved to Washington, to the house on Q Street in Buzzard Point. She got a job as a clerk at Lansburgh's warehouse working six days a week and earning sixty-two dollars a week.

Charmaine, who was six at the time, said her childhood ended at this point. "It's just like I had to grow up *fast*. My mother was working, so that meant I had to take over her chores of keeping house while she worked to support us. At that age, I knew how to do everything that a grown-up did. I was doing things that older kids were doing, like sweeping the house, folding clothes, washing dishes," she said. Donald, on the other hand, was not expected to do household chores. "He never had to do anything. He was pampered."

Although he was two years older, "I was sort of raising my brother." Donald, who later dropped out of school, was left back twice in elementary school, and Charmaine caught up with him. In the sixth grade one day Donald got into a fight at school. "The teacher came to me with it," said Charmaine. "I guess I was mature for my age." The teacher asked Charmaine to relay the message to her mother or have a talk with Donald. "I had an influence over my brother. I told him he shouldn't be fighting in school, and he wouldn't do it after that. It's changed now! Can't tell him anything now!"

Donald got much more freedom than Charmaine, who was required to stay inside or within sight of the house. When Charmaine became a teenager, she started to complain to her mother about the difference. Her mother told her, "You a girl. That's the reason."

The restrictions on her social life were imposed shortly after Charmaine turned thirteen. They were identical to the rules that had chafed Rosalee a generation earlier. "I was not allowed to step beyond the front porch after I got home from school," recalled Charmaine, the resentment still clear in her voice. "I always had to stay around the house, if not out front, out back. I couldn't even go next door. That's when I started reading horror books. It was an escape. I still do it a lot. It's like being in another world by yourself."

Charmaine said she knew that her mother was afraid she would get pregnant, but found her mother's restrictions unreasonable. Yet they never talked about sexuality. Charmaine said she and her mother had many discussions, but not about sex. She said, "Mother really didn't tell me anything. My mother wouldn't talk about babies. She wouldn't talk about [menstrual] periods" even after Charmaine began her menses at fourteen. "Nothing. She was probably afraid that if she did tell me I would go out" and experiment.

Charmaine's sex education came from conversations with friends and a course called Personal Family Living that she took in the seventh grade at Randall Junior High School. She remembered how friends used to tease her about her sexual inexperience, telling her, "Girl, you don't know what you're missing."

Something else had happened to Charmaine by the time she was thirteen. She had learned to be afraid of men. One incident stands out in her memory:

Late one summer night, on an unlit playground near Charmaine's house in Buzzard Point, five youths attacked a nine-year-old girl as she took a short cut across the playground on her way to a store. After the girl was raped and her assailants fled, she began screaming; people heard her cries as they sat on their front porches, a common pastime on warm nights in Buzzard Point. Some rushed to help her, unaware that it was too late. Some time later, Charmaine said, she learned that the girl was pregnant.

This incident, along with others, made Charmaine wary of men, and her experiences since then have only heightened her fears.

THE TRANSITION TO ADULTHOOD

When I met her, it had been fourteen years since Charmaine's rebellion against her mother, but she still remembered when she was fifteen and met the twenty-year-old man who became the father of her first child. Her brother was dating one of the man's sisters. Charmaine's mother allowed the young girl to leave the house if she was going out with her brother, so Charmaine tagged along with Donald to his girl friend's home. It was there she would run into the father of her first child.

At first she did not like him. "He thought every woman wanted him." The man flirted with her although he was dating someone else. "It seemed like every place I went" with Donald, the man would be there. "If I was leaving out of someone's house, he'd be coming in. No matter where."

As the months went by, they began to talk. Her initial reaction to him changed. "He liked the things I liked and, you know, so on and so on. So we started seeing each other." He was her first boyfriend. He had money and would spend it on her: He was a snappy dresser who wore suits, owned his own car, and had a steady job as a maintenance man.

When her brother would go to see his girl friend, Charmaine would go to see her boyfriend. Donald and his girl friend would go off together alone; Charmaine and her boyfriend did the same. "Far as my mother knew, I was going with my brother to see his girl friend. She didn't know about [my boyfriend] until after I got pregnant."

While Charmaine wanted to break her mother's hold on her and wanted to grow up and be able to act like a woman, she was frightened when her adult boyfriend made the first sexual approach. They were at the Maryland nightclub. "It's a combination disco downstairs and a motel upstairs," she said. After dancing and drinking, "we went upstairs" to one of the rooms. "Then we kissed. He started feeling all over me. I got kinda scared because I didn't know what to expect. I didn't know what to do!"

The man sensed her fear. He told her he would not hurt her, but Charmaine was not convinced. She told him that she was not ready. He said he would not rush her. She was relieved. They went out together several more times, and he did not approach her sexually. She began to relax with him again.

She was baby-sitting at the home of her boyfriend's older sisters one night. After Charmaine had gotten all six of the woman's children to bed, her boyfriend joined her at the house. They made love. They did not use contraception or discuss it. "I didn't worry about it. It didn't weigh on my mind that I would actually get pregnant. He wanted a baby, but I told him at the time that babies were the last thing on my mind."

Charmaine had known from her family-life course three years before that she eventually would get pregnant. Deep inside of her, she wanted a baby to hurt her mother, to show her mother that the "choke chain" had not worked, to show her mother that the harsh confinement had failed.

She and her boyfriend made love as often as they could see each other. Most of those occasions were in the rooms over the disco. "We were making love like twice a day, sometimes. He still was not coming to my house 'cause he didn't know how my mother would react, by him being a lot older."

Two months after the first time they made love, Charmaine noticed that her menstrual cycle ran for only two days, instead of the normal week. She did not think about it too much, she said. A month later, the same thing happened. She told her mother. Rosalee responded calmly, "I think you're pregnant." Charmaine denied it. "To me, as long as I saw blood, that told me I was safe." She told her mother, "I'm not doing anything."

Mother and daughter went to the free city clinic near their home. On the way, Charmaine began to work through in her mind what she would do if it turned out she was pregnant. She was no longer thinking about her resentment toward her mother. "If I am, [my boyfriend] has told me plenty of times that he wants a son. I said to myself that it would be nice to have a baby. I was really feeling kinda lonely. I was mostly to myself, except when I was with my brother, [my boyfriend], or something like that. I just felt that a baby would fill that gap" of emptiness.

At the clinic, a doctor confirmed that she was two months pregnant. Charmaine's mother asked her what she wanted to do and told her than an abortion was an option. Charmaine rejected the idea of an abortion. "[My boyfriend], he wants the baby." It was the first time her mother had heard her boyfriend's name. "So, do I get to meet this [boyfriend] finally?" her mother asked.

Her boyfriend came over to meet Rosalee that evening after Charmaine called him with the news of the pregnancy. "He asked me to marry him and I told him no. I just didn't want to marry him. To me, the only reason he wanted to marry me was because of the baby, and I didn't want that. If we got married, both of us might have been miserable. He didn't love me. I was infatuated with him. He helped me get out. Get away from my mother, but I didn't love him."

After an obviously pregnant Charmaine was turned away from high school in September 1971, "I started ironing people's clothes and fixing hair." She charged twenty-five dollars to wash, straighten, and curl a woman's hair. She charged thirty-five dollars to iron an "eye-measured" large bundle of clothes. A man's haircut was five dollars. "I done that for quite a while. About a year," earning as much as two hundred dollars a week.

Charles was born on February 27, 1972, and Charmaine applied for public assistance four months later. In October, she got a job as a waitress for seventy-five dollars a week at the soda fountain of a chain drugstore. She began receiving a monthly welfare check of one hundred fifty dollars in November. The father of her son "would give me sometimes seventy-five, sometimes one hundred dollars, every two weeks. We managed pretty well off of what he made, what I made, and what I did. Every now and then, on my day off, I would fix hair."

Charles was a year old, his cerebral palsy already diagnosed, when the family's income suddenly was reduced. Charmaine's mother was laid off from her job at Lansburgh's warehouse when the company went out of business. Moreover, Rosalee, who did not have health insurance, had developed significant health problems—a crippling bursitis in both arms and her right hand and dangerously elevated high blood pressure. Rosalee was certified as physically disabled and went on the public-assistance rolls. Even so, there was less money than when Rosalee had worked. "Life was a little hard then," Charmaine recalled. Her mother was too sick to take care of Charles, and Charmaine had to stay home from her waitress job. Their welfare checks, food stamps, and help from Charles's father barely got them through from week to week.

Fortunately, Rosalee recovered her strength by the summer of 1973. Charmaine taught her how to handle, bathe, feed, and change Charles and went back to her waitress job. Then Charmaine found a second job in the fall as a cashier at a McDonald's fast-food restaurant. Between the two jobs she brought home three hundred fifty dollars every two weeks. With great pleasure she informed her welfare social worker to drop her from the rolls. She no longer needed public assistance, although she continued to receive money for Charles's care and her mother still received a disability stipend.

The ability to work two jobs restored Charmaine's self-esteem and rid her of what she said was the most degrading experience of her life—receiving welfare. "I was used to working. I didn't really want the hassle of public assistance because they do drive you crazy! They would have you to come down [to the central office] every six months to get recertified. They would ask you a lot of questions that you have already answered when you go down there to first apply. It was always something they wanted you to bring in or to have or to go and get."

She was unable to make any material improvements in her life as a welfare recipient. "They keep sort of like a tight rein on you. You weren't allowed to have bank accounts. If you did receive public assistance, you have to spend the money and show for what you spent it. You wasn't allowed to save none of it. I just got fed up with it. I liked having my own money every week or every two weeks." She worked both jobs for three years, until the drugstore closed its soda fountain. At McDonald's, she was accused of pilfering money from her register, angrily walked off the job, but was later exonerated when the true culprit was caught. She was asked to return. She refused; her pride told her they should have accepted her word that she had not taken the money.

Charmaine met the father of her twin sons on a 1974 blind date arranged by a girl friend. Charmaine was a woman of nineteen, seeking the something she felt was missing in her life; she was still searching when I met her a decade later. They dated for several years before deciding to have a child. Their relationship remained close until a month before Lawrence and Lionel were born on August 31, 1976. The pregnancy brought out feelings of possession on the part of the father of her twin boys, feelings that both frightened and angered Charmaine, feelings that led to the man slapping her, feelings that brought back memories of her mother's sufferings at the hands of her father.

The man had begun to act as if he "had [marriage] papers on me. He had got real domineering. I wouldn't stand still for it. He acted like he was more my father than my boyfriend. He would say I didn't have no say whatsoever over what I'm going to do with my own money. When I asked him what was he going to do with his, he'd say, 'You ain't got nothing to do with what I do with my money.' One time he slapped me. He got mad because I wouldn't do something he wanted me to do. I told him, 'Get your ass out of my house!' I said, 'Well, I see we're not going to get along so bye-bye.' " They split up.

The father of her twin sons had not seen them since they were two years old. "He doesn't come to see them. He doesn't call." She would call him when the twins needed something, and he would send money. Otherwise, she did not hear from him. "We really planned for this child. He wanted a child, didn't care if it was a boy or a girl. I wanted a little girl since I already had a boy. No, I wasn't in love. I wasn't planning to marry him, because he didn't ask me to marry him. We never really mentioned marriage. I probably would have turned him down, because I feel to marry someone I have to love him and I couldn't say that I did."

Charmaine said she never considered marrying Lawrence and Lionel's father. "I just wasn't into marriage. I know when my mother was married she had it pretty rough. I guess that's another reason that I don't really trust men all that much. Most of my girl friends are married, and they're miserable."

Her girl friends who married when they were pregnant in order to give their children their fathers' names told her they regret the decision. "No love was involved. In my case, my kids have a name. The name is Ford. It's a good name. It might not be their fathers' names, but they have a name. So, I'm not going to jump up and marry no man for his name. I know who my babies' fathers are. They know who their daddies is."

Charmaine enrolled in a nurse's training course in an antipoverty program in June 1977. Charles's father had a car body shop "so he helped out a lot. No, I didn't get back on public assistance. I lived off of him." Charles's father had continued to ask Charmaine to marry him, even after she pulled the gun on him, and she had continued to turn him down. She finished the course in November and worked as a home nurse for elderly people.

Another relationship followed in 1979, this one with a Vietnam War army veteran. Charmaine moved into his apartment, just three doors away from her mother's home in the Buzzard Point community. Significantly, despite the proximity of her new place to her mother's, she was finally out from under her mother's roof. Her relationship with the veteran was one of friendship and harmony, if not love. Charmaine had given up looking for love. She did not think she had any in her to give; she did not feel there was any man who would love her.

The veteran helped with the bills; her twin boys idolized him; he was good to them; he treated them as if they were his own sons. Charmaine was happy. She felt secure and settled. Then her world collapsed. Her male friend had come back from Asia with a carefully hidden secret, a secret that broke into the open one day, a secret that destroyed their harmony: He was a heroin addict.

The relationship was a year old; her twin boys were four. "He had put his works into the bathroom and walked out. I went looking for the boys because they were too quiet. I didn't hear them playing." She looked in the bathroom. "Lawrence had the needle in his hand. Lionel had the rubber in his. And I *went* off! I poured it down the toilet. I stood on the syringe and broke it. I was feeling disgust for him. At that moment, I even hated him for bringing stuff like that into the house, knowing that I have small kids there."

Her friend came back to the bathroom, saw what had happened, and flew into a rage. "He hadn't shot up yet. He was getting ready to. When he first went into the bathroom the twins were standing right there at the door. Playing in the hall. They was crazy about him. Everywhere he went, they followed him. So when he set down the [heroin] works and walked out, they went in to see what was in the box."

"You know how much money I paid for that?" her friend asked.

"Yes, matter of fact, I probably do," Charmaine replied. "Maybe about two, three hundred dollars. Maybe more."

"I spent my whole check buying that," he continued.

"I don't care."

"You don't know what you done. I need it!"

Charmaine told him he would have to choose between her and the heroin. He chose her. She offered to help him overcome his addiction. He promised to seek help. Weeks later she found out that the heroin habit still came before her; it was the day she went Christmas shopping.

Charmaine set her pocketbook down next to the sofa; she told her friend she was going Christmas shopping for her sons; before she left, she went over to her mother's to share the excitement of the shopping trip; when she returned home, the boyfriend said he had to go out; she picked up her pocketbook and left right behind him. "So I got on the bus and I got halfway downtown. Something hit me and said, 'Look in your pocketbook!' I looked. He had stole all the money. All of it! I had about two hundred dollars. I was so mad and so upset. It hurt to think that he would steal from me."

She got off the bus and started walking back home. She got as far as the Fourth Street police station in Southwest Washington before she started crying. She went into the station and reported the theft. She told the officer who took the report that the police had better find him before she did. When she reached home, "I just sat in the dark." He was arrested a couple of weeks later. Charmaine declined to press charges, and the police released him. A week went by. One evening, when she had returned home from work, Charmaine found an envelope stuffed under the front door. He had put it there. Inside was two hundred dollars in cash and a note. "He asked for my forgiveness. We stayed together, but the chemistry wasn't there like it had been. He just kept on doing the same thing over and over again."

Fed up, she ended the relationship. Charmaine found the three-bedroom apartment on Condon Terrace in Washington Highlands and moved on a hot day in July 1980 while he was at work. "He wasn't serious at all" about ending his addiction. "He was just bull-crapping!" Her mother moved with her. He found out where she moved to and came uninvited to see her several times, begging her to return. She told him their life together was finished. After several months of his asking Charmaine to come back to his home, he finally stopped. She did not hear from him again.

Her father's terminal illness with cancer was the next stressful period in Charmaine's life. When William Ford was hospitalized in La Plata, Maryland, Charmaine would call him. "What do you want? What you calling here for?" is how she remembered his response when he realized it was Charmaine calling. "Well, I just called to see how you were doing," she told him. "I'm doing fine," Ford answered and cut the conversation short. "Everybody else call there, he talked to them in a civilized manner. Everybody except me."

Weeks later, the day before Ford was released from the hospital, he called Charmaine. "How you doing?" Ford asked Charmaine. "That's how I knew something was up. He never had spoken to me in a pleasant way." Her father "cried the blues" about not having anywhere to go. His sister had told him he could not come back to her house. His girl friend of many years said he could not come to live with her. He had two other sons besides Donald and two other daughters besides Charmaine, but they all had told him they had no place for him. He ended up calling the daughter he had rejected all of her life and her mother, the woman who left him twenty-three years before because of his mistreatment, and asked them to take him in. They did.

"Of all people," Charmaine managed to laugh. "He needed *me!* His feeling for me still didn't change. He still treated me the same way. He still rejected me the same. And I never disrespected him. I never talked back to him."

One of Ford's sons brought him, together with a hospital bed, to Charmaine's apartment on Condon Terrace. "He was like a baby, really. I had to diaper him, feed him, bathe him. The cancer affected his legs. He could not move his legs. Every time he had a doctor's appointment, I would take off from work and I would carry him. Every time he took sick and had to go to the hospital, I had to go. Every time he felt bad at night, I had to set up with him knowing I had to go to work the next morning. I did all this stuff, and he still acted the same way. Silly man!"

What Charmaine hoped and prayed for while caring for her dying father was his love, a last-minute change of heart on his part, an acknowledgment that she was *his* daughter. Ford's other daughters visited him at Charmaine's apartment. "He would always say, 'My daughters are coming to see me!' It hurt, but I would never show it. My mother, she knew how it hurt me."

Rosalee still thought of herself as William Ford's wife; they had not divorced. She was not a person to bite her tongue, especially now that Ford could not punch and kick her anymore. Rosalee would get right up in his face to say, "How could you say something like that when Charmaine is taking care of you? Them other girls that you call your daughters don't do anything for you!" Rosalee said she would get so angry, she would shake her fist in his face, threatening to beat and kick him the way he had abused her in the past. She laughed at the memory, saying she had only been joking, but the fear on Ford's face had told her that he had not been too sure.

William Ford, sixty-six, died in Charmaine's apartment on December 15, 1983, without ever acknowledging that the woman who took him in and cared for him in his last days was his daughter. Charmaine still carried the pain of that rejection whenever she talked about her father. "I was just hoping that things would have been better between us."

Charmaine's experiences with violence and her fears about neighborhood crime dramatically influenced the way she raised her family. Following her mother's lead, she imposed her own set of rules on her twin sons. They could not leave the apartment without an adult. They could not play outside, not even on the grounds of the apartment building, unless an adult was with them. They could not go to the store, or play ball in the street, or go to the playground alone. They were escorted to school in the morning and picked up at the end of the day. They spent most of their time inside, watching television.

Charmaine realized that she could not shelter them forever; one day, as she did, they would tug at the chain and try to break free. But she believed she was making the right choice—perhaps, as she saw it, the only choice.

CHAPTER NINE

THE STORIES OF THE six Washington Highlands families illustrate how we are in great part but the sum total of our parents' collective experiences.

Charmaine Ford's life, for example, illustrates how a consistent method of controlling children was followed through three living generations, in spite of a consistent pattern of adolescent rebellion growing out of the restrictions.

In 1947, Charmaine's mother, Rosalee Mae Ford, rebelled against her grandparents' control over her social life. Rosalee remembered her adolescence as a time when teenage children in rural Charles County, Maryland, dared not talk back to their elders. So, in protest, the eighteen-year-old Rosalee stayed out all night with an adolescent boy, a youth who, when he had asked Rosalee's grandparents if he might "keep company" with their granddaughter, was turned down by them. Rosalee's grandparents' reason: she was too young.

Rosalee saw it differently. Most of her girl friends were married and had been mothers for several years. She experienced her first sexual encounter that night of protest, and did not get pregnant. But a generation later, Rosalee controlled her daughter Charmaine's actions exactly the way her grandparents had controlled hers. And Charmaine rebelled in the same manner.

The first Rosalee knew of Charmaine's rebellion was the unwelcome news that her sixteen-year-old daughter was pregnant. It was years before Charmaine was able to tell Rosalee that she had gotten pregnant out of spite, in resentful reaction to Rosalee's "choke hold" on her social life.

Charmaine exercised the same restrictions over the movements of her preadolescent twin sons, although she acknowledged that one day they too would rebel. Only the manner of rebellion remained in question.

Sheila Matthews's exceptional academic abilities counted for little among her Washington Highlands peers, the majority of whom were school dropouts. Most of them were first- or second-generation offspring of sharecropping migrants from the South. For these adolescents' parents and grandparents, segregated schooling had held a secondary place to the year-round work on their landlords' farms. Children grew up at an accelerated pace and were expected to take on adult responsibilities early in life. Once an adolescent girl married or delivered a child, she acquired the status of a woman no matter what her age!

Many of Sheila's Washington Highlands girl friends and boyfriends saw pregnancy as an avenue to the same end: the tangible achievement of adult status. So, fifteen-year-old Sheila decided that having a baby would improve her social standing with her friends. To have a baby was even more important than her dream of becoming a pediatrician.

Her parents had migrated to Washington, D. C., directly out of North Carolina's sharecropping culture. Both parents earned little in their employment, the mother as a domestic and the father as a general laborer. In their endless struggle to rise a notch above the poverty of Washington Highlands, the couple managed to hold on to integral elements of their rural childhoods, one of which was the concept of the sanctity of life from the moment of conception.

In Sheila's early weeks of pregnancy, she often cited the sanctity of life as the reason she could not have an abortion. Sheila was very much aware of this family attitude before she got pregnant.

Theresa Williams's decision to become pregnant was the clearest link of a family's past influencing the motivations of a younger generation. Theresa was the eldest of Lillian Williams's four daughters. Because Theresa was eighteen and childless, she was teased "as a barren woman" by younger adolescent cousins who were already mothers. She felt pressured to prove her self-worth by having a baby. So she got pregnant. When her daughter was born, Theresa moved up in status from infertile adolescent to woman and mother.

I wondered if Theresa's actions were not an archaic family need that had been passed from parent to child. The female cousins who were cruelest in their teasing of Theresa had become mothers by age fifteen and sixteen. They were explicit in their self-description as *fertile women*! There was a lot more going on here than just the patterns of early childbearing evident in the Williams family. From my extensive interviews with Theresa, her mother, and her grandmother, there emerged a consistent pattern of early childbearing that went back generations. It was a pattern shared by neighboring North Carolina sharecropping families whom Theresa's mother and grandmother could name. Importantly, it was a pattern of economic survival that had been documented among living sharecroppers by a black scholar fifty years before I met Theresa.

Long before the Williamses migrated to Washington, early childbearing had provided the *economic* basis of survival for poor North Carolina sharecroppers. Theresa's underlying motivation for having a child revealed how a resilient social custom, born out of necessity, had persisted past its economic utility through the generations. The pattern, passed by parent to child from the family's origins in the tobacco-growing regions of Lenoir County, North Carolina, was brought by them into Washington, D. C.'s blighted Washington Highlands community.

The journalist in me wanted to know more about why some urban adolescents were unknowingly acting out rural customs formed generations ago. So, I decided to travel south to interview elderly black sharecroppers who had been young when sharecropping was at its peak. I wanted to learn more about the demands sharecropping had made on them. I wanted to know if the coping patterns established in Theresa Williams's family were common or unique experiences.

I discovered that early childbearing was a common practice, but more often within the legal sanctions of marriage. I also discovered some surprises. A number of habits, attitudes, and actions I had thought were peculiar only to the Williams family of Washington Highlands turned out to be modes of behavior practiced by landless black farmers in widely separated parts of the South. It became clear that the cultural patterns within Theresa Williams's family were a communal response to the poverty, harshness, and segregated isolation of the sharecropper's world.

I made contact with elderly sharecroppers through Henry Jackson. I was introduced to Jackson by William "Bill" Manley,

Theresa's maternal uncle. Jackson knew several families of retired sharecroppers living in and around the town of Oxford, the seat of Granville County, North Carolina.

Jackson gave me the Oxford telephone number of one of his cousins, Essex Lazzlo Hester. I called Lazzlo, and he agreed to introduce me to some of the Oxford community's retired tenant farmers. During April 1987, Lazzlo and his wife, Charlotte, introduced me to nine people, aged eighty-three to ninety-seven. Most of them had tenant-farmed from childhood until retirement. I interviewed the members of seven families, including Lazzlo's.

A month later, I visited the dean of black American history, John Hope Franklin, at his Durham, North Carolina, home, thirty miles south of Oxford. Franklin, as active in retirement as he was when he was lecturing full time, was teaching a course in constitutional history at Duke University Law School. He was interested in the work I was doing and introduced me to Charles Spurgeon Johnson's 1934 book about black tenant farmers, *Shadow of the Plantation.*

Johnson, the son of an emancipated slave, was a distinguished sociologist as well as a civil rights leader and the first black president of Fisk University.

In *Shadow*'s foreword, the late influential sociologist Robert Ezra Park wrote poignantly about the endurance of cultural forms past their utility: "Customs persist and preserve their external forms after they have lost their original meaning and functions."[5]

The "Negro peasant family" living under the South's tenant-farming system had undergone a profound change after its emancipation from slavery, continued Park. In slavery, "natural maternal affection" had created the bonds that tied the family together.

"It was not until freedom imposed upon the Negro tenant the necessity of making his farm pay [however] that the Negro farmer began to reckon his children as a personal asset. The effect of this was that parents began to discourage the early marriage of their children, the consequence of which would be to deprive them of their children's services."[6]

Children were not, therefore, a barrier to an adolescent mother's chances of marrying. Women earned status and value in the eyes of other women, their husbands, and the landowners for whom their husbands worked by the number of children they bore. A tally was kept of all the children born, including the many who died in the first moments, days, months, or years of life. The labor of the sharecropper's children provided the security, barring a disastrous drought, of land to live on and food to eat.

I was excited by Johnson's observations in *Shadow.* His comments were based on interviews in the early 1930's with 612 black tenant-farming families of Macon County, Alabama. Their life-styles duplicated the information I had gathered about Theresa Williams's family with its roots in Lenoir County, North Carolina. Many of the experiences and choices of the elderly sharecroppers I would interview in Granville County were identical to those described in *Shadow* and paralleled what I already knew about the Williams family. After my first reading of *Shadow,* I carried it with me during my weekly shuttle trips back and forth between Oxford and Washington, D.C. I read the book over several times while finishing my Oxford interviews in August.

The South's economic and social conditions produced parallel coping mechanisms among families of black tenant farmers. These strategies were identical despite regional distances and differences. They shared patterns of early marriages, large families, and households containing several generations, the same pattern of family life found in the home of Theresa Williams's mother in Washington Highlands.

In the course of my Oxford interviews, I also learned that the different types of tenant farming made dissimilar demands on landless black families, within a relative framework of poverty, throughout the South. Not all were sharecroppers.

There were tenant farmers called "fourthers," who were paid with three quarters of the crops they raised. Fourthers owned their livestock and farm equipment, which included mules, horses, cows, plows, wagons, and harnesses. They used the livestock and equipment both for farming the land and growing the family's food. They received payment for the crops they raised after they "paid out" on the debts they owed. The debts accrued from goods and credit plus interest extended during the year before the fall harvest. The remaining one fourth of the crop went to the landlord in payment for using his land.

There were "thirders," who earned two thirds of every crop because they owned their equipment but no livestock. They had to pay for using the landowner's plow mules.

At the very bottom of the tenant-farming system were the sharecroppers, who worked "shares." They owned no livestock or equipment and paid the landlord for the use of both. In turn, they ideally received 50 percent of the crops after they paid their debts. Sharecroppers were the least independent, the most desperate, and the most vulnerable of the black tenant farmers.

Theresa Williams's forebears were sharecroppers. In the family's childbearing patterns, Theresa's great-great grandmother and great-grandmother each gave birth to two babies as young girls *before* they married. Only *after* Theresa's great-great grandmother and great-grandmother gave birth were the two girls *seriously* courted by the young men they eventually married. These men were not the fathers of the children. They were young adult black men, the sons of sharecroppers, looking for sharecropping arrangements with white landowners. They were young men who preferred to marry women with proven fertility. They were men who knew they needed children if they were to live on and work the land.

Theresa Williams's great-great grandmother and great-grandmother grew up in homes that included three generations—relatively young grandparents, adolescent parents, and grandchildren, plus the adopted children of relatives.

Johnson found similar households in Macon County, Alabama. "The makeup of households which sociologically may be regarded as families often constitutes a confusing picture. Mary Grigsby, of Hardaway, is head of one of the oldest families of the county. She gives an account of the present structure of her household. It contains some of her own children, her children's children, and a half brother's and sister's natural and legal children. It is, however, as stable as most of the others."[7]

The marriages of Theresa's great-great grandmother and great-grandmother were loveless unions of convenience rather than couplings born of any avid attachment. Their world was not one where there was much time or room for romantic love to flourish. Marriage for the sake of survival was not uncommon. Survival for sharecroppers always came back to large numbers of children. Theresa's great-great grandmother had twenty children *after* she married. Theresa's great-grandmother had nine children *after* she married.

When Lillian Williams, Theresa's mother, was a child of ten growing up on her grandmother's sharecropping homestead, three of Lillian's adolescent aunts had eight children between them. Lillian Williams remembers the aunts' adolescent childbearing as appearing normal to her. Her grandmother made no comment about it, as Lillian recalls. All three aunts eventually married.

Johnson noted the same patterns in the early thirties among the Alabama sharecroppers. "Whether or not sexual intercourse is accepted as a part of courtship, it is certain no one is surprised when it occurs. The girl does not lose status, perceptibly, nor are her chances for marrying seriously threatened. An incidental compensation for this lack of censuring public opinion is the freedom for children thus born from warping social condemnation. There is, in a sense, no such thing as illegitimacy in this community."[8]

Johnson felt that some of the Alabama black sharecroppers' social practices had evolved among slaves on southern plantations and persisted when blacks became tenant farmers.

"The tradition of the plantation, its relation to morals, sex relations, and marriage never has conformed to that of the world outside. Unique moral codes may develop from isolation. It has happened elsewhere. Even in America there have developed patterns of sex relations among white communities not very different. In rustic villages of Bavaria, Austria, Norway, and Switzerland the presence of illegitimate children is not a handicap to women who wish to marry, but the conditions there have been different.

"In the families of this study the customary courtship period is observed, but in conformity with a tradition older than the country itself, when pregnancy follows this relationship it is not socially imperative that marriage follows.[9]

"Sex, as such, appears to be a thing apart from a marriage.[10]

"In a system which requires the labor of the entire family to earn a living, children of a certain age are regarded as an economic asset. They come fast, and there is little conscious birth control. The coming of children is 'the Lord's will.' The number of miscarriages and stillbirths is extraordinarily high and the infant mortality great. There is pride in large families. 'Good breeders' are regarded with admiration. For men the size of the family is a test of virility and for women fecundity has tremendous weight in their valuation as mates. Interest in children and in large families, and the high fecundity rate, may indeed carry over from the period of slavery when social status among Negro slave women was an important measure based upon their breeding power. Again it may reflect adjustment to a high mortality-rate which demands a correspondingly high birthrate to insure a balanced survival in the population."[11]

I was surprised when Theresa told me that she desired her two children but had no interest in marrying their father. I thought her attitude was an eccentric exception. I was wrong. A woman's desire for children, but a disinterest in having a husband, is not unique or new, according to what Johnson found.

"Again, there are competent, self-sufficient women who not only desire children, but need them as later aids in the struggle for survival when their strength begins to wane, but who want neither the restriction of formal marriage nor the constant association with a husband. They got their children not so much through weakness as through their own deliberate selection of a father."[12]

Within the Williams family there were other behavior patterns, aside from sexuality, that were linked to the sharecropping past.

For instance, when I first interviewed Lillian Williams, Theresa's mother, she left me confused about her age. In September 1984, Lillian Williams told me her birth date was August 28, 1944, that she was forty-one, and that she had been fourteen when she gave birth to her eldest son, Kenneth Earl Williams. Earl, as everyone in the family called him, had turned twenty-three on May 22, 1984.

I told Lillian that her birth date indicated she was forty, and if she was sure about how old she had been when Earl was born, then she had to be thirty-seven. "I don't know," she answered in frustration. "The midwife [who delivered me in North Carolina] died before she made out a birth certificate. I'm just going by what my mother says."

Eight months later, I interviewed Lillian's mother in her Baltimore home. She brought down the family Bible from her upstairs bedroom to clear up my confusion. The birth dates of all five of her children were written on one of the opening pages. Lillian had been born on August 28, 1943, was forty-one when I met her, and had given birth to Earl when she was seventeen.

Johnson encountered the same confusion in Alabama. "One of the first circumstances encountered . . . is the confusion about ages. Those who lacked the continuing relationship with a single white family would have them set down the most likely age or date of birth in a Bible. If the white folks died, or the Bible was lost, their ages were also lost and this was counted as irrevocable, not to be troubled about further. After all, ages are only needed at rare intervals, when a census is being taken or the even less exacting requirement of an obituary and death certificate."[13]

Allie Downey was one of the first retired tenant farmers I interviewed in Granville County, North Carolina. His life's story reinforced everything I read in Johnson's *Shadow* and heard from the Williams family about their sharecropping ancestors.

Allie Downey was born in his parents' weathered plank wood house on the Watkins family tobacco plantation twelve miles north of Oxford. Downey has lived all his life in the shadow of the plantation. His generation was the next to last of four generations of Downeys who were born, lived, farmed, and died on the Watkins's land from the end of the Civil War. Downey was one of six surviving offspring of seven children. The children had come quickly and were a year apart in age. The last two children were a year and two years younger, respectively, than three-year-old Downey when their father died.

Downey's childhood ended with his father's death, an event he can still recall. In his mind's eye, Downey can see his dead father stretched out on a bed in his parents' bedroom. Tom Downey was cut down in the prime of manhood from a fever caught while cutting summer wheat in the North Carolina sun. There was a hushed silence in the crowded bedroom. An older cousin reached under Downey's armpits and lifted the child up. It was Downey's last look at his father's face.

Tom Downey's death drastically changed life for his widow, Martha, and the couple's six children. The year was 1900. Martha, with the help of her young children's labor, was able to get the family through the fall and winter, the next spring, and even a couple of additional tobacco-growing seasons. But it was hard work for a lone, proud woman heading a tenant-farming family of fourthers. She turned down most offers of help, but accepted those that made a crucial difference. There was not much idle time for the Downey children to play and no time at all for school.

Downey and I talked often during the spring and summer of 1987. I was hoarse after each session from yelling my questions over the whirring sound of the living-room ceiling fan. Downey had grown hard of hearing when he reached his mideighties.

I always enjoyed the drive from Oxford through the Granville County farmland to Downey's house. The verdant North Carolina landscape rolled past over the hills and "bottom" grasslands on the banks of fast-flowing creeks. There were patches of woodlands broken by flat, cleared fields of corn and tobacco plants. But that summer, the corn and the tobacco were noticeably stunted. It was obvious that the harvest was going to be a poor one. There had been too little rainfall.

The stunted crops meant painful memories for Downey. He recalled friends and family not fortunate enough to farm land owned by the too few "decent white folk." A drought represented instability and fear for many of the tenant farmers he had known.

"Yeah, in the old days, with a drought like this one, sharecroppers were put off the land 'round about now," said Downey on a stifling July afternoon. "If you were living on the white man's farm, this time of year like this, he'd be scared. He'd think he can't get his money [out of the tobacco crop] so he'd put the sharecroppers off his land. That way, he didn't have to pay them. Whatever little money he got was his. A drought meant real trouble for the sharecropper." The farm owners also cut the food rations and reduced the amount of credit they extended to the sharecroppers, and their large families.

"No, there wasn't much sense going to court about it. It didn't matter if you'd worked the land for months and months. In court, you could say what you want to, but they were going to take the white man's word every time."

Other memories crowded in on Downey whenever we talked. Some of these memories made him uncomfortable and uncommunicative. Some of the pain of past memories showed clearly in his eyes. Some of the memories were still so raw that he would fall silent as he thought about them and then decline to discuss them.

If he harbored any bitterness, it did not come through. The aching experiences of the past, both his own and those of others, were not evident in his dialogue. He was a God-fearing Baptist, but not at all preachy about it. He laughed often, at his own jokes, the jokes of others, and mine. He liked to tease and took it well when he was teased.

In the first weeks of our meeting, he became confused about my name. Before my first revisit, I called him long-distance to tell him I would be down to see him in a couple of days. He told his daughter, Maria Hannah Royster, that Leon Spinks had called. Hannah corrected him and told him that I was not a boxer but a reporter named Leon Dash. He asked her not to tell me, but she did anyway. Afterward, whenever I called to say I was coming down, I would tell him it was Leon Spinks calling. He laughed and laughed. It became our joke.

Downey's gait is slow and deliberate, about the pace you would expect from a ninety-year-old man with bowed legs and a slight stoop. His complexion is dark brown. His face is oval shaped, and he wears horn-rimmed eyeglasses under a floppy brown hat, the kind of hat that looks right on a man who has farmed nearly all his life.

Downey said his mother took his father's place in all respects after Tom Downey died. Martha Downey even fulfilled her husband's fourther's farming arrangement with the Watkinses, getting behind the mule-drawn plow and turning the earth for the spring planting as her husband had always done.

Planting and cultivating acres of tobacco for sale guaranteed that the family could stay in the three-room house the Watkinses provided for their tenant farmers. Planting and cultivating acres of tobacco guaranteed that the family's basic needs would be met by the Watkinses during the cold winter months—at five-percent interest on a dollar's credit.

The Downey children worked from before the sun rose to long after the sun set. Their childhood experiences were not unique because their father died. All the children of tenant farmers worked the same hours.

Tenant farming, in the best of circumstances, demanded children's labor. While their father lived, the Downey children's labor had been an important contribution to the family's survival. After their father's death, their labor became a crucial contribution to the family's survival.

Just how important children were is evident in Martha Downey's second marriage to Bob Harris several years after her first husband's death. Martha Downey was still a young, attractive woman when she married Harris. She gave birth to fourteen additional children, nine of whom lived, which meant that fifteen of her children worked the Watkins land, at one time or another, from the turn of the century until Allie Downey retired in 1974.

Tenant farming was a way of life that prompted parental-child conflicts when an adolescent wanted to marry. Many tenant farmers tried to hold on to their youngest children's labor to guarantee themselves a place on a white farmer's land. Children in a household meant the parents would be able to stay on the land when they began to weaken with age, when bending over to weed the tobacco required concentrated effort for older adults.

Some girls eloped, especially the youngest at the end of a long string of children, to get away from possessive parents. Net, the last child of Martha and Bob Harris, eloped when her parents balked at the idea of her leaving home to marry. Net was the same age as her older sisters who had married and left home before her "without a fuss," remembered Downey.

There also were young girls who gave birth to children before they married, but given the value of children, the birth of a child to an unmarried adolescent was not a major traumatic event. In most instances, the children of unmarried adolescent girls were easily incorporated into the large families, which included several generations under one roof. All children were valuable. These children either stayed in the household of the girl's parents, or were adopted by the families of nearby relatives and friends, particularly by those couples who were childless.

There always was room enough and food enough for children, and the circumstances of their birth mattered little to most adults. These children were not stigmatized as illegitimate. To what earthly purpose? Would they be in line to inherit acres of rich farmland when their parents died? No, not if they were the offspring of tenant farmers. Generally, they were raised by their grandparents and thought of them as their parents. They treated their young mothers as older sisters.

The tenant farmers' need for children's labor did not mean, however, that all of them were sanguine about their daughters bearing children outside the bonds of marriage. Allie Downey's mother, for instance, took in her young niece and raised the niece's child as one of her own children after one of Bob Harris's brothers, furious with his unmarried daughter for getting pregnant, expelled her from his house.

After the South's slaves were emancipated, the overwhelming majority of freed blacks were landless and lived in agricultural areas. There was a minority of freedmen who were able to buy land and some who were given land, but most ex-slaves did not have the means. They had farming skills, their labor, and little else with which to survive.

White farmers, on large and small expanses of land, were desperately trying to recover from the ravages of the Civil War. They needed the former slaves to tend acres of labor-intensive cash crops —the less demanding cotton and the more profitable tobacco—to get back on their feet and maintain a profitable edge once their fields were back in full production. The South's system of tenant farming evolved from this mutual economic need, although tenant farming was little more than a postslavery peasant's life for the families of the freedmen.

Landowners worked at keeping the tenant farmers ignorant, in debt, and available as a cheap pool of labor. The children of tenant farmers were explicitly included in the unenforceable "handshake" agreements. The agreements were not binding on the landowner, and tenant farmers were resigned to being cheated and abused, knowing that if they showed too much intelligence or inquired too deeply into the true market price of the cotton or tobacco they raised, they would be forced off the land.

"As long as you're poor, you're working for him," said Downey. "But if you got as much as he got, you would not work for him. [The landowners] didn't want to lose you. If you didn't owe them nothing, they figured they might lose you."

During the hard times and the good times, the survival or prosperity of the tenant farmer was tied directly to the labor of his children. The more children a tenant-farming couple had, the larger the landlord's profit.

A childless couple had little chance, if any at all, of getting a tenancy with a landowner unless they brought with them the adopted children of family and friends or perhaps the adopted children of several unmarried nieces. Tobacco and cotton demanded months of bending, kneeling, and careful picking, work that children did best.

The Downeys were relatively well off because the Watkins family treated them with a benign paternalism, as long as the Downeys did not challenge the Watkinses' postharvest figures on what the Downeys owed to the Watkinses. Sam Downey, Downey's brother, and Sam's son successfully disputed the figures one day in the late 1950's. Sam was told, "You've gotten too grown," and was booted off the Watkinses' land. Sam moved to Oxford to live with his son.

In Oxford, on Sundays when Irene Winston Taylor feels strong, she attends Oxford's First Baptist Church at West Front Street and Granville Avenue, just a short walk from her house. Lazzlo Hester was First Baptist's treasurer and knew Taylor well. He introduced us on my first visit to Oxford.

Taylor is a small woman with an impish smile. Her cheeks, round and prominent, dominate her face. She does not look like a woman of eighty-four, but more like a woman in her fifties, just settling down to enjoy her first set of grandchildren. She is stubborn and suffered a mild heart attack in June 1987 when doing housework, which long ago had been forbidden by her family doctor.

Taylor remembered with a deep, lingering resentment being forced to grow up early. She had baby-sitting responsibilities when she was just a child herself. Children as young as five were given the responsibility of looking after younger brothers and sisters.

I found several instances of the same custom among families living in Washington Highlands.

Taylor was born and grew up on a farm where Route 96 meets Wilton Road, fifteen miles due south of Oxford. Alan and Mary Jane Winston, Taylor's parents, were tenant farmers on land owned by Eugene Moss. Some years the Winstons did well and worked fourths. Some years they suffered setbacks and worked shares.

There were seven children in the household. The two oldest were by Winston's first wife, who died shortly after the second child was born. Mary Jane, Winston's second wife, gave birth to six children and five lived. Taylor was the second born of the second set.

The farm work was something everyone did and was never seen as a major chore by Taylor when she was a child. She remembered pulling grass out of the tobacco-plant beds and carrying the foot-long plants in a basket on the day the tobacco plants were transplanted to the fields. "Somebody would be in front of us making the hills with a hoe. I'd drop a plant on a hill. Somebody going to come behind you then, push a peg into the hill, and put the plant into the hole."

For four months of the year—October to January—Taylor was able to go to school regularly, "but then after a while, I had to go whenever I could because my two sisters and brother younger than me had to be looked after when the adults were in the fields working."

The baby-sitting would not have been such a burden, recalled Taylor, if the children she had cared for were limited to three. "What made it so bad was the neighbors 'round wanted to leave their children also. I was baby-sitting for the neighbors' children and the white children. Never was no less than twenty, twenty-four children. Something like that."

When the children got into mischief or hurt themselves, which happened just about every day, "I'd get a whipping just like they would. It's a wonder I even got any skin on my legs."

When Taylor was eleven, her father died of a heart attack. "Momma just kept right on doing as we had been doing," raising hogs and cultivating sugarcane, rye, wheat, and tobacco. Several years after her father died, Taylor's mother came down with pneumonia in both lungs. Taylor bathed and cooked for her mother and took care of the younger children during her mother's months-long illness. "She always used to have to wrap up heavier than anyone else in the winter. My mother was small and caught cold easily."

Mary Jane was unable to rebound from the pneumonia, as she had from her previous illnesses, and she slowly grew weaker. "Toward the end, she would look at me and hold my hand and squeeze. The morning she died, she tried to sing a gospel song but did not have the strength. Her eyes closed. It was close to Christmas 1918. I missed her so bad!" cried Taylor in her sitting room seven decades later.

After their mother's death, the children lived on the Moss farm for a couple of months. The oldest person in the home was Early, Taylor's sixteen-year-old brother. Taylor was fifteen. The younger children were Geneva, Willie, and Ruby. The older sister and brother by their father's first wife had married and left home before her mother died.

Taylor felt her two brothers and two sisters expected her to replace their mother. She felt overwhelmed. "The least little thing that come up, Early or Willie or Geneva or Ruby, they would all cling to me. Early was older than me, and I felt, being the man, he should have headed up the house, but still, I couldn't make myself tell him so. I don't know why. He would come to me as if Momma and Daddy were still somewhere around and I was suppose to look after him as well as Willie and Ruby. To see that he was well fed, clothes ready for him. Just like Momma would have done. That put a lot on me!"

Eventually, Willie, Geneva, and Ruby were sent to live at the black-children's orphanage on the outskirts of Oxford. Early went to work on a nearby farm, and Taylor moved to the federal experimental tobacco farm southwest of Oxford, where Eugene Moss was working as manager.

Immediately after Taylor arrived on the experimental farm, she was enlisted to read the Bible every Sunday morning and every Wednesday night to Ransome and Caroline Hargrove, an elderly couple who were emancipated from slavery. The Hargroves worked on the experimental farm and lived in a small house near the Moss family's house.

From the Hargroves, a shocked Taylor learned that it had been dangerous for slaves to learn to read, even to read the Bible. So they had come by their Christian faith with difficulty but were steeped in it, and they taught Taylor a lot of what she came to live by as an adult.

The Hargroves entered Irene Taylor's life at an important and painful juncture. It was a time when the orphaned adolescent was in mourning for her parents. It was a time when she was separated from her brothers and sisters. It was a time when every day she felt the ache of not seeing her family.

The Hargroves were able to lift some of Taylor's suffering through their warmth and concern for the young girl. Taylor felt that the Hargroves, and the couple's deep Baptist faith, gave her the strength and stability to face each day. Perhaps the Hargroves were so surefooted in their belief, as Taylor remembered them, because they had won it through surreptitious struggle. As slaves, the Hargroves had risked a cut in their rations and other persecutions for stubbornly pursuing their religious preference without so much as a "by your leave" to their masters.

Taylor knew little of slavery except that it had existed sometime in the foggy past. Her mother's mother, she knew, had been a slave, but Taylor was too young when her grandmother was alive to ask her what her life had been like in slavery.

On her first Sunday morning at the Hargrove home, however, the adolescent Taylor got her first lesson on the customs of slavery. She had begun to thumb through the worn pages of the Hargroves' Bible, searching for the section the couple had requested, when Uncle Ransome suddenly stood up from his chair, grabbed the iron washpot by its bowed handles, overturned it, and set it down with its three legs in the air in the dirt entrance of the front door.

Taylor knew about the conventional uses of a washpot. On wash day, she and her mother would set a washpot's legs on a set of stones, fill it with creek water, and build a fire under it. They used the hot water to wash clothes, or they added lye to it and boiled the especially dirty farm clothes. The fat of a slaughtered hog was cooked in the washpot to make lard, which was stored and used all year for frying chicken and other foods.

After he turned the washpot over, Uncle Ransome returned directly to his chair. Taylor saw his action was deliberate, but she was perplexed about the purpose.

"Uncle Ransome said back in slavery times they had to put the washpot outside the door and turned it down to cut their voices," said Taylor. "If the white people heard them praying, they would punish them one way or other. They were not allowed to sing gospel songs loud enough for the white people to hear. Back in them days, they had to get their food from the white people. The white people would give them so much flour, so much [corn] meal, so much sugar, coffee, and stuff like that. If they heard them pray, they wouldn't give but enough food for two meals a day. Cut their rations. Cut them down little by little. They didn't want the slaves doing nothing unless they asked them first."

After hearing the rationale, Taylor protested. Slavery ended long before she was born, and there was no longer any need to "turn down the washpot" outside the door. That was all right, she said Uncle Ransome told her, but he and his wife felt better with the washpot outside the door when they prayed and sang gospel songs inside the house.

"They would always turn the washpot down on Sunday morning so that [the Moss family] wouldn't hear them pray," recalled Taylor. "Uncle Ransome said this was the way they did it back in slavery time, and this was the way he was going to do it then."

Sixty-eight years later, Irene Winston Taylor recounted in an interview the "turning of the washpot" as her first encounter with an acknowledged "slavery-time" custom. It was a custom that was practiced, at least in the Hargrove household, well past its utility. Indeed, the Hargroves continued to "turn down the washpot" every Sunday morning and Wednesday night until their deaths shortly after Taylor married in 1927.

"It was just something they had gotten accustomed to doing all their lives, and they continued to do it," said Taylor.

Before she told the washpot story, Taylor pointed out to me the washpot that sat in the front yard of her house. The bottom of the washpot had been broken out years before by one of Taylor's six children. Red and white flowers bloomed in the earth-filled washpot in the summer of 1987. Whenever Taylor remembered to look at the washpot, she was reminded of the Hargroves and someone else she still missed. The washpot in the front yard had belonged to Mary Jane Winston, Taylor's mother.

Rachel Brandon Peace, ninety-one, was another person Lazzlo introduced me to in Oxford. She was a large, tan-skinned woman who moved around slowly with the aid of a cane and impatiently waved away anyone who tried to assist her. She kept her pure white hair parted in the center and swept up into a bun at the back of her head. Her piercing brown eyes looked like an eagle's when she was serious and twinkled when she chuckled. When she laughed, Peace's whole body shook.

Unfortunately, Peace died on July 2, 1987, before I finished interviewing her.

Peace's parents, Osh and Sarah Brandon, did fourth cropping around the town of Kittrell, North Carolina, in Vance County, the next county east of Granville. Peace was born in Kittrell, the thirteenth of seventeen Brandon children, on October 30, 1896.

"I chopped cotton. Picked corn. We didn't do much tobacco in Vance County. It was all cotton when it came to making money. I picked cotton as I got older. Sometimes you didn't finish and had to pick after Christmas. Picked many a lock of cotton after Christmas. Go through the winter."

Peace and her husband, George Peace, ninety-six, lived in the rural community of Antioch on Oxford's eastern edge just back from Orphanage Road.

On every one of the many visits I made to their house, two of their seven daughters were there. The daughters, who themselves were grandmothers, looked after their parents in organized shifts. One of the Peaces' two sons was dead, but the surviving son, Morris, visited his parents each morning.

As Rachel Peace moved through the narrative of her life, she began to chuckle when we reached the period in 1910 when she met George. "We went together three years before we married. He came to see me on Wednesday nights and had to leave the house by nine o'clock."

The couple also saw each other at the Ilong Baptist Church both their families attended in southern Granville County on Fairport Road. Before Rachel Peace was born, Ilong was given its name when it was just a tent pitched on land owned by her husband's uncle. "In those days, there was a woman who would say, "*I long* for the day when we have a building to hold services in. When the church was finally built, they named it 'Ilong.' Like everything else, it was built far back from the [Fairport] road in the woods. The white church was up on the road."

Rachel Peace was the eldest child at home when she turned sixteen. There were four younger ones behind her, but her parents relied on her to help them with a lot of the farm work. Leaving them was not going to be easy, Peace thought. Osh Brandon resisted her desire to marry. She understood her father well enough to know that his resistance would stiffen and turn to an outright prohibition if she confronted him, although Osh Brandon liked George Peace well enough.

So Rachel eloped with George on August 4, 1913. They were married on the Granville County–Vance County line by the Ilong pastor.

"My father like to have a fit. My brother knew. He was there. He went back and told" her parents. Her father said, in shock, "My Rachel?" Then he cried.

The couple moved to the Dickerson community in Granville County, where George got a sharecropping agreement with a white farmer. Seventeen-year-old Rachel Peace gave birth to the first of their nine children in February 1914.

Children were essential assets for the survival of adults, said Charlie Jones, ninety-seven, the night Lazzlo introduced me to him in the Zol-Mar Rest Home, eleven miles northwest of Oxford. "Without children, the grown people were put off the land by the white folk," recalled Charlie.

Charlie came to realize how important children were when he and his three brothers and sister went to live with an uncle after his father died. Charlie's youngest brother was the last child to leave the farm that the uncle sharecropped. Soon afterwards, the uncle and his aunt were put off the land by the landowner because all the children had grown up, and moved on.

When we met, Charlie's mind was still clear, and he would tease the women who worked at the Zol-Mar Rest Home about going out on a date. He was a thin man with a thin face, and both his legs had been amputated. His one active pleasure was snuff, both the mild and the strong types, and he sent me to the store to get a two-week supply each time I talked with him.

Two years after Charlie was born on April 4, 1890, in Brunswick County, Virginia, his father died of pneumonia. His mother, Neal Jones, moved with her five children—four boys and one girl—to Granville County to live with her sister and brother-in-law, Corena and Jim Bumpers. The Bumperses had only two daughters, and welcomed the addition of Neal Jones and her children. Jim Bumpers sharecropped a farm near the town of Berea, ten miles northwest of Oxford.

The two families totaled ten people in a three-room house. There were a kitchen and bedroom on the first floor, and a bedroom upstairs. "Adults slept downstairs and children slept upstairs. The house was unpainted dry board. Snow blew into the house in the winter. We'd wake up and find snow way up on top of the bed. Would be so warm under there. Three children to a bed. You didn't have a blanket. You had quilts. Three or four."

Charlie was the second youngest of Neal Jones's children and remembered pushing a fertilizer planter for the corn crop on the farm at age three. "My uncle grew corn, tobacco, [sugar]cane, and wheat."

Charlie left his uncle's farm at thirteen when he got his first job as a cook in Creedmoor in southern Granville County. His older brothers had already left. Charlie's older sister had already married and moved away. His mother had remarried and moved to another farm. That left Jim Bumpers, his wife, and two daughters on the farm after Charlie's younger brother left in 1904, the same year the farm owner put the Bumpers family off the land.

"The white man wanted more help, and Uncle Jim did not have any children to help him. Anytime you're ready to farm, the plants would get away from you if you didn't have children. You needed to have children right there."

We last talked in early July before Charlie became ill. A nurse at the rest home called me in Washington to tell me that he died on July 29, 1987.

I met Catherine Clack Mitz, eighty-seven, through one of her daughters who worked at the Zol-Mar Rest Home. At age fourteen, Mitz had thought of herself as old enough "to court."

When there was a cooling breeze, Mitz and I would talk on her front porch overlooking Easy Street, just inside Oxford's eastern border. On hot days, we would sit together in front of the blowing floor fans in the front room of the house she and Arthur Mitz built in 1950. Mitz died in 1970, and Catherine's youngest daughter and son-in-law lived with her.

Occasionally, I pushed her out onto the porch in her wheelchair if the weather had cooled enough during one of my visits. She seemed more at ease when we were on the porch than when we were inside the house.

Catherine was dependent on her wheelchair. Her left leg had been amputated. Her right foot had been weakened by several operations and could no longer take her weight if she stood on it.

Catherine's white hair was usually brushed straight down below her ears. She is a brown-skinned woman and has been slim all her life. Whenever she remembered something unpleasant, her nose wrinkled up before she began to talk.

In the spring of 1910, shortly after her tenth birthday on February 26, Catherine entered the fields to work the long hours of an adult sharecropper. "I worked like a *boy*! I did everything everyone else did" except plow.

"My daddy didn't grow cotton, and I'm glad he didn't. Cotton was an easier crop, but you made more [money] from 'bacca."

Within a year of entering the fields, Catherine knew intimately the steps required to get tobacco from the winter plant bed to the fall warehouse auction. Her labor was an integral part of the long process.

"You cleared the ground for the plant bed in the winter, mixed the 'bacca seeds with fertilizer, and sowed the bed. Then you covered the bed with canvas.

"You removed the cover in the spring. After a short time, you had to get on your knees, honey, and weed out the small grass blades in the plant bed to keep them from killing the 'bacca plants.

"By time I was eleven, my daddy would hire me out to pick plant beds. The farmers didn't pay me, they paid my daddy, and I don't know how much they paid him and I'd better not ask, either! You had to pick it over about twice.

"Then the seedlings, about as tall as your hand, were put [transplanted] in the field. After you put the plants in, you had to weed the field once. Then hill off [each plant with a small mound of dirt at its base]. Then you had to top it [so leaves would spread out] and break off the suckers [plant buds between stalk and leaf]. By time you broke off all the suckers, you had to start at the beginning and worm the 'bacca. Go through the plants, pull them worms off, and break them in half with your fingers. That's the reason I'm afraid of 'bacca worms today. They were green. Sometimes, two and three worms on a plant.

"You start getting in 'bacca in July. When I was small, 'round eleven, people cut 'bacca. They stopped that after I got married. They'd cut the leaves off and leave the stalk in the field.

"Then you'd fill the barn with leaves and burn a fire under the hanging leaves. Had to stay up all night to keep the fire going and the heat at a particular temperature. This was done for three or four days until all the 'bacca was cured.

"After it was cured, you laid it out on a flat. Then it was taken to the landlord's stack house. It was graded, tied in bundles, and stored there until the warehouse opened at the end of August. Carted to the warehouse and sold at the fall auction.

"You worked that 'bacca from winter to fall!"

Two years after Catherine entered the fields, the Clack family moved to another farm. It was the third and last move Catherine would make while living with her parents. James Clack had worked himself up from sharecropping to working fourths. He had two mules, two horses, two milk cows, and hogs.

James and Nanny Clack were strict and religious and did not allow their children to go to parties where there was square dancing or the drinking of alcohol. In her midteens, Catherine was permitted to go to friends' birthday parties with her father's adult male cousin acting as escort and chaperon. "I was a great, big courting girl of fourteen."

This was the same year that Arthur Mitz came striding up the path to the Clacks' home. James and Nanny Clack now had sixteen children, but Catherine's eldest sister was married and living in her own home. The only girls of courting age at the Clack house were Catherine and her second-oldest sister, fifteen-year-old Roseanna. Both girls immediately understood the reason for Mitz's visit.

Catherine whispered to Roseanna, "Hummphh! I don't know what in the world he come here for. Don't nobody want him!"

After Catherine's fifteenth birthday, Mitz asked her if he could come around to see her. She told him no, that she did not want him to come to see her. He came anyway. "So after a while, I started talking to him." They were married on February 16, 1916, three weeks before her sixteenth birthday.

Catherine and Arthur Mitz had fourteen children, twelve of whom lived. The first child was born in 1917 and the last one in 1941.

In the early years of their marriage, Mitz followed the sawmill. The sawmill operator would buy a "seat" of timber and cut the trees until all the quality timber was finished. Then the sawmill would be dismantled and moved to another seat. In the first eighteen years of their marriage, they moved eight times, including back to Mitz's South Hill birthplace and several parts of Granville County.

Catherine was unaffected by the moving. She had understood what her life was going to be like when she married a sawmill man. And she worked in the tobacco fields wherever they lived. Mitz was earning as much as six dollars a week in the sawmill and did not want his wife to work, but Catherine refused to stop working.

"I know I was young, but I was grown," said Catherine. "I wanted him to know this. When I left my mother and father, I didn't have no more bosses. Now, we'll work shoulder to shoulder, but no boss.

"I was making twenty cents an hour weeding 'bacca. I thought I was making something. The children would be on a quilt under a shade tree" on the edge of the field. "I'd get there as early as I could and work as late as I could. I earned as much as nine dollars in a week. That was *big* money! Couldn't nobody tell you *nothing*! A pair of shoes cost forty-nine cents. If you paid a dollar for shoes, you had the *best* of shoes."

In 1934, the price of processed wood fell below the cost of the timber, and the sawmill closed. Catherine was pregnant with their twelfth child.

The family got a sharecropping arrangement with a Granville County farmer named Seymour Hart. "He was a landowner what did not like colored people," remembered Catherine. "He said if he had to go to heaven with colored people, he didn't want to go there."

There was no rain in the early summer of 1935, and everyone was afraid the tobacco was going to die. "I had two cows. Hart wanted my husband to give him one of the cows." Catherine refused, saying, "We half-sharing and he ain't got nothing to do with my cows." Hart was afraid that the tobacco crop "was not going to bring enough for us to pay him out. If he got the cow, he'd have something on us."

Hart next reduced the amount of beans and flour he gave to the Mitzes. He suggested to Arthur Mitz that he reduce the food rations for the smallest Mitz children and keep the children who were working on full rations. Hart told Mitz that the previous sharecropper who had worked his land had done that during another dry period. Hart's suggestion "made Arthur real mad. He was going to move on away from there," but again Catherine refused. "We have done too much work to leave," she told her husband.

Catherine began walking to houses as far as three miles away to do washing. She was paid by the number of people in a family. A one-dollar wash would be for a family of five; she charged the same fee to do the ironing. "I strung tobacco pouches" with drawstrings. "Seven thousand in a sack. Got a dollar seventy-five for stringing one thousand tobacco pouches. We still accepted the little food the land-owner gave us," she said.

"There was a country store not too far from us. My husband would go to that store every Saturday and buy food for those children. My children did not go hungry and never did cry because they were hungry.

"It wasn't too long then that it commence to raining and that crop come out." Hart wanted to give her husband everything they agreed to before the dry spell. Catherine refused. She wanted to keep their debts to Hart as low as possible. After the 1935 tobacco crop was sold, "we paid that man all we owed him and then we moved. It seemed like to me, it was the most money we ever made working shares on a 'bacca crop." They were able to afford shoes and clothes for all their children, and there was money left over.

"That was the hardest time. That was the hardest year. Even when I was a child" and her father worked shares, "I didn't have no time like that. I got on a scale. I weighed 105 pounds," down from her normal 125. "Arthur," said Catherine laughingly at the time, "I done work my fool self to death!"

Charlotte Hester, Lazzlo's wife, introduced me to her oldest brother, Joe "Bubba" Green, Jr. Bubba said that the lives of black tenant farmers were the same up until the mid-fifties. "That ain't too long ago," he said. "A few things have changed, but people's attitudes and habits haven't changed that much."

Bubba was born in 1942, the eldest of his father's thirteen boys and two girls. Bubba, therefore, was the first child in his family to labor in the fields his father sharecropped. The first to walk ten miles one way, as he grew older, to the only high school a black child could attend; the first to endure the jeers of the white children as they rode past him on the bus.

He did not think of it then as a hard life. "It was just a way of life as it was the way I was growing up."

If you knew the answer to a problem, "it was best to keep your mouth shut. A white man did not want a black man to know as much or more than he did. There were no laws to protect sharecroppers. A farmer did not like you if you did a lot of questioning or wanted to write down every time you borrowed twenty dollars. That is why you had the migration out of here. People went north looking for a better life."

Not all the landowners cheated their sharecroppers. "My daddy made more money working shares than people doing thirds and fourths."

There was one consistent expectation among most landowners, Bubba said. "If you were a small household, you couldn't get no farm 'cause there wouldn't be enough equity in the white farmer's pocket. The bigger the family, the better the white man would like it. So it was better off for you and better off for him, too, if you had a big family."

Bubba's father moved the family to the Dickerson community in southern Granville County in 1958. Bubba was sixteen. He went with his father the day Joe Green, Sr., approached a local farmer about sharecropping on the man's land. "Daddy told [the farmer] that he had six boys and man, [the farmer] just about had a fit. That was just the thing he wanted to hear."

The farmer immediately showed Green the house he was to move into with his family. The quality of the house was considerably above the average available to sharecroppers. The farmer's son lived in the house before the son died in 1950.

While Bubba listened to the farmer and his father talk, the farmer's daughter interrupted her father. "Daddy, ain't no Negroes ever lived in that house," she said. "You going to let colored live in there?"

The farmer replied, "The house ain't doing me no good and here's Joe, got all these boys, and I got a lot of land to tend!" Green moved his entire family into the house several days later.

Most of my time in Oxford was spent with Lazzlo Hester and his wife, Charlotte. Besides providing the necessary entrée I needed, they and Charlotte's brother, Bubba, provided invaluable interpretations of the material I gathered from the older persons I interviewed.

During candid moments, Lazzlo revealed brief glimpses of his life. He and his older brother had managed to claw their way out of poverty. But Lazzlo was reluctant to flesh out his story with details. The little that he revealed was still a valuable contribution to understanding the past.

Lazzlo, thirty-nine, and his older brother, Robert, grew up in the small town of Oxford, but they remembered spending many weekends and summers months working in the tobacco fields of Granville County. Lazzlo was unable to look back over his life without anger at the way he and his brother were exploited as children.

"My brother and myself were used," said Lazzlo, sitting at his glass-top dining-room table. "My great-uncle used the family ties to get labor from us. I hate the whole thing because I put a lot of hours in, and I was underpaid all the time. We were under ten."

Lazzlo complained to his mother, Rebecca Hester, about the long hours their uncle made them work and the little money he paid them. "She had mixed feelings. We were poor. My mother did migrant farm labor. The little money we would make on the farm, we put right back into the house. It was my way of buying my own socks, my own pencils, and things for school. We never skipped school to do this."

Lazzlo's mother separated from his father when he was an infant. The father moved to New York City and never sent any money to help his former wife raise their sons. Rebecca Hester and her sons were taken in by Catherine Mitz until Rebecca Hester was able to rent her own place. When both boys reached school age, Rebecca Hester's strictest rule was school attendance. "Even when we were sick, we had to go to school. She didn't want us laying out. I appreciated it. The days I was really sick, I saw how much I missed."

Both of Rebecca Hester's sons graduated from high school. Lazzlo later earned an associate degree from a two-year community college and today works for a large textile manufacturer. His older brother finished a four-year college and did postgraduate studies. "My mother was *high-minded,*" said Lazzlo. A high-minded person was prideful and, if they were poor, did not let others know what their true circumstances were, explained Lazzlo and his wife, Charlotte.

"There were Sundays when we did not have food in the house to eat, and my mother would insist that we put on our Sunday clothes and go to church. Me and my brother had better not let anyone know that we were hungry! I think my mother's attitude saved us."

Today, Lazzlo understands why his labor was exploited when he was a child. "The black farmers were always in debt. I understand it today, but I couldn't then." Several of the family men of his grandfather's generation had lost their land when they put it up for collateral to cover loans.

One sharecropper, Arthur Standback, stands out in Lazzlo's memory. Lazzlo was twelve and was one of the dayworkers Standback hired when it was time to bring in the fall tobacco crop. After they had harvested enough leaves to fill a tobacco barn, Lazzlo asked,

"Mr. Standback, how much is this tobacco barn going to bring?" He asked the same question many times, but Standback never gave him a straight answer. Instead, Standback would turn to the other adult men present and turn Lazzlo's question into a joke. "They'd curse. They'd laugh. They'd joke. Everything was a joke."

Bubba explained Standback's joking, cursing, and laughing in response to Lazzlo's questions. "The pain was too deep. You were caught up in a system in which you had no redress. You had to hide the pain by joking and laughing."

Years later, Lazzlo understood Standback's need to joke, laugh, and curse. "He couldn't answer those questions. He didn't know, but he didn't tell me that. As I got older, I found out he never knew. If he'd known those facts, he might have given the white man trouble."

When it was time for Standback to pay Lazzlo for his work, "he always fell short. 'Well, I can't pay ya'll,' he'd say. Even though I was suppose to get two dollars a day, five days a week, I didn't get it [all]. In fact, he's dead now and still owes me money."

There are lessons to be drawn from Lazzlo's experience. Despite the financial odds the family faced, their mother insisted that her sons attend school and do their school work. Rebecca Hester's single-mindedness provides a well-known answer to some of the problems of poverty for our society, and for the parents and adolescents trapped in urban communities like Washington Highlands.

Rebecca Hester's unyielding command on education made all the difference, for the better, in both men's lives. They both have moved up into the middle class.

Two hundred miles north of Oxford, Lillian Williams's family remains trapped in cycles of adolescent childbearing, perpetual underemployment, and welfare dependence in Washington Highlands. Lillian's eleven children never got the elementary school academic foundation they needed to do their junior high school and high school work. The youngest of her children who are still in school are all several grades below where they should be. Who is to say that they will not seek a tangible achievement for themselves in another arena? By becoming an adolescent parent, for instance.

The life of Lillian Williams's younger brother, Bill Manley, presents us with another answer to this urban dilemma.

When Manley migrated out of Lenoir County, North Carolina, he carried the same educational deficiencies that burdened his sister Lillian. But unlike his sister, Manley landed a job as a clerk-courier for Washington's city government. The job changed his life and his outlook. He is married, has one son, and is buying a house in the Maryland suburbs.

The job interrupted the old family-life patterns for Manley, while these customs still dominate the welfare-dependent existence of his sister, her children, and her grandchildren. Manley's life-style and attitudes were altered because of a significant accomplishment: steady, secure employment.

EPILOGUE

SHORTLY AFTER MOVING into Washington Highlands, I realized that so much of what people I interviewed told me about their decisions was the result of low self-esteem. I reached a point of being able to tell many things when I walked into anyone's house by the expression on a person's face or a person's body language. If they were happy, I knew they were working. The unemployed and recently laid off were always sullen and hostile, both adults and adolescents.

I began to think about how many middle-class professionals take their jobs and careers for granted. They don't recognize how much their employment fulfills them. A lot of the negative behavior I saw and learned about grew out of a person's inability to earn an income. The teenagers I spent a lot of time with saw their economic futures as limited. Selling death-dealing drugs, for example, was a possible avenue out of Washington Highlands, and the income provided status and prestige for adolescent boys.

Enormous pressure was put on the young men by their girl friends, regardless of whether the young women were mothers, to be providers. A male who could not bring money into a relationship was "triflin'," lazy, and no good. Many of the young men were unemployed and, therefore, by the young women's measure, considered trifling.

Education might provide an escape. But education was not a priority in their homes; survival was. The school system had failed them. All of the adults and adolescents I met started elementary school as enthusiastic children, but by the second grade academic deficiencies appeared and remained uncorrected. Instead, they passed on to the next grade. By the sixth grade these children knew that they would not finish school.

Wesley Williams, one of Lillian Williams's sons, was seventeen when a junior high school official told him that he was too old to be in the seventh grade and should drop out of school. Wesley did so with a sense of relief. Seventh grade had just become too difficult for him to pass. He had not received the foundation he needed in the first six years of school.

Only marginally educated, Wesley and countless youths in the same predicament often lose motivation to continue their studies past the junior high school level.

I met youths in Washington Highlands who did not know how to fill out a form or who asked me to interpret the plain language of a classified employment advertisement. The thought of talking to government and school officials intimidated many adults. For some young adults, getting past the written exam for a driver's license was a major task. The lack of a license was a significant obstacle to getting a job.

My seventeen months in Washington Highlands brought me to a crucial realization. It took me six months to reach a point at which people would begin to talk to me honestly about their lives and the motivations for the decisions they made. I am a well-paid newspaper reporter who had the luxury to indulge my interest in this issue. There are people in government institutions who are trying to turn this complex problem around, but they are not as well paid and do not have the incentive or time to win the trust of people they want to help.

Individual trust is what is needed. The people of government and private charitable agencies donate food and clothing and offer jobs. But they have not made a dent in the wall of problems imprisoning these young people.

Up to the point when the series appeared, I functioned as a reporter. Later, I dissolved the wall I put between me and the friends I made while working on it. There was not much that I could do, but I made an effort to make a difference in three of the girls' lives, to be available to do what I could.

Today, I listen to their problems, give advice, and intervene in their lives when I can make a difference.

* * *

I received a large volume of letters in reaction to *The Washington Post* series. Included here are parts of several of them.

One letter that I received in early February 1986 from a suburbanite living in Columbia, Maryland, went to the core of the subject of adolescent childbearing as a human problem that crosses lines of class and ethnicity. In the following letter and all the others reproduced here, I have made editing changes to hide the writers' identities and made minute changes for clarity; otherwise, they are as they were written:

January 31, 1986

Dear Mr. Dash,

> *Having just completed the reading of your six-day series in* The Washington Post *"At Risk: Chronicles of Teen-Age Pregnancy," I feel compelled to share with you excerpts from my own entrance into motherhood at the age of eighteen. I am a white female, age thirty-six, of European descent.*
>
> *Like the black women in your study, I knew the ramifications of sex without "controls." Neither my then boyfriend and future husband nor I cared if I got pregnant. We both wanted to escape the talons of sick, repressive middle-class parents. I saw pregnancy as a means to that end. I also was incredibly lonely and unloved. I wanted desperately to have someone to love. Having sex with my boyfriend seemed to be a way to get him to "love" me (I might add I did not enjoy sex during that part of my life). And the conceived child was a captive for me to love.*
>
> *Marriage and parenthood seemed to be the right and only future for me. I was not encouraged to see life any differently. Eighty to ninety percent of my understanding of relationships was gleaned from TV. I truly believed . . . someone [would] magically appear in my life to rescue me from my parents or the boredom of life. In some ways I still fantasize about this savior, but I am mature enough to know that I must save myself!*
>
> *In their own way maybe the parents of the teens who eventually got pregnant were no different from my white parents. My dad started work at age five as a courier for a Jewish jeweler in Philadelphia. His Hungarian mother, who spoke no English, was dependent on his earnings to survive in the Slavic ghettos of*

Philly. My mom is the daughter of a German immigrant who was a tenant farmer in Westchester [Pennsylvania]. Both of my parents knew extreme poverty and discrimination. They both became harder for it. They were both from broken homes. My grandfather disappeared in the streets of NYC shortly after deboarding from Budapest, leaving my pregnant grandmother to fend for herself. My maternal grandfather escaped the Nazi army in WWI as a teenager and married my Quaker grandmother. They were later divorced since my grandmother turned out to be quite a runaround.

My parents hadn't planned for children. They were careful. After ten years and a slipup I was conceived. My mom made sure I knew how I ruined her life. Throughout my childhood and adolescence I was undisciplined and unguided, often locked out of the house. I roamed at will. Only by the grace of God did I grow up at all. Once I entered my teen years my folks suddenly became very demanding and strict. A complete turnabout. You must be in by . . . You better not . . . , etc. I am surprised that I didn't "get in trouble" sooner. I was always throwing myself at boys from the age of twelve on. I lost my virginity at fifteen.

Today? I, too, am divorced. I have raised two daughters singlehandedly since 1975. I have worked at a local college since 1977. My eldest daughter is completing her freshman year at ———, and my younger daughter is a junior in high school with aspirations of college in Texas.

How did I get here? I used men when I needed to. And I will again if I have to. I pray. And I am determined that my children will enter the work force, as in my words "productive members of society." I give them emotional support and love to try to see them through. Yes, I am determined because I will not permit them to join the one-in-three statistics that appeared in The Post *today regarding children receiving welfare.*

What I have attempted to do is to show you that the attitudes of these young blacks don't differ so dramatically as one might think from the attitudes of young whites. I totally understand their thoughts. I was lucky. I was born white. Had I been born black, I too may have been trapped in the cycle unable to break free.

Please continue your work. Perhaps the friendships you started may be the impetus in the youth of Highland[s] to find the self-esteem and self-love which was lost.

From an Alexandria, Virginia, high school teacher:

> *It was with great interest that I read your series of articles on teenage pregnancy. But, Mr. Dash, are you sure you were writing about Washington Highlands? Were you, perhaps, writing about the students I work with in a suburban Virginia high school where the minority population is 25 percent? I was sad when I read about the people you interviewed and wrote about—and even more sad when I thought about how much they are like many of the families I work with. Our school community may not be as impoverished, but many of the attitudes and values are exactly like those you described.*

From a Bethesda, Maryland, pediatrician, engaged in research at the National Institutes of Health, who worked with adolescent mothers in Houston and Los Angeles:

> *As you know, the problem is not one of race but circumstances, and I entirely concur with your assessment about the complexity of the issues involved. To me, the most compelling aspect then, reiterated in your recent articles, was the sense that parenting establishes adulthood among these adolescents, a pernicious cycle that reinforces the lack of opportunity these young women face.*

From a licensed Silver Spring, Maryland, social worker specializing in counseling adolescents:

> *Self-esteem and feelings of self-confidence are truly wrapped up in this vicious cycle of self-defeating behavior that you so accurately describe. No one can succeed unless they feel that they can; and no one can bounce back unless they have the emotional courage to do so or without the support of another person.*
>
> *Fifteen years ago, [Senator Daniel] Patrick Moynihan wrote a piece about the erosion of the black family amidst much controversy and criticism. Look where his findings are today, and look where the American black family is today. I hope people heed your words (they won't) rather than rebuff them as they did Moynihan's.*

From the president of a Washington, D.C., advertising firm:

I enjoyed your articles, but quite frankly I read each one with a strong sense of anger and embarrassment. Embarrassment because you quite accurately and necessarily snatched the covers off of all of us (comfortable and secure black folks). As Jesse Jackson has been preaching for some time now, the struggle is not over and in fact we need to arm ourselves again with the knowledge of our not-so-distant past.

From a Cleveland social worker:

Mr. Dash . . . , thank you for your frank, humanist approach to a very real problem. One that will not go away and one that is not "one of youthful ignorance and male exploitation of vulnerable, emotionally needy girls."

My job is so much like the year you spent in gathering your information. I am a home visitor for the Metropolitan Housing Agency of Cleveland, low-income housing for the poor and disadvantaged. I am that personal link between the agency and the applicant, the closest they come to an authority before they are actually housed. And, I see the problem every day, day in and day out. Some days I think I cannot go to work, and do what I must because it is so depressing. Especially when you see a nineteen-year-old girl, pregnant and with three other children the ages of one, two, and three. And when you ask why, they shrug and or say, Why do you ask? "I love my children." Yet, the kids are hungry, in need of medical care, poorly dressed, underdeveloped mentally, and really have not the communicative skills that they should have for their age group. But if you are a child and have come from the same environment, what can you pass on to your children?

But for the grace of God and a pair of loving and caring parents all of this could have been me!

From an aspiring Washington writer:

February 9, 1986

Depending on how strong of character you are, I would think that you may be in need of some moral(e) support. I sincerely believe you, at least, have reached a very correct solution to the dilemma of "what can I do?" I could almost see you mature and grow as you wrote this series. I'm happy that you wrote this final summation of your experiences.

I am no one in particular whose name you would recognize, or maybe I am all the black female, single head-of-household, ex-teenage mothers. I've been there. I may be, still. I'm writing to you because it seems I recognized somewhere in your articles an appeal for help from where it should come—us. Having a writer's heart, I recognize the anguish one can get from undertaking such a task as this, only to be attacked by those whose approval is most important to you.

Moreover, your description of your friend in the suburbs is a very compelling incentive for me to write. He is the epitome of all the middle-class blacks I've met in this area. I, too, am from Brooklyn, New York, by way of North Carolina, as are many of those same "middle-class" blacks here in Washington. A sad fact, however, is that those "gains" they are so afraid of losing came off the backs and at the expense and exclusion of folks just like those whose stories they'd rather see stay in dark corners. Many of these people mark their relative "successes" by taking an ostrichlike approach to helping others of their kind. They are actually embarrassed by other blacks who take a course less accepted by whites. Doesn't it seem strange that we don't seem to have a sense of love of our total selves; no sense of duty to uplift the whole of our race. That's what you have been hearing from your colleagues and peers. Perhaps this defect is rooted in our history. We were never really freed, you know; we were turned loose.

"Black middle class" is a misnomer. How can we be of different classes when what separates "us" from "them" is a job, and often, a public-service job? I know [people] who consider themselves middle class who are living from paycheck to paycheck, have no interest income, and no valuable assets to liquidate. So don't take what the nonexistent "black middle class" has to say too seriously.

If there was anything or anyone I felt you were remiss in dealing with, it was the sister who worked real hard to give her kids a better chance. Many of us are articulate, well-read, educated by night or hook or crook, and have made unbelievable sacrifices to accomplish belated goals interrupted by early preg-

nancies or other misfortunes. Some balance is needed with regard to this saga. I would personally, face-to-face, critique your story by stating similar concerns as those of the psychiatrist who called you. However, you are certainly right that she should be doing something to help one-on-one; for if not people like her, then who?

I am working on an original play about black men and women affected by the Vietnam conflict. Be strong.

ENDNOTES

[1]National Center for Health Statistics, *Vital Statistics of the United States* (Washington, D.C.: annual volumes).

[2]Ibid.

[3]Kristin A. Moore and Martha R. Burt, *Private Crisis, Public Cost: Policy Perspectives on Teenage Childbearing* (Washington, D.C.: The Urban Institute Press, 1982), p. 20.

[4]Ibid.

[5]Charles S. Johnson, *Shadow of the Plantation* (Chicago: The University of Chicago Press, 1934), p. xv.

[6]Ibid., p. xxi.

[7]Ibid., pp. 29–30.

[8]Ibid., p. 49–53.

[9]Ibid., p. 58.

[10]Ibid., pp. 66–67.

[11]Ibid., pp. 17–18.

[12]Ibid., p. 4.

[13]Ibid., p. 57.

FOR THE BEST IN PAPERBACKS, LOOK FOR THE

In every corner of the world, on every subject under the sun, Penguin represents quality and variety—the very best in publishing today.

For complete information about books available from Penguin—including Pelicans, Puffins, Peregrines, and Penguin Classics—and how to order them, write to us at the appropriate address below. Please note that for copyright reasons the selection of books varies from country to country.

In the United Kingdom: For a complete list of books available from Penguin in the U.K., please write to *Dept E.P., Penguin Books Ltd, Harmondsworth, Middlesex, UB7 0DA.*

In the United States: For a complete list of books available from Penguin in the U.S., please write to *Dept BA, Penguin,* Box 120, Bergenfield, New Jersey 07621-0120.

In Canada: For a complete list of books available from Penguin in Canada, please write to *Penguin Books Ltd, 2801 John Street, Markham, Ontario L3R 1B4.*

In Australia: For a complete list of books available from Penguin in Australia, please write to the *Marketing Department, Penguin Books Ltd, P.O. Box 257, Ringwood, Victoria 3134.*

In New Zealand: For a complete list of books available from Penguin in New Zealand, please write to the *Marketing Department, Penguin Books (NZ) Ltd, Private Bag, Takapuna, Auckland 9.*

In India: For a complete list of books available from Penguin, please write to *Penguin Overseas Ltd, 706 Eros Apartments, 56 Nehru Place, New Delhi, 110019.*

In Holland: For a complete list of books available from Penguin in Holland, please write to *Penguin Books Nederland B.V., Postbus 195, NL-1380AD Weesp, Netherlands.*

In Germany: For a complete list of books available from Penguin, please write to *Penguin Books Ltd, Friedrichstrasse 10-12, D-6000 Frankfurt Main I, Federal Republic of Germany.*

In Spain: For a complete list of books available from Penguin in Spain, please write to *Longman, Penguin España, Calle San Nicolas 15, E-28013 Madrid, Spain.*

In Japan: For a complete list of books available from Penguin in Japan, please write to *Longman Penguin Japan Co Ltd, Yamaguchi Building, 2-12-9 Kanda Jimbocho, Chiyoda-Ku, Tokyo 101, Japan.*